THE
REINCARNATION
LIBRARY

AEON PUBLISHING COMPANY

MAMARONECK · NEW YORK

FOUR

· · · · · · · ·

GREAT

· · · · · · · ·

OAKS

Mildred McNaughton

First Published 1946

This edition has been designed and typeset
exclusively for The Reincarnation Library.
All rights reserved.

ISBN: 1–893766–12–8

Library of Congress Control Number: 99–80171

The Reincarnation Library is a registered trademark,
and Æ is a trademark and service mark
of Aeon Publishing Company, LLC.

PRINTED AND BOUND IN THE UNITED STATES OF AMERICA.

For my mother

CECILIA CHARLOTTE McNAUGHTON

who is a descendant of Sir Francis de la Warre

one of the characters

in this book

PART

· · · ·

ONE

Chapter One

❖　　❖　　❖　　❖

AUTUMN SUNLIGHT POURED THROUGH THE GREAT ORIEL
window, flung a transparent golden veil over the near-by paneling and floor of polished oak so black with age that it looked
like still woodland water, glinted here on a picture frame of
massive gilt, there on a rich Venetian brocade or Persian rug,
and deepened the shadows that gathered in the curve of the
west wing staircase.

The sounds outside—the crooning of doves, the cawing of
rooks, the sharp bark of a dog, followed by the clip-clop of
horses' hoofs on gravel, seemed to make the stillness in the long
gallery of Sudbury Court more profound and more tense.

The tall boy who stood near the window, intently watching
the shadowy head of the staircase, was as still as the painted
faces of his ancestors. His coat of stiff, dark-purple corded silk
gleamed where the sun caught it; the cravat of Mechlin lace at
his throat was touched to creamy richness; the silver buckles on
his soft leather shoes glittered, and sparks of green fire flashed
from the large square emerald of his signet ring. John, Baron

Beausire of Sudbury, gave no outward sign that he had just returned from a ride over his vast estates, a ride as dangerous as any of the adventures undertaken by any of the brave figures in the portraits.

Hearing sounds on the stairs, John Beausire stepped forward eagerly. The sunlight flashed on his thick bronze hair—worn uncovered by a wig, in defiance of the fashion of that year of 1685—turning it to the color of an autumn leaf. His long ivory face, with its chiseled features, had in the recent weeks of terror become the face of a man. The heavy-lidded hazel eyes, deep-set beneath level brows, gave promise that, whatever came, the boy would face it with dignity.

An elderly man in the livery of the house, wearing a carefully dressed white wig, and about his neck a silver chain of office, appeared at the top of the stairs and peered cautiously down the gallery, signaling to someone behind him to stand back as he did so. Thomas, the steward, was frightened as never in his life before, and he was not averse to letting his master know it. It was bad enough when his Lordship attended the trials, paid fines for the prisoners, scattered bribes to obtain clemency for the condemned; but when he rode out and personally brought in a fugitive for whom the dreadful Judge Jeffreys had had special search made, it was almost more than his devoted servant could stand.

"My Lord," he said, as he became aware of his master's presence, "the fugitives are upon the staircase." He bowed low: his lips trembled and his voice shook as he added, "I beg that your Lordship will observe all possible caution, and hide them as quickly as may be."

John Beausire laughed. It was the laugh of a boy, gay, carefree and confident. It was good to realize that Giles, friend of his childhood and boyhood, husband of his dear Sarah, was

FOUR GREAT OAKS
By Mildred McNaughton

Can it be true that love and life endure? Is there a pattern of Justice which compensates right action with good, and bad action with suffering?

Four Great Oaks is a story of love and life, taking you from the tragedies of the Monmouth Rebellion of 1685, to the ominous clouds preceding World War II. Author Mildred McNaughton weaves a rich tapestry of insight and experience along the way.

John Beausire, Lord of Sudbury, is caught up in a web of treachery and betrayal that leads to his being stripped of his title, his home, and his family. The terrible Judge Jeffreys, holding unlimited power of life and death, ships him to the West Indies as a slave.

Two hundred and fifty years later, his descendant, an American also named John Beausire, travels to England to look at his ancestral lands. The new John looks remarkably like the original and, in Sudbury, he meets a girl who rekindles a love in him that he dimly remembers.

Bit by bit the two incarnations begin to fit together like the pieces of a well crafted puzzle. Some players from the first act are easy to place; others will keep you guessing until the end. Along the way, you'll be charmed as old enmities are softened, and old loves rekindled, in this marvellous book.

safe at last in Sudbury Court. And he was also glad to extend it to the miserable waif whom Giles had picked up on his headlong flight and protected during the weeks of hiding in ditches and thick coverts by day, and by night creeping ever nearer home.

"My good Thomas, you make too much of this business," he said. "Giles is no longer a fugitive. He is as safe as a lord in his castle, and the poor lad, also. Go tell him to come down, then fetch the food and bring it to me in the library."

The steward bowed again, then went back to the stairs, descended into the darkness and in a moment reappeared, followed by a tall and heavily built man with the ruddy face and work-hardened hands of a farmer, and a pale boy, thin and ill-formed, with a shock of wild straw-colored hair and blue eyes whose vacant stare looked as if the clamor of the battle of Sedgemoor, the flight from the soldiers of the King, the weeks of hiding, had taken from him the few wits which he might once have had.

Farmer Giles looked down the gallery with a quick glance of overwhelming relief. He had not thought to see the inside of Sudbury Court again. Many times he had come up the west stairs to talk in the library with his Lordship on some matter concerning the home farm, of which he had charge. His thoughts flew back to the day nearly nineteen years ago when he stood here, and his wife Sarah came down the gallery from her late Ladyship's rooms, the infant heir on one arm, their own first-born son on the other—for Sarah, good healthy countrywoman that she was, was nursing the pair of them and living at the Court for the time. That day she said she did not know which child she loved more dearly.

John Beausire motioned sharply to the steward, who disappeared down the stairs, still muttering under his breath of this tremendous risk undertaken for witless fools: they had had no more sense than to be beguiled by the Stuart beauty and charm of his late Majesty's natural son, the Duke of Monmouth, when that unfortunate young man—who was as deficient in good sense as he was rich in good looks—raised his ill-fated standard, proclaimed himself King of England and gathered his tatterdemalion army of shopkeepers, peasants and small farmers, to take the throne by force. The absurd adventure lasted but a few weeks. The Duke was already dead, beheaded in the grim Tower of London, and many of his unhappy followers had followed him by way of the hangman's rope or the headsman's ax, or had been transported to slave labor in the Indies. Others were languishing in prison, or still cowering in some hidden place, with the net which the senselessly cruel Judge Jeffreys boasted none could escape tightening steadily about them.

Thomas hurried to the buttery to prepare food and drink for the secret guests of the Court. He would not dare assign an underling to that task. The servants were loyal to his Lordship: there was not one who did not know how he had ridden about the county, not to speak of his own estates, urging all who would hear him to have no part in this senseless venture. But in these evil days walls had ears and eyes, and the very wind seemed to whisper tales of the hiding-places of fugitives to that evil-faced judge—more devil than man—who held his mockery of trials in the grim Castle of Taunton, less than seven miles away. As he cut thick slices of good roast beef and packed loaves of fresh bread, butter from the home farm, pasties and pie from the housekeeper's table, into a basket that could be prudently covered with a cloth, visions of corpses hanging from Somerset trees, twisting slowly in the breeze, rose before his eyes. His hand shook as he drew a jug of the rich amber cider of Somerset from a cask. It was to the Tower that his Lordship would go, if Jeffreys caught him at his work of helping fugitives fly the country. His rank would prevent transportation or a quick hanging, such as had been the lot of lesser men—aye, of women even, who had been caught, or even suspected of such a thing.

Thomas uttered something between a prayer and a curse. Not Giles—even for Sarah's sake—not all the blockheads who had risen with the Duke put together, were worth this risk. Why, it was but a month ago that the sons of Giles had been hidden, just as their father was being hidden now. God grant that this business would go as well, that there would be no hitch in the night journey to Minehead, the wait behind the casks in the cellar of the Plume of Feathers, the wary boarding of the *White Heron* when her master was ready to sail again for France without attracting too much attention. Today the message had come that he had put into port after a safe journey. He had landed the Giles boys in France. It would be a week before he would dare sail again. Thomas hoped devoutly that his Lordship would not decide to keep Giles and the lad hidden here until the sailing. They should go tonight to Minehead. The moon was waning and rose late. The dark night would be a welcome cover.

The basket was heavy, but Thomas did not dare ring for a lackey to assist him. His Lordship desired the food brought to the library. That meant the secret room of Sudbury Court must be somewhere near. Since his boyhood the steward had wondered where it was. He remembered hearing his mother tell tales of the days when it had been a criminal offense to hear Mass or to give sanctuary to a hunted priest, and of a small hidden room, somewhere under the eaves of the Court, where

Mass was said, and of how those who gathered at the Court were led blindfolded to it.

✦   ✦   ✦   ✦

Farmer Giles and the boy followed Lord Beausire from the gallery to the library in silence. At the heavily carved oak door, with its massive knob of silver, the lad drew back in terror; he looked as if he would break and run like a hunted hare, and Giles grasped his arm firmly and pulled him through the door.

"Steady, la-ad," he said, "ye-re sa-afe now. His Lordship'll ta-ake care o' we."

John smiled and put his long white hand on the rough fustian sleeve of the clean coat in which the boy had so lately been dressed, saying, "Have no fear, all will be well with you. You shall go with Giles to France for a while, and then, when all is safe, you will come home."

The boy smiled but did not speak. John wondered how much he understood, and marveled at the courage of Giles in keeping the lad with him on the perilous secret journey. "Who is he?" he asked, turning to the farmer. He knew every soul on his own estates and for miles around it. This boy was a stranger.

The sense of security given by the familiar room with its ceiling-high shelves of books, its carved panels bearing the arms of the wives of the Barons of Beausire, and the heavy old furniture, loosened Giles' tongue. He explained that all he knew of the lad was that he was an ostler's boy at an inn near Bridgwater, that he had not the wit to know who the Duke was or why he raised an army to fight the King, but had been swept into battle with his master, and of how he, Giles, had come upon him later, cowering in a ditch. Knowing that the boy had no hope of escape if let alone, he had taken him along on his own flight.

John listened with interest. "That was good and brave of you, Giles," he said. "He will go with you to France, where you will join your sons. Directly the trials are over I ride to London with my Lord Stawell, Sir Francis de la Warre and others, to speak with his Majesty, demand amnesty for the transported and imprisoned, and acquaint him fully with the mockery of justice, the horror of cruelty, that has been perpetrated in his name. When he returns the boy will find a good home here."

The words of praise brought a mist of tears to the farmer's eyes. "My Lord," he gasped, "it's thee a-as is good and bra-ave." He had no other words to say, though the enormity of the thing that had been done for him and for this nameless stranger, not to speak of his two hotheaded young sons, and certainly others, now broke over him with terrifying force. He could only stare helplessly into those clear hazel eyes and wish he had the ready tongue of his good wife Sarah. Sarah had been against the Duke. Her sons had joined the rebel army against her will. Sarah would find it hard to forgive this risk his Lordship was running for those who were so lacking in good sense as to have acted contrary to his urgent advice.

"I run but little risk," John said calmly. "It is to the future we must look, not to the past. I would that you had not ridden out with the Duke, but that is over and done with."

John wished desperately that he could really think it was over and done with, that there were no more trials to attend—the issues of which were determined before a word of evidence was heard—that the hangings, the burnings, the transportations and imprisonments, the merciless fines that spelled ruin, were over and done with. But it was not so, he knew. Yet, as it had done all day since his talk with his cousin Mark early in the morning, joy broke through his gloom like sunlight breaking from dark clouds.

Impulsively he turned to the farmer and added, "You have come home on a happy day, Giles, a day made even happier for us by your safety. Today my cousin, Mr. Beausire, gave his consent to my marriage with his sister, Mistress Rosalys. On St. John's Day, the twenty-seventh day of December, we are to be wed."

"The little ma-aid," Giles exclaimed joyfully. "Aye, it's a ha-appy day."

The soft Somerset drawl, with its long broad a's, had never seemed more lovely to John than as they talked eagerly of the changes that were to be made: of how Mr. Beausire and his wife, the Mistress Diana, would leave the Court and live at the newly restored Manor of Combe St. Philip; of the arrangements Thomas had made for a larger staff of servants within, and of the plans for the wedding.

As he listened the dark mist of terror that had for weeks past enclosed the boy Jerry dissolved slowly. His pale eyes wandered about the great room and lighted with pleasure as a white dove perched upon the sill of a window, then entered, glimmering upon the dark wood of the embrasure, its coral feet and snowy plumage in bold relief. Of human creatures the half-witted lad had learned to be afraid, but he loved all birds and beasts. Now something new and strange, love and trust, was rising within him. He knew that the splendid figure in the purple coat, whose sheen was like the plums on the great tree near the inn yard, represented safety from that unspeakable evil that had broken over him in shouts, screams, charging horses, roaring cannon and swinging swords, all shrouded in mist and night, the horror that seemed to have happened so long ago that he could remember nothing before it, yet that seemed to be with him still. This great Lord had been kind to him, as none but the man who had found him in the ditch had been in all his lonely and unhappy life. Jerry was uncertain why this should be. He was not quite sure why he was here. But he knew that he wanted to serve his Lordship, that gratitude almost choked him.

When John Beausire bound his eyes with a handkerchief the boy did not flinch. He saw that the eyes of the farmer had been bound also. It was all a part of this strange new world that had opened to him.

"The entrance to the hidden room of Sudbury Court has always been a secret," John said. As he tied the knot, he saw with a sense of infinite pity that the boy's back was deformed. "It must remain so. I warrant you are as safe there as if you were guarded by the King's men. You can sleep in peace. I shall bring you food and drink myself."

Through a door in the east end of the library he led them. The famous Queen's Room of Sudbury looked somber now that the sun had left its one circular window. It was a completely circular room, paneled from floor to ceiling in black walnut, heavily carved with a design of pomegranate trees.

For a moment John thought of the sad Queen Catherine, wife of Henry VIII, who had been a guest at the Court and had given the paneling to the Baron of the day. It bore her emblem, the pomegranate. John remembered now that it was an emblem of sorrow.

Directly facing the fireplace, which—now that the library door was closed—was the only break in the paneling, he knelt and touched a carved pomegranate that appeared to have just fallen from its tree. Many times lately he had opened the panel, and the movement was familiar to him. Grasp the knob formed by the fruit firmly, push it up, slide it along the deeply cut trunk, pull. The whole panel slid inward. A small stone staircase was disclosed. A lamp burned on a ledge cut into the wall at its head. John closed the panel, took the bandage from the eyes first of the farmer, then of the boy.

"Go up," he said. "The room is prepared for you. You will find mattresses and blankets and a lamp burning. I shall return with food, and later, when I have talked with Captain Pollard, who rides from Minehead tonight or tomorrow morning, I will tell you when you can go farther. But have no fear, you are safe."

The thought of his old friend Pollard came like a ray of sunlight in a dark place to Giles. Pollard had taken his boys to France and safety aboard the *White Heron*. Some day, when all this was over, he would tell his Lordship that it was only to bring back the boys that he himself rode to Bridgwater, that never for a moment had he been misled into thinking that the foolish Duke of Monmouth held a solution for the country's woes. But that would do later. Now he could only say, "God rewa-ard your Lordship, for ma-an ca-annot."

Then he went up the little twisting stairs, followed by the boy, who at the top turned and looked back at the tall figure still standing below. The splendid coat was dim in the faint lamplight, the shining hair dark. Jerry remembered an old woman who had once talked to him of God. He had liked to hear her, though he did not understand much of what she said. He thought now that his Lordship must be something like God.

John went back to the library, and sitting at the long table near the west window, opened his journal to make his entries for the day. There must be no break in the usual routine, no hint that anything out of the ordinary had happened. If a lackey came upon some errand, he would find the master of the house quietly at work, as was usual at this time of the day.

The leather-bound book lay open at a fresh page. John

wrote the date. It stood out boldly upon the parchment. October 1, 1685.

It had been an eventful day. Laying down his plumed pen, John reviewed it. . . . It began auspiciously. At sunrise, while riding, he came upon his cousin Mark. Mark was seldom abroad so early. Indeed, it developed later that he was not setting out but returning from a night at cards with their neighbor, Sir Samuel. Mark had been in luck and was in high good humor. They rode on to Combe St. Philip, and he showed Mark the work lately done upon the ceilings by a famous gild of plaster molders. Mark was full of praise of the restoration. They talked of how once a great Abbey Church had stood where now the orchards were, and of how the house had been the Abbot's house and still retained traces of its former beauty. Now it was restored, and was as gracious a manor as any in the county of Somerset, famous for its manors.

Then quite simply he said to Mark that it was for him that the house had been restored, for though he, John, might have to wait for a year or two years, the time would come when he would marry his little maid, and she would be mistress of Sudbury Court, and Diana would want her own house.

And quite suddenly, as if he saw the matter in a new light, Mark withdrew his objection that his little sister Rosalys was too young for marriage, and gave his consent that the wedding should take place at any time after she reached her fifteenth birthday, which was but a few weeks away.

There was joy at Sudbury Court, in spite of the grief and fear that hung like a dark cloud over all the West Country. It almost seemed that the great Tudor house was secure against the common evil.

Later John rode to Taunton, to attend the trials in the Castle. Jeffreys was at his worst, yelling and screaming, cracking vile jokes, shrieking obscenities, condemning utterly innocent men and boys to the gallows, to years of slave labor in the Indies. It was said he had grown rich on the money he received for them. He had imposed fines that meant ruin to many a prosperous farmer for no greater offense than that the victim had been suspected of giving a night's lodging or a change of clothes and food to a fugitive.

John had barely reached his own door when a white-faced groom leaned close as he took the bridle of his master's horse, whispering that Farmer Giles had been seen in the south wood at daybreak by a charcoal burner who knew him well and would not have made a mistake.

John knew that to his life's end he would remember every detail of that ride. . . . He immediately remounted and set off, scouring the south wood and several other woods and coverts before he came upon Giles and the boy Jerry. They were famished, tattered, weary to exhaustion. Slowly, from cover to cover, he brought them in, riding ahead to see that the way was clear. At last they reached the west door. Thomas was summoned, and spirited them to his own quarters to be washed and clothed. . . .

He had told Giles that as soon as the trials were over he would ride to London to see the King. That he meant to do. He had little doubt that, once the matter was settled, James II would realize how his name had been blackened by the maniac he had appointed to judge the rebels. John thought now with pity of James Scott, Duke of Monmouth, son of Charles Stuart and beautiful, stupid Lucy Walters. The Duke had been blessed or cursed with an almost unearthly beauty. He could charm a bird off a tree, but he lacked any quality of kingliness. Moreover, he had not the shadow of a claim: there had never been a marriage between King Charles II and his mother, before his birth or after it, though the King had acknowledged him, created him Duke of Monmouth, and been intensely fond of him. Well, he had paid the price of his folly upon the block in the Tower of London. The tragedy was that he had wrought such ruin among the simple folk who were persuaded that he would right all their wrongs—and, as God knew, those wrongs were many—and turn back the tide of Popery they so ignorantly but honestly feared would be let loose by James II.

The King had been much frightened, and he was a bitter and hard man. But the weight of public opinion must in the end force justice from him.

A clock chimed the hour. John felt again the golden glow of joy that not even the horror of the morning trials had been able to blight. Soon it would be time for him to go down to ride with Rosalys, his cousin, his little maid, who would so soon be his wife.

He made a few more entries. Then he began to think of that dim-witted hunchbacked lad, now sleeping his first peaceful sleep in weeks in the secret room of Sudbury Court. Why were lives so utterly different? What had life brought to Jerry, what could it bring? The best he could ever hope for was enough to eat and drink, rough clothing, a place to live, and such kindness from his masters as was given to a valued dog. The beauty and richness of the world—books, art, travel, knowledge, even the joy of an earthly love—would be denied him.

As if because of its contrast, his own life rose up before him. He had had from his birth everything that the world could give. His parents had given him adoring love. They had waited nearly twenty years for a child, and he came to them as a miracle of the infinite goodness of God long after they had laid by the hope of an heir and had accepted Mark, his father's

nephew, son of a younger son of the house who had stood
stanchly by the Stuart cause and who had gone into exile with
the widowed Queen of Charles I, marrying one of her French
ladies. The elder Mark Beausire had died in France after an
exile of many years.

For four years now he had been Lord Beausire. His parents'
death had been a bitter grief. But soon after their going—so
close together that it had seemed one sorrow—the great light
of his life burst upon him. How well he remembered the day
when his cousin told him that he, Mark, had a little sister, born
but a few months before their mother's death. She was then a
child of ten years, living in the convent in Provence where she
had been born and cared for all her life.

John laid down the pen again. It was impossible to work. It
was better to let this flood of happy memory have its way with
him. From the moment Mark had spoken that name, Rosalys,
a burning excitement gripped him. It seemed an interminable
time while Captain Pollard prepared the *White Heron* for the
voyage to France. At last he sailed out of Minehead, bearing
the letter Mark had written to the Lady Abbess, requesting
that his sister, the Mistress Rosalys Beausire, be sent home to
Sudbury Court, where her cousin, Lord Beausire, wished to
receive her.

And then the word came at last that the *White Heron* lay off
Minehead once more. How gladly he rode out to meet her!
Mark had been hunting that day and would not go. Diana was
too near the birth of her child.

And it was as he had known it would be. From the moment
he saw her, her red-gold hair shining against the dark habit of
the lay sister to whom she clung, her lovely little face lifted to
his, her wide gray-green eyes misty with tears, he knew that
now his life was full and perfect. For an instant the terror of the

new life, the new faces, was with her; then she smiled and slipped a small hand into his.

Then they were so happy. The only cloud was that for the past year he so greatly desired their marriage, and Mark said she was too young. But they knew that with the kindly passing of time that barrier must go down.

The misery brought by the Monmouth Rebellion and its aftermath in some strange way made their happiness more full and deep, for as the sorrow of others touched them, they came to a yet deeper understanding. Childhood fell away from them, and they entered into the fullness of life. . . .

The almost blank page of the journal caught his eye. Resolutely John took up the pen again. Today he would write only of happy things, so that in the long years to come he could read this page and remember the day as a landmark in his life.

So he wrote nothing of the trials he had attended, but in his neat handwriting: "This is so far the happiest day of my life, for this morning, my cousin, Mark, gave his consent to my marriage with his sister, Rosalys, and the Feast Day of St. John, December 27th, was settled upon for the wedding."

He shook sand over the wet ink, then added, "An old friend returned, which added to our joy."

The thought of Giles brought memories of the many things they had planned and done together. It was Giles who helped him select the best spots for a new orchard, who planned the crops, supervised the raising of livestock on the great estate. Giles had been a wise and willing helper to the boy of fourteen, who came into a great responsibility at an age when most lads were still thinking of their play.

It was Giles who had suggested a cherry orchard at Markscombe. John wrote: "Returning from Taunton at midday I looked down from the hilltop into Markscombe. The

young cherry trees are growing well. When they are in full
growth and bloom they will be a fair sight."

As if it were spread in a vast panorama before him he saw
his heritage, the Sudbury valley, and lands far beyond it. But it
was the valley he loved, the valley with its four villages named
for the Evangelists clustering around the wide park in which
was set one of the loveliest and greatest houses in all England.
Sudbury St. Matthew, with its fine farms; Sudbury St. Mark,
behind which the deep combe struck into the hill, where
Markscombe lay, with its ancient farmhouse and the water-
mill that had been recorded in the Domesday Book in 1085, for
there were already Beausires at Sudbury then; Sudbury St.
Luke, with its fifteenth-century inn; and Sudbury St. John,
whose church was old when the Conqueror came, bringing
with him the young Norman knight who had become the first
Baron Beausire.

Life lay before him like a shining road. How splendid it was
going to be, how gloriously happy! To live in this house he
loved, with his little love, Rosalys! To till the rich earth, and
make ever more beautiful this most beautiful place in all the
wide world!

His thoughts turned to the broad meadows beyond Combe
St. Philip, stretching down from the hillside to Taunton Dene.
He saw them white with blossoming pear trees, and a mill for
the making of the perry the country people loved beside the
stream. He wrote: "Combe St. Philip, though it is on the far
side of the hill, has always seemed part of the valley to me. I
have decided to settle it upon my cousin, Mark Beausire, but I
was happy when he told me today he would leave its care to
me. Next year I shall plant—"

There was a knock on the door. John turned quickly and
called, "Enter." It flashed through his mind that he no longer

need fear lest any unexpected messenger bring word that Giles had been taken by the King's men.

The lackey who entered was almost as white as his powdered wig. "What now?" John thought, as he bade the man speak.

"Your Lordship's pardon," he said. "Master Thomas said we should tell you at once that Sir Francis de la Warre has sent word by his body servant, to say that he would be vastly obliged if you would join him, as soon as is convenient to your Lordship, at the White Hart in Taunton."

"Send the man to me at once," John said sharply. This was no light matter. He did not doubt for a moment that it was evil news, for Sir Francis would not have called him back to Taunton today unless the affair was pressing.

A man in hodden gray riding-clothes stood in the doorway. John saw that he crushed the buckled hat in his hands nervously and that his eyes were wide with horror.

"What news?" John asked, and his hand rose to the lace at his throat.

The man bowed. "Sir Francis begs that your Lordship will understand that he had no time to write. My Lord, he begs your assistance. It is Mistress de Lisle."

John nodded encouragement. He had known all his life the old lady who was now imprisoned. Because of her great age he had little fear but that after her trial she would be released with a fine.

"Today Judge Jeffreys called her from her cell after the trials for the day were over and there was none to protest or to demand justice. She has been condemned, my Lord, to die at the stake. Sir Francis would speak with you, with my Lord Stawell, and others, that you may together contrive a way to save her."

For a moment they stared at each other. Then John spoke slowly, as if unable to believe that Sir Francis had been informed correctly. "Dame Alice is eighty years old," he said, "a gentle lady, widely known for her charity and good works. She did but give shelter for the night and a meal to two poor lads who fled after the Duke's defeat at Sedgemoor. That is the only charge against her."

The servant nodded. Silence hung heavy in the long room. The white doves on the sill seemed to be moaning.

"I will ride out within the hour," John said.

When the door opened, John called to his lackey, who was standing without, to have the bay mare Nicolette saddled at once and brought to the west door.

He picked up his plumed hat and the sword that lay across a chair, and walked down the broad and shallow steps of the west staircase, through the west hall, and out into the little enclosed court beneath the library windows, dispatching a footman in search of Mistress Rosalys.

The water splashed merrily in the fountain beneath the tall statue of St. Francis, and the court was still gay with late summer flowers, so mild had the weather been. John looked around it wistfully, loathing the thing he had to do. He had built this court for his little maid: it was an exact replica of the one she had played in as a little child in the Provençal Convent. How delighted she had been when she returned from the trip to London, planned for no other reason but that she might not see what the workmen were doing beneath the library windows!

John sat down on a carved stone seat to wait for her. The white doves she loved circled about the cowled head of the statue or dipped their dainty feet into the crystal water.

Tall and straight the Michaelmas daisies lifted their myriad starry faces to the sun. A few pale gold leaves drifted down to lie on the fountain water like tiny boats. John Beausire felt for the first time that the terror stalking the west country had at last penetrated his home.

◆　◆　◆　◆

Almost before the sound of his footsteps died away from the west staircase, Diana, wife of his cousin Mark, came to the library door and called, "John." Receiving no reply, she entered the room and looked around it anxiously. Mark had spoken of attending the trials on the morrow, but Diana wanted John to persuade him not to go. Mark might lose his temper. He had not the cool self-control John displayed. His wife sat down to wait, nervously opening and shutting her great lace and pearl fan. Soon guests would arrive, and there would be no opportunity for a family argument. Mark must not be seen at the trials. Anything he said would be noted, and Mark usually spoke first, and thought, if he thought at all, afterward. He might express an opinion of the injustice and cruelty of the whole wretched business, and Diana was determined that he should remain in favor with the King. It was already said that the King was much displeased by what he had heard concerning Lord Beausire's interest in the rebels.

Diana Beausire had been one of the great beauties at the Court of the late King, Charles II. She was well versed in the ways of courts, and she knew something of the Duke of York, who had but lately ascended the throne of England as James II. He was very different from his late brother. He would never forgive one he suspected of being disloyal.

Diana was the only child of a ruined Cavalier family. Her beauty and her name had been her only heritage, and when she was seventeen it had appeared to be a sufficient one, for she was betrothed to one of the wealthiest peers in England. Her elopement a few weeks later with Mark Beausire, a handsome and well-born courtier with no fortune of his own, was a nine-days' wonder at the Court. There were few who did not predict that she would regret it. The King made a witty remark and sent them a handsome present, and then the matter was forgotten.

But Diana did not regret it. Her love for her husband was a consuming passion. They came to make their home with the boy cousin who was Lord Beausire, whose unexpected birth when Mark was sixteen had ended Mark's hope of being his uncle's heir. At first she was very happy. All her life she had been burdened with her parents' memories of poverty-stricken exile in Holland, with the hardships of having insufficient money to live in the manner to which she had been born. She was delighted with the beauty and splendor of the home of the Beausires. The generosity of John was prodigious. He paid all Mark's debts and provided them with every possible luxury.

Diana immediately slipped into the role of mistress of the great house, as Mark accepted the easy and pleasant life of a wealthy country landowner with no responsibilities. It was not until after the birth of her son that she realized they were no more than guests, the superb estate would never belong to their son, and all John's generosity and pleasure in having them with him could not make it otherwise.

Her boy, Mark, was four now, the little Diana nearly two. Every day made her more bitter. She was very near to hating the tall boy who was so gentle and who had done so much for them.

Diana began to hope that John had not returned from Taunton. It was possible that the servant who told her he was writing in the library had been mistaken. She would then be able to do the honors of the house with a better grace. The guests were important ones. She was richly dressed for the occasion. Her yellow satin dress became her dark beauty to perfection. Her thick, almost black hair was piled in natural curls, into which were twisted the pearls that had been John Beausire's wedding gift to her. Pear-shaped pearls hung from her ears, and a pearl necklace fell into the frothy mass of fine Honiton lace at her breast, lace that rose in a great wired collar behind her head and fell in cascades from elbows to wrists.

Diana stared up at the finely molded ceiling. How splendid the house was! The whole valley, with its farms and houses, was superb. She no longer tried to hide from herself the fact that she coveted all this wealth for Mark, for their son after him. It made no difference that she knew Mark was quite satisfied with things as they were. Lately that, too, had become a trial to her.

It had seemed a joke when John declared within a few weeks of the child's arrival from France that he would marry Rosalys. She had then been able to push from her mind any thought of the time he would marry and beget heirs of his own.

Now Diana thought with fury of the approaching marriage. How could Mark have been so weak as to give his consent? Yet, deep in her heart, she knew that Mark merely faced the inexorable fact that if it was not this year, it would be next year, or the year after; that if it was not Rosalys he married, it would be some other girl who would also provide heirs.

She sprang up nervously and walked to the window. Her face hardened so that it almost lost its loveliness at what she saw there. John and Rosalys were sitting in the court below, their hands clasped, their heads bent close together. A dark cloak was flung over the girl's pale dress, and her masses of red-gold hair escaped in riotous curls from a tiny lace cap and hung in a cascade of shining color down her back.

A few months ago Rosalys had seemed a child, occupied with her lessons, her pets and her flowers. Then, suddenly, she had seemed to grow up and was now a tall young woman, no longer a child, looking more like eighteen than the bare fifteen years of her age. John had aged, too, since the Rebellion. A boy, they called him, but the men in Taunton knew they had to reckon with a man. Mark had said that with a certain pride that maddened Diana: he had advanced the remarks made by several of his friends who had attended the trials, as an excuse for giving consent to an immediate marriage.

Turning from the sight, her eyes wet with angry tears, Diana saw her husband beside her. She had been so engrossed by the scene in the court that she did not hear him enter.

Mark Beausire was an exceedingly handsome man. At thirty-five his tall, broad figure and fine-featured face might have belonged to a man ten years younger. His dark hair and brown eyes had been inherited from his French mother. There was little of the Beausires about him. It had been a disappointment to Diana that neither of their children had red hair, a mark of so many of the Beausires. She felt that in some mysterious way it would have made them more truly heirs of the house.

Diana forgot her concern about Mark's attending the trial: only one thing was in her mind.

"Mark," she exclaimed, "you must postpone this marriage—it is absurd, a crime for those children to marry!"

Once she had embarked upon the subject, all the thoughts with which she had tortured herself through sleepless nights came back to her. Mark sat flicking the long white hairs of a too affectionate dog from the crimson silk of his gold-laced coat. He had known for some time what was in his wife's mind, and as he did not know what to say he said nothing.

Diana's heavily ringed hands were clutching the oaken edge of the table, and her words poured out as if she had at last lost all self-control.

"John has not even been educated. He should go abroad for at least a year. It is a scandal that a young man in his position has not made a grand tour. Then he should spend another year at Oxford. It is humiliating for one of his position not to have been abroad, or studied at a University. Why, he has barely been to London, and is quite unknown at Court."

Mark knew the thing might as well be faced now. There was no chance of evading it.

"My love," he said, "I see your point of view. But John has had the best of tutors from England and the Continent. He speaks French as well as we do, who were brought up to the language, and Italian into the bargain. He is a Latin and Greek scholar of no mean attainments, and 'tis said his knowledge of literature is amazing in one so young. Master John Locke, the philosopher he dotes on, but whom I must confess I find as dry as dust, told me he could hold his own with the savants in a discussion of philosophy. And he knows and appreciates every stick and stone upon the estate, which is more than can be said for your humble, devoted and adoring husband, my dear."

Mark stooped to pat the deerhound that had burst into the room and was excitedly licking his Spanish leather boots, then looked into his wife's angry face and let loose his final shot, which was more to the point of the argument.

"Moreover, John is a born farmer—which I am not and

never will be. He's quite old enough to marry, my dear, and so is the little one."

Diana flung her fan to the floor, herself into a chair. Mark picked up the fan and laid it by her hand.

"What does that signify?" she exclaimed. "Is it necessary for Baron Beausire to be a good farmer?"

Mark smiled good-humoredly. "It seems so, from the stew my Lord Venner has got himself into lately. 'Tis said he's dodging bankruptcy and fast losing the chase, and that he must now choose between finding himself a rich wife and a debtor's prison. And that because he spent his youth at Court and knows nothing of farming. I do solemnly protest that were John a poor man with but a few acres to his name, he'd soon be well to do. It seems that he loves the land, and the land returns the compliment with richness."

"Don't be a fool." Diana's face flushed. It was a relief to be speaking to Mark about this thing, to admit that it was John's position, not his forthcoming marriage, that troubled her. Her eyes were bright with tears. "Mark, are you going to stop this marriage?" she said, choking down sobs, despising herself for her weakness. When her voice was again under control she went on, "If you don't, within a year there'll be no more hope that our son will ever be Lord Beausire."

It was out now. Mark was staring down at the dog, stroking the long head lying across his knee. He did not speak.

Diana continued: "Rosalys is a child. How can she preside over this great house? The servants will laugh at her. Do they not speak of her as the little maid? She also should see something of life before she marries. I do declare, John is the only man who has paid his addresses to her. Within a year they would both blame us bitterly for our lack of judgment."

Mark spoke firmly. "I think not," he said. He wished with

all his heart that Diana would accept the situation as philosophically as he had done. He went on with a note of desperation in his voice.

"My sweet, what if I did refuse consent? Not that I could now; it was given definitely this morning, as I have already told you. Nothing would keep them apart and, God knows, there is no reason that they should not wed. As well soon as late, I say."

Diana knew what he said was true. Her temper having ebbed, she faced the cold fact mercilessly. She would within a few weeks have to hand over the management of the house to a fifteen-year-old chit.

"There is something else," she said. "It is becoming common talk that John is backing the rebels, that he has paid huge sums in fines. Why, it is even being whispered that he is smuggling them over to France. It is possible that he will soon have to appear before the King to defend himself, and in the mood in which his Majesty now is, he may have to cool his heels for months in London before he is summoned to Whitehall."

"Then he'll need a wife for company," Mark said lightly, "and I'll warrant he'll find better employment than cooling his heels, however long it may be before His Majesty condescends to command his presence."

Diana tossed her head.

In a moment Mark was serious, more serious than was usual with him. "They speak of him already as in the old days they spoke of saints," he said. "I think that for a long time his charity will be remembered in Somerset. His loyalty could not be questioned. Why, Sir Francis, Lord Stawell, Phelips, many others, would testify how he rode the county, begging all who would hear him not to be led into such foolishness. He was out as soon as we had word that that brainless idiot Monmouth had landed at Lyme and raised his standard. No, there is nothing to fear there."

Mark lifted his head proudly and added, "The King himself would not dare impugn the loyalty of Beausire."

The dark thought that had crept into Diana's mind would not be denied utterance. "Jeffreys would," she said sharply, "and Jeffreys hates him. You forget that Judge Jeffreys has a warrant from the King to condemn whom he will—without question or appeal."

"A warrant he has used to the full—curse him!" Mark stood up, saying, "Come, my sweet, we will forget the matter." He pulled her to him and kissed her lips and long white throat. For a moment Diana stiffened and drew back; then she moved to him and returned the kiss with passion.

Mark took a dark curl and twisted it about his fingers. "Life has been good these five years, has it not?" he said.

Diana nodded. She had no words. Yes. Life had been good, but it could be perfect. Mark went on speaking quietly.

"We are better provided for than we thought possible when we bolted from my Lady Allingham's rout together." His face lighted with laughter. "And our babes are provided for, too. John was ready with his deed of gift to land the very day each was born. When he gave me the papers for Diana I told him that at this rate I'd warrant I'd have half the valley from him— with your gracious help, my love. He laughed and said he'd take the risk: he was vastly happy to welcome another Beausire; there was plenty for all who might come. And, as if that was not enough, now he insists that he will settle the Manor of Combe St. Philip upon me and my heirs forever. It is a fine house. He has spared neither money nor care upon it. The land is rich and well tilled. Why, when I said I hoped he would continue to see to its care, as I knew nothing of such things and prefer to meet the products of the land for the first time upon the dining table, you would have taken your oath that it was I who had just bestowed upon him a princely gift!"

Mark paused. There was no response in Diana's face. "And a princely gift it is," he added.

"He will be less generous when his own children come," she said coldly.

Mark was glad when a servant came to announce the unexpectedly early arrival of the guests, and to say that his Lordship was obliged to return to Taunton upon an urgent matter and would be forced to dine there.

Diana was gay that night. To the delight of the elderly Sir Samuel, who declared he had come for his revenge at cards, she sang gay French songs in the manner that had been so well received at Court. Mark assured Sir Samuel that if he understood the words his periwig would rise in air, so shocked would he be. For the first time in his nearly seventy years Sir Samuel regretted that he had neglected to study the French language in his misspent youth.

Diana watched carefully for her opportunity, for the time when she was alone with Sir Samuel. Then she asked lightly, as if really the matter interested her but little: "Sir Samuel, is it your opinion that a man of rank, believed to be giving succor to the rebels, would be attainted?"

Sir Samuel shuddered almost imperceptibly. He had had enough of the Rebellion and did not relish its ugly trail being brought into this delightful assembly, but he answered the question, to the best of his belief, honestly.

"Sweet lady, such grim matters should not trouble your pretty head. But since you ask, yes, I am sure that he would. His Majesty is in no mood for mercy. But, thank God, there is no man of high rank involved. This time it is the common people who have made fools of themselves. A few gentlemen, of course, but none of conspicuous rank."

Diana ran her slender fingers over the keys of the harpsichord. The thought that had entered her mind as a little trickling stream was now a dark river. Soon it would flood her whole being with one sinister intention.

Chapter Two

◆　◆　◆　◆

THE MARE NICOLETTE PAWED THE GROUND IMPA-tiently as John reined her in upon the bridge that spanned the main drive, and looked back at the house. The groom behind pulled up his own horse nervously, his hand instinctively seeking his sword hilt, but he saw no suspicious strangers. The long sweep of the drive was empty: its bordering elms had carpeted it with the pale gold of their first fallen leaves. Thomas the steward had admonished the man never to be more than ten paces behind his Lordship, but, Frank thought ruefully, it was easier to command than to do, for his Lordship liked to ride on alone and had no fear of any untoward happening.

The cawing of the homing rooks set up a mighty clatter. To John it was a friendly and a lovely sound, inextricably woven with the memories of his happy childhood. It was a strange and beautiful thing to know that in a few years children of his own might hear them and raise small hands toward the tree-tops, hoping to entice them down, or to catch them upon the wing if they swooped but a little lower.

Joy that was as bright and fiery as the flaming sunset swept him. Unheeded were the warnings of Thomas that a visit to the home farm today might stir up gossip that he had news for Mistress Giles, and when two and two were put together, it was not hard to make four, and perhaps the charcoal burner, pot-valiant at the Beausire Arms, had said that Giles was within the valley and, should Jeffreys spread his net ever so cunningly, would slip through it to safety, with the help of his Lordship. Thomas had even imagined that as the fatal words were being spoken, Captain Moffet—the King's man who lodged at the Inn with a troop of soldiers to watch the valley and particularly the comings and goings of the great house in its center—would be passing the door of the common room and hear them.

John remembered Thomas' gloom with pitying amusement. He felt there was no room in all the world for grief and fear today and decided, on a sudden impulse, to pay a visit to Sarah. He would stay but a little time, then put Nicolette to the gallop and be in Taunton in short order. Sarah would almost certainly be beside the pond, feeding her ducks and geese.

He turned Nicolette's head toward the grassland of the park, flicked her into a trot. She responded with a toss of her head and was soon skimming over the springy turf so lightly that her dainty feet hardly seemed to touch it.

The old gray tower near the little river that wound through the park was also lit with sunset splendor. The tower and some fifty feet of crumbling wall were all that remained of the great castle the first Lord Beausire began to build in 1067. The wall led to a small church which once stood within the fortifications but was spared by the great fire that ruined the castle in 1497. This church was still the burying place of the Beausires.

The sunset brought out all the color in the turning leaves of the four magnificent oaks, the pride of Sudbury, that stood apart from other trees. John pulled Nicolette into a walk, the better to admire them. He would remind Thomas that the Beausires were under supernatural protection. But alas, Thomas was too filled with fear to draw comfort even from an ancient superstition.

As he drew nearer the great trees he thought of the legend that was woven into the history of his house. Now, looking at the majestic oaks, he could almost believe it as simply and as wholly as his mother had done. It was during the Third Crusade that it happened. The Baron of Beausire, in that year of 1191, joined Richard the Lion-Hearted in his effort to wrest the holy places from the infidel. The Lady of Beausire besought him not to attempt the perilous and thankless venture. She was bitter and grief-stricken when he rode out to join the King at Dartmouth. A monk from the great Abbey of Our Lady and St. Philip near by strove to comfort her, offering a priceless gift, a splendidly illuminated copy of the Gospels but lately finished in the Abbey scriptorium. She flung it aside but later turned the brightly colored parchment leaves, murmuring, just before she slept the sleep of exhaustion, the names of the Evangelists. She had a strange dream that she walked in the meadow outside the castle walls and saw there the four saints haloed in heavenly light, dazzling in their glory. They promised her protection for her house, as long as the tenets of the Gospels they had written down for men were kept. From that day, through seven years of almost hopeless waiting, she had no fear. At last her husband and her son—her only child, who had been but a lad when he left her—returned safely. The Baron, with all the pomp of Holy Church, placed the House of Beausire under the protection of the Evangelists and swore for himself and his heirs forever to keep the laws they had made clear to men. As a memorial of his oath, he planted four acorns where in his lady's dream she had seen the Evangelists stand, that the trees might grow and through the centuries remind those who came after him of the promise he had made.

Through the centuries the legend had grown. It was misty now, but the symbols of the Evangelists were borne in the arms of the house. Their names were given to the sons of the house. Generation after generation, with but few exceptions, the Beausires had to the best of their ability tried to keep those few simple commands given to men: to mete out justice and charity, to help the needy, to do good in the world, to regard all men as the children of one Father.

For nearly five hundred years the trees had stood there: they were enormous now. They would outlive the gray tower at whose narrow window she who had the vision sat as she fell asleep. They would live yet for many hundreds of years, growing, increasing in size and beauty.

Now, in the evening light, the message of the legend was clearer to John than ever before. It was so simple. If those tenets had been kept, the evil now abroad could not have come upon the land. There would be no wars, no want. Death would come, with its darkness of loss and separation, but if the words of the Lord were truly believed, even death would be touched with brightness. That he knew. His mother had believed those words, and how joyously she had gone into the darkness, believing it but a door into glorious light! Perhaps even disease, with its agony and ugliness, would be vanquished. Was it not said that those who believe would do even greater works than He who healed all who came to Him with trust that He had the power and the mercy?

But how did one obtain that faith? John realized suddenly that he did not know whether he believed or not. He had never been tested. His life had been easy and pleasant. It had been easy to be generous to those destiny had placed in his power: it had required no sacrifice.

Matthew, Mark, Luke and John, the village folk called the trees. Since the Reformation, people no longer sought the prayers and protection of saints in glory. Yet it had come to be understood that the trees were in some way connected with the luck of the house, that while they flourished the house would stand, but if they fell, the end of the Beausires would be in sight.

John wondered with a touch of amusement whether any of the older folk had been watching them anxiously since he started to attend the trials and openly take the part of so many rebels. As the thought crossed his mind he noticed a tall hooded figure standing with her back to the trunk of the farthest tree—St. Luke, they called it—her face upturned to the thick whispering leaves.

Pleasure lighted his face. He sprang from his horse, and beckoning to the groom behind him to take the reins, ran toward the tree, calling, "Sarah, Sarah."

As she bent to kiss the hand he held out to her, John knew that Sarah felt but little relief. Fear still covered her like a dark cloak.

The groom stood between the two horses, waiting for his master to remount. He was safely out of earshot.

"Sarah," John said, "have you no smile to greet this marvelous day? Think of it! Since sunrise my wedding day has been set, and so soon I hardly dare to think of it, lest I think of nothing else. Word comes from Minehead that the *White Heron* is safely in port, having accomplished the mission upon which she flew, landing Dick and Hal at Calais in the safe keeping of my good friend Dupuis, and then, to crown it all, Giles is safely hidden and before the week is sped will be another guest at the hospitable board of Monsieur, and the poor lad he saved from the carnage at Sedgemoor also."

Slowly they walked from the shelter of the trees, the groom following at a respectful distance. Sarah raised her clear blue eyes, trying unsuccessfully to blink away the tears.

"My Lord," she said, "well you know that what brings happiness to you brings it to me also. Today has been to me as if I had risen to find the land changed while I slept from the dreary gloom of winter to all the flowering of spring. Like an angel from heaven Mistress Rosalys burst into the dairy as I was at the churning—God knows she is as lovely as any angel there can be—and shooed my maids away, saying with blushes and smiles that she had news Sarah must be the first to hear, and they went laughing, guessing well what the news was. Then she flung her arms around me and told me all in one breath that Hal and Dick were safe and that on St. John's Day she was to wed her cousin John."

Sarah was smiling now. "And when we went out to find the girls gathered, waiting to hear the news as hungry chicks wait for their food, she had already promised that I should dress her in her bride clothes. As the maids clustered around her, she told them of the silks and laces that would come from France, and it was for that that the *White Heron* came and went, wines for the feasting being needed also. I felt in my heart then that Giles was safe."

Sarah had been the village beauty in her youth. Now she was a comely woman, though John saw for the first time the fine lines about her eyes and mouth, and the threads of white in the nut-brown hair as her hood slipped back.

"And he was safe," he said. "Even then he was being freshly clothed and fed by our good Thomas, the peril of his flight past."

Sarah's sun-browned hands clenched convulsively.

"His peril may be over," she whispered. "God grant it is, though it seems to me to be a long way from this valley to the deck of the *White Heron*. But, my Lord, my very soul sickens when I think of the risk you ran in bringing him in."

John took her arm reassuringly. "Think no more of it, Sarah," he said. " 'All's well that ends well' is a wise saying. I would pledge my word that none saw me, but if they did, who is there hereabouts who would do me a mischief?"

"If there should be, no curse would be black enough for such a one," Sarah responded. Fear, horror of the thought that caused that fear, respect for the name of the one she most doubted, battled within her. Then into her mind flashed the picture Thomas conjured up as he described the last hours of the Duke of Monmouth to her—he had had the tale from a gentleman who attended the execution. She saw the slender graceful figure entering the dreadful Traitor's Gate of the Tower; her mind followed through the grim days until the beautiful head was laid upon the block, to be severed by one stroke of the flashing sword. As Thomas talked she would have stopped him had she been able. Now fear brought every word back to her. She felt as if the gushing blood had splashed her white apron, and she knew suddenly what it was she had seen then and saw now. Not the head of the Duke upon the block, but the head of John Beausire, whom she had nursed at her breast and loved as she loved the son she had nursed with him, the son he had but lately saved from a traitor's death.

Fear choked her. It was all she felt now. What would it matter to the hardhearted King that John Beausire had but helped a few poor wretches flee injustice? The Duke had been a traitor—perhaps he deserved his fate, son of the late King though he had been—but the gallows and the block, the prison ships and cells, had taken many who were guilty of no more than common charity.

She turned sharply, her handsome face taut with misery. The sun was sinking, a ball of glowing crimson flame. For a moment it seemed as if in its dying it had spilled blood over all the valley. They were in view of the home farm now; its windows glowed redly, and the pool between the park and the farm garden—last remnant of the old Castle's moat—seemed filled with blood. The hills dripped blood; the little river winding through the park, and under the great stone bridge that spanned the drive was a broad slow stream of blood between its grassy banks; every bush and tree had reddened. Nothing could stop her now. She would out with it. Each sharp look, each tightening of the lovely lips of the Mistress Diana that she had noted and remembered came back to her. Almost incoherently the words poured from her.

"My Lord, my little Master John," Sarah gasped, her fresh face gray now, her full lips colorless, even the blue of her eyes dimmed as she faced him. "It is because I love you, because lately gratitude has been added to that love, that I dare speak. Remember that evil beast Jeffreys hates you because you have stood up to him and many times balked him of his prey. Remember also that should you be—"

Sarah paused, for she saw the astonishment in John's eyes, but she forced herself to put the dreadful thing into words, and went on boldly, "Should you be dealt with as the Duke was—and he the late King's acknowledged son—or should you be attainted and transported, as poor Mr. Thelwall of Winchester was, remember that all you hold would pass to other hands, that a word, a hint, would be sufficient for Jeffreys. Had he cause to think a fugitive was hidden at the Court, he would find the unhappy wretch though he tore the house down, stone by stone, to do it. And it is you who would pay, you who would walk through the Traitor's Gate, to the Tower and the block."

John faced his nurse and friend calmly. "Whom do you fear?" he asked, wondering if it was Thomas, who on rare occasions had been known to drink a mite too deeply, though he would die for the welfare of the House of Beausire.

Sarah did not flinch as she replied. The narrowed eyes and bitten lips of the Mistress Diana, as she had seen them a week past when Lord Beausire and his cousin Rosalys rode out together, were before her.

"I fear the Mistress Diana."

Then, as if to get the words out before she was bidden to stop, she spoke what was in her mind day and night now. "She dreads your marriage. She will leave the Court, where she has been mistress for five years now, with ill grace. Mr. Beausire is good at heart, but she is the stronger of the two. God forgive me, but I must say out what I feel. I do with all my heart believe that did she know what you have done, what you are now doing, and what, because I know you, I know you will continue to do while this evil business lasts, she would send word to the King that the Baron Beausire of Sudbury, Peer of England, is a traitor to the King's Grace. Then she would wait, those dark eyes of hers shining, for the time to come when her husband, and her son after him, could step into your shoes."

Sarah hid her face in her hands, and sobs shook her. She did not see the anger that flashed over John's face and vanished as quickly as it had come. Pity seized him. This madness was understandable. Sarah, in an agony of fear, had awaited for nearly three months the news that did not come until hope itself seemed dead. She had seen corpses hanging like awful fruit from wayside trees, like new and terrible signs from the posts of inns. No wonder Sarah was unstrung. It was common gossip that it was Diana who had opposed an immediate marriage, Diana who had insisted that Rosalys was but a child, when all the country folk knew that a maid of almost fifteen was full ripe for marriage.

Gently he laid his hands on her shoulders. "Sarah," he said, "God knows that what you have had to bear of late is enough to make you see the whole world awry. But let me hear no more of such nonsense. Mistress Diana only protested what she thought was best for our little maid. She herself had a gay girlhood, surrounded by suitors and courtiers, and thinks it but dull for a lady as lovely as Mistress Rosalys to marry so soon. I think she would have liked to show the beauty of her husband's sister at the Court of Whitehall, but now she sees where the heart of the lass lies, she will go happily to her new home at Combe St. Philip."

"God grant no evil comes of what you have done today," Sarah whispered. "If the life of Giles caused you grief in its saving, it would be a greater burden than I could bear, though I have not the courage to face what life would be if he or our boys were lost in this miserable business."

"Try to think only of happy things," John said. "Think of the wedding on St. John's Day. Giles, with Dick and Hal, will be back from France. His Majesty will not deny me amnesty for them, and many others for whom I shall demand it. Mr. Beausire, who knows the new King well, will accompany me to London. I must go now. Go in and rest. Tomorrow, at eight of the clock, come to the Court. Say in the servants' hall that Mistress Rosalys sent for you to assist Mrs. Allison with the spicing of pears. I promise that during the day, between the putting up of many succulent jars of fruit, I shall give you a word with Giles. We will know then when the *White Heron* sails again: two days hence, I think. There is no danger in the journey to Minehead. Thomas will conduct the wagonload of casks Captain Pollard is to take to the French vineyard to be filled. No soldier of the King will dare demand to inspect the casks of Lord Beausire. Thomas would first demand a warrant signed with the King's own hand."

Sarah curtsied deeply. John signaled to the groom and in a moment mounted and was off across the park on his way to Taunton.

The sun had gone down: the gray stillness of autumn twilight was over the valley. Sarah went slowly toward the great sprawling mass of the farm buildings.

By the new barn she stopped, looking up at it with the warm sense of delight it always gave her. It was a copy of the great barn that still stood untouched, though the Abbey to which it had belonged was in ruins. A Beausire had built the Abbey barn, long ago in the thirteenth century. Now, in the seventeenth, another Beausire, needing a new barn, had had it built in the image of that building of the Abbot Adam of Sudbury, who had done so much to beautify and ennoble the Abbey, already so old that its founding was almost lost in the mists of time.

The doors of the huge cruciform building would have graced a nobleman's house. Set in the arms of the cross, they were high enough for a loaded wain to enter. In the gathering shadows Sarah turned her eyes upward to the space under the gables where the emblems of the Evangelists were carved. The angel of St. Matthew, the lion of St. Mark, the ox of St. Luke, the eagle of St. John. Fervently she hoped that the luck of the Beausires would hold now.

✦   ✦   ✦   ✦

The darkening Taunton street was almost deserted, but John had a sense of being watched, of frightened eyes peering from the small leaded windows in the overhanging top stories of the timbered houses, of whispered conclaves behind the shut doors.

In the common room of the White Hart the men seated at a long table rose respectfully. The landlord advanced and bowed low.

"Sir Francis de la Warre awaits your Lordship," he said. "He and some other gentlemen are in a room abovestairs. If your Lordship will allow me, I will conduct you to them."

The landlord's face, once round as the full moon, looked pinched and worn. It was said that he faced ruin because of the fine that had been imposed upon him, for no other fault than that a potboy, since vanished in terror, had given a mug of ale to a thirsty lad who cheered for the Duke when he was proclaimed King of England in the Market Square. The lad himself had swung for three dreadful days from a signpost of the inn.

A cheerful fire burned in the grate of the low, paneled room. At a table in its center sat six men who represented some of the greatest houses of Somerset. Wine glowed with the color of rubies and topaz, crystal glasses shimmered in the candlelight, which fell softly on the fine silk of the gentlemen's coats, found points of light in the jewels of their rings and laid a fine gloss upon the curls of their fashionable wigs. But as John Beausire took the oak chair reserved for him he knew that there was no good cheer at this meeting; that they were come together upon grim business.

Sir Francis spoke first. His deep pleasant voice was harsh with anger. "Beausire, there's little time to lose. At eight of the clock tomorrow, Dame Alice goes to the stake. A jailer, whose mother she befriended in times past, smuggled a letter to me. A pitiful little missive it is, too. 'Sblood, to think that this can still happen in England, and in the county of Somerset! I swear it is time the Peers of England reminded His Majesty that there is an island in the Thames upon which another King of England was forced to sign the Magna Charta. History often repeats itself, 'tis said."

Phelips, hotheaded as usual, and never one to question a scheme when it appealed to him, burst in with a plan of riding at top speed to Whitehall, all of them here present and as many of the gentlemen of the West Country as they could rouse at short notice, to force the very gates of the palace, if need be, and demand of the King that justice be done and Mistress Alice and other victims be released forthwith.

John took the parchment leaf obviously torn from some book of devotion and read the message faintly scrawled upon it. Sir Francis had spoken truly when he had said it was a pitiful thing. As he read, anger flamed in John until he could have mounted and ridden with Phelips without more ado. But in an instant cold sense touched him with the remembrance that, long before the best horses could reach London, Dame Alice would have perished at the stake. What was to be done must be done here.

Dame Alice wrote that she did not fear death, that the King's Grace was welcome to the poor remnant of her long and happy life, but that, with a lack of courage she made no shift to hide, she feared the flames. She begged for the mercy of one swift stroke of the ax and sent this message in the frail hope that her friends might yet obtain that mercy for her.

The eyes of all at the table were fixed upon John Beausire. Though not one of them had voiced the thought, their hope was in him. Had they not more than once seen Jeffreys break off in the midst of a vile, furious outburst, turn his eyes from the unfortunate wretch cowering in the dock and try to meet the steady gaze of the tall young aristocrat, as though he feared it?

Just before his arrival they had been discussing the curious power Beausire had more than once seemed to exercise over Judge Jeffreys, the almost visible wave of relief that broke over the prisoners' pen at the end of the castle hall when he arrived to take his place in the big carved chair reserved for him, the way the whisper that he was in the hall would pass from group to group of the terrified relatives of prisoners gathered in the Castle courtyard. "Lord Beausire is here" were words of hope, and revived a belief in justice that had died when they saw the evil face of the Judge as he passed on his way to the castle.

"We shall have to act tonight." Lord Stawell's voice was bitter and angry. He knew the value of time. A week past he had ridden to Bath to sign a petition to the King for mercy that was being written by some gentlemen there, and upon his return had found that two of his favorite servants for whom he had begged amnesty were beyond the saving power of His Majesty. Their corpses swung from the tall gates of Cothelstone, a warning to himself that Judge Jeffreys would brook no interference with his merciless decisions.

John laid the torn page with its hastily scrawled message upon the table. "I am going to the lodgings of Judge Jeffreys," he said. "If he refuses the mercy of the block, we ride tonight for Whitehall."

There was a clamor of voices. Phelips was convinced they should all go and, as gentlemen of Somerset, speak their minds about this outrage, giving warning in no uncertain terms of what they intended to do should their demand be denied.

It was quickly decided there was little hope of a reprieve. Dame Alice had freely admitted what she had done; moreover, she had protested that if given the opportunity she would do the same again.

Sir Francis de la Warre tried to weigh the merits of a joint demand, which would inevitably attract attention as they entered the house where the Judge lodged, or of falling in with John Beausire's desire to go alone, thereby compromising himself only and leaving the others free to make arrangements for the possible ride to London. Nothing so roused the devilish fury of Jeffreys as an attempt to thwart his power. Sir Francis remembered almost with a shudder the dreadful finality of the warrant the Judge held from the King. There was no gainsaying his power. For the sake of the helpless old lady who so pitifully confessed she feared the searing flames, discretion would certainly, in this case, be the better part of valor.

Sir Francis took up his sword. "Beausire and I will go," he said. "Let the others remain here. We may have to ride tonight for London. Beausire shall make the demand. I shall stand witness of all that passes."

No lights showed in the dark street. Great clouds scudded across the sky before a rising wind. The signboard of the White Hart creaked dolefully, as if in remembrance of a burden lately borne. When the waning moon slipped from behind a cloud, the dark mass of the Castle loomed up. Somewhere a dog howled, and far off there was a sound of horses' hoofs on a cobbled street.

Lord Beausire and Sir Francis de la Warre walked in silence, their men behind them. It took but a few minutes to reach the house they sought.

"Seek only to save her from the flames. All else is hopeless," Sir Francis said in a low voice, as his man mounted the steps before a house whose lightless windows looked as if all life within had long since departed.

It was some time before a surly manservant opened the door. He peered out into the darkness, dimly silhouetted by the light of two candles burning on the table in the narrow hall. He expected the usual desperate suppliant, a wife or mother, making a last hopeless effort to obtain mercy.

"His Worship sleeps," he said gruffly. "Begone, there is no mercy here for traitors to the King."

John Beausire stepped forward, quickly followed by Sir Francis. The man in the doorway bowed obsequiously as he recognized them. This was another matter. Such gentlemen could not be kept waiting upon the doorstep.

"Tell your master that Lord Beausire and Sir Francis de la Warre wish to see him immediately upon a matter of great urgency."

John spoke quietly, but the words seemed to echo through the gloomy hall. The candles flickered as the night breeze caught their little flames.

"Enter, my Lord, and pray be seated. I shall tell his Worship at once. He will be honored to receive you."

The man's echoing steps died away. A heavy silence was broken only by the ticking of an unseen clock, which presently struck the hour with such sadness in its muffled chime that it seemed a sentient thing, aware that every hour dropped into the dark well of the past was one of the few remaining to certain unhappy souls within the Castle. Then the booming notes of the Castle clock struck the door like the knocking hand of doom.

The sound had barely ceased when the shuffling footsteps could again be heard. There a look of fear upon the peaked face of the servant as he came forward and announced, "His Worship will receive Lord Beausire and Sir Francis immediately."

The groom Frank stepped forward, beckoning to the servant of Sir Francis to follow him, but John waved them back.

"Wait here," he said, "We shall return shortly. This business will take but little time."

Frank watched them go. He wondered what Thomas would think of this. But it was impossible to disobey his Lordship. He consoled himself with the thought that it was but a small house. A call would be heard from end to end of it.

If the hall could be considered gloomy, it was bright compared to the room into which the two seekers for mercy were ushered. Sir Francis looked about him anxiously, expecting to see some horrible sight that would explain the evil and despair that could be sensed hanging about the somber curtains and heavy oak furniture. At first glance the room appeared empty; then Sir Francis saw that John's eyes were fixed upon the far corner.

He had an instant's sense of having seen some loathsome beast rise from its lair, then realized they were already in the presence of Judge Jeffreys, the man whose merciless use of the power given him by the King would blacken that King's name forever and make his own synonymous with evil as long as the Monmouth Rebellion was remembered.

The flaccid face was heavily lined. Deep-set dark eyes seemed lost in a maze of cobwebby wrinkles. The thin cruel lips were twisted into a parody of a smile.

"You honor me, my Lord." The Judge spoke in the low and gentle voice that he used to pronounce the most cruel of his sentences. Though he had bowed deferentially to both his visitors, Sir Francis knew that he concerned himself with but one of them. His black slits of eyes under their heavy brows were fixed upon the man who stood so tall and straight before him, returning his gaze steadily.

The Judge's great curled periwig bent humbly before the proud red head of John Beausire. The young man's pale face looked now as if a light shone behind it, and the emerald on the long hand touching the edge of the table gleamed with green fire.

"How can I serve your Lordship?" The thin voice seemed to come from far away.

Not for an instant did John Beausire turn aside his gaze. "The sentence passed upon Dame Alice de Lisle—illegal according to the law of the realm—is preposterous in its cruelty. We have come here to demand an amelioration of it. Dame Alice is highly regarded. Were she to be burned at the stake, I give you my word there would be such an outcry through the West Country that the sound of it would reach the ears of his Majesty, however well he may guard them from such sounds."

Almost unconsciously, Sir Francis nodded approval. John Beausire was speaking well.

Jeffreys leaned forward and answered, "The woman is a traitor. She is equal in guilt with the rebels she fed and sheltered in her house. The punishment of traitors is death. Death."

As though the word fascinated him, the Judge repeated it, his voice rising until his listeners expected to hear that unearthly scream that so often rang through the Castle hall as he poured a tirade of hatred upon his victims.

"I repeat what I have said. If this woman burns, the King's Grace will know shortly that there are things that cannot be done in England, however great the power he is willing to grant his servants."

The narrow evil eyes dropped before the clear hazel ones. There was a cringing note in the Judge's voice as he replied, "My Lord, the position of his Majesty's servant in this case is an unhappy one. The treachery to the Throne he has encountered is unbelievable."

The Judge paused, then went on hurriedly, his voice rising as if he felt the excitement of a chase, saw the panting quarry in view.

"There are lordly houses where it is said that the stable doors are left open through the night, with horses saddled, their saddlebags well stuffed with food and money and with a change of clothes, yes, even the livery of that house. For what would this be but for the aid of escaping criminals?"

"That house." Sir Francis felt his throat constrict. There was no doubt now as to whom Jeffreys referred. He had only one house in mind. Only John Beausire had dared to do that. Sir Francis knew. Leaving Sudbury Court late one night, he had seen it with his own eyes, and he had known that his host had wished him to see it, as a silent hint as to what might also be done at Hestercombe.

It was soon obvious that Dame Alice must die. So great a tide of feeling had been raised by the word of her sentence that Jeffreys for the sake of his own authority would not dare remit it. All that remained now was to settle the question of the way in which she would meet her death.

Sir Francis watched anxiously. Often he did not hear the words that passed. They seemed to mean little. He could sense the battle of minds, the slow breaking down of the Judge's will.

At last the grudging consent came. A clerk was summoned. His pen scratched upon parchment and he handed the writing to his master with a covert glance at John Beausire, who still stood beside the table, unwilling to be seated in this house.

The Judge affixed his signature and seal and held the parchment a moment, as if loath to the last to admit himself vanquished; then, handing it to John Beausire, he said, "My

Lord, since you have constituted yourself defender of this woman, I give you this deed. Present it to the Chief Warden. Dame Alice will die upon the block."

John took the paper and read it by the dim light of the candles. "I shall go at once to the Castle," he said, and turned toward the door.

"My Lord," Jeffreys said, and there was again that hint of excitement and desire in his quavering voice, "I must in justice and charity tell you that it is but because of the great age of this rebel against the King's Grace that I grant this mercy." He paused, and John Beausire, standing in the center of the room, met his gaze again, a half-smile upon his own face, as though he knew what Jeffreys wished but did not dare to say.

"When other traitors are apprehended—as they will be, so well is the net spread—there will be no mercy." The Judge clenched his hand as he uttered the last words.

"He is thinking of Giles," John reflected. "He would be less sure of the catch his net would haul in if he knew where Giles slept tonight."

The Judge bowed again. Dark shadows seemed to hover about him. He watched them go, then sat down, his eyes still on the closed door. He was not thinking of the farmer, Giles— though for days the man and the hope of his capture had been in his mind, since the death of Giles would hurt John Beausire as no other capture and death would. Now that meat was not rich enough. The servant would not be sufficient recompense for John Beausire's contempt, for his attendance at the trials, for the lives he had snatched from death, the victims he had bought from prison. He rubbed a finger over his lips as he thought of having John Beausire himself within that net. There must be a way to prove that he had gone beyond the law in aiding the rebels. That he had done so the Judge believed with utter conviction, but to prove it was another matter. Not even the King's warrant would cover the arrest and punishment of Baron Beausire of Sudbury without conclusive proof of his guilt.

"I must have proof," the Judge murmured. Soundless voices, heavy with hate, seemed to whisper back, "Proof—proof— proof," until the curtains stirred as if touched by unseen hands.

◆　◆　◆　◆

The warden read the commutation with relief. "My Lord," he said, "this is evil enough, God knows, but, on my oath, I lacked the courage to see Dame Alice burn."

"I would like to speak with her," John said. "Sir Francis will not intrude upon her now. He knows her less well than I."

The warden hesitated but a moment. "I will escort you myself, my Lord," he said.

When the door of the cell opened, the old woman seated on a bench at the foot of a rough pallet started up. Her face lighted with joy as she recognized her visitor.

That joy did not diminish when she knew what the sunrise would bring for her. She laughed almost gaily.

"I fear it not, my boy," she said. "When you have reached the age of eighty years, you have walked for a long time with Death beside you, and those who know him do not fear him. I spoke the truth when I said I feared only the flames. Tonight will be peaceful for me. Why should it not be, when tomorrow I hope to see many from whom I have been separated for long years?"

They talked quietly of the state of affairs in Somerset. Dame Alice nodded approval when John told of his plan to demand audience of the King.

"I shall take with me the message you wrote Sir Francis,"

John said. "I hope it will shock him to an understanding of what has been done in his name. Your death may save others, Dame Alice."

As he spoke, John realized why the old lady, who had known him all his life and his parents and grandparents before him, had written to Sir Francis in her need. She did not wish to compromise him further, knowing full well that Jeffreys hated him and would on any pretense do him mischief.

Dame Alice smiled. "Had I known it would meet the eyes of the King's Grace," she said, "I had written it more carefully, with more attention to spelling and penmanship."

She added, "The leaf was torn from a book of Psalms," and pointed to a book upon the pallet. "It has been a comfort to me. The Psalmist had great wisdom, and a deep knowledge of God. But I long for a Testament. It is forbidden that books be given the prisoners, or I would ask the warden for one. I would like to read again the words of the Lord, and of those who knew Him best. But it is a small matter. Many of those words are written in my heart."

John thrust his hand into a pocket inside the full skirt of his coat and drew out a little book, so small that it lay within the palm of his hand.

"Take this," he said. "It is the Four Gospels. The print is small, but it is singularly clear."

Eagerly the old woman reached for it. "My eyes have served me to the last," she said, "for which I have never ceased to thank God. Tonight I shall be more grateful than ever."

John heard the warden moving anxiously about the corridor. He knew that he must go. It seemed an awful thing to leave this splendid soul alone now.

Dame Alice seemed to catch his thought, for she said in a voice that rang with courage, even with joy, "John, I regret nothing. There is only an infinite gratitude in my heart. At best I had but a few years, perhaps those burdened with the infirmities of age I have so far been spared. I have had a good life. I go in the sure and certain hope the Lord will not forget that I did what I could, and will weigh that in the balance against my many sins. God bless you. Go now. If it be possible, I would like to lie beside my husband and the children who have gone before me."

"I will myself attend to the matter," John said. "It shall be as you wish."

As he bent to kiss her forehead, Dame Alice put her slender, almost transparent hands on his shoulders. Looking at those hands one could see how old she was, though her face belied it.

"There is no need to pity me," she said. "Tomorrow for me will be a day of happy meetings. Your book will carry me safely through the night."

As John followed the warden down the bleak stone corridor he felt curiously oppressed by the gloom of the Castle. The enormous thickness of those gray walls—beneath one side of which the river Tone slid so quietly—became almost visible to him. He longed for the hilltop wind that always seemed so fresh and pure as he felt it before descending into his own valley.

The White Hart was a babel of voices, a seething mass of faces. As he passed through the common room John heard a man speaking in a low, determined voice. The words echoed in his mind as he ascended the stairs. "My great-aunt, Elizabeth Poole. The Deane brothers. Taunton, New England. Settlers wanted there. What remains to me would fetch sufficient money."

So they were planning to leave England, to seek a freer life in that New England beyond the seas. Elizabeth Poole, a spinster of great courage, had left Somerset many years ago, and with the Deane brothers, Taunton men, and a group from the West Country, founded a new Taunton in New England. One could not blame these men for wishing to follow her.

There was bitter disappointment when Sir Francis disclosed the result of their efforts. After all, Dame Alice had to die. Those who had waited understood at last how hopeless it had been to expect greater clemency.

John was eager to be on his way. He could not tell them that there was nothing tragic in that death, that it was a glorious end to a happy life. He only asked that they would all meet him in this room at nine of the clock on the morrow, to escort the body of Dame Alice with due honor to her home.

For a time John Beausire and Francis de la Warre rode in silence, their men behind them. John felt he was awakening out of a dreadful dream to the reality of day. In less than an hour he would be supping in the Queen's Room with Rosalys, his little love. She knew nothing of the sadness of his errand, and she must not know. This happy day had already been darkened for her. They would be happy together, and he would know that Giles was sleeping peacefully and safely above them.

The twisted face of Jeffreys, as it had looked when he swore to trap and punish those who had helped rebels escape, rose out of the darkness before him, but he thrust it from him, thinking of the firelit, candle-bright room he would soon enter and of how the light would be reflected from the gold hair of the little maid who waited for him so eagerly.

It was not until he had to turn off the road to reach his own Hestercombe that Sir Francis spoke of what had lain like a heavy weight upon his mind ever since they left the Judge's lodging. He pulled his horse nearer to John and said in a low voice that rang with anxiety, "My boy, have a care. That devil hates you. He would glory in doing you a mischief. Trust nobody. He has his own ways of extracting information. God grant your Giles slips the net, but take no great risk to help him do so. I tell you you are being watched."

John smiled. One more hill, and he would descend into his own valley, that place of peace and joy and security.

"Every soul in the West Country is being watched," he said, "I have done nothing that I would not do again."

As soon as he spoke he knew he had unconsciously repeated the words of Dame Alice. He wondered whether, if faced with the price she had to pay, he would be able to say them so boldly. Well, she would have been the first to say that she was eighty, with a happy life behind her, while he was nineteen, with all life's glory ahead.

Sir Francis and his man disappeared into the darkness. The ascent of the Sudbury Hill began. Nicolette quickened her pace, knowing she was near home.

As they entered the deeper darkness of the South Wood on the other side of the hill, descending the steep road into the valley, John thought of the strange isolation of the human soul. Even now, surrounded by grief, he was filled with his own joy, but not because the sorrow of others did not touch him.

They were out of the South Wood now. Far off, deep in the valley, the lights of home gleamed through the trees of the park.

Chapter Three

✦　✦　✦　✦

CANDLELIGHT TOUCHED THE LAST ROSES OF THE YEAR, giving their yellow petals the soft bloom of a moth's wing, striking an iridescent rainbow from the deep bowl of Venetian glass that held them. It gleamed on the polished surface of the table, reflected from silver and crystal, and made of the red-gold hair of Rosalys an aureole of living flame.

Her eyes, which could look as green as seawater, or as coldly gray as a stormy sky, were now black fathomless pools in which were reflected the light of stars.

Watching her, John wondered once again how one so lovely could be real. The ivory satin of her long gown, with its deep, low-cut berthe of shadow-fine lace, was not more silken-soft than her bare arms and shoulders. Clasping the stem of her wine glass in slender pink-tipped fingers, she raised it and sipped the wine.

The light danced down the curls that fell to her waist and touched one of the roses in the bowl, giving it a deeper tint against the whiteness of her hands.

"Captain Pollard's man was here," she said. "He said that tonight there would be a storm, so I cut what flowers I could."

John nodded. Slowly he peeled one of the big yellow pears from the walled garden. Its rich juice dripped to the Sevres plate. He remembered the mournful sound of the rising wind as he rode through the South Wood on his return from Taunton.

He did not want to think of storms, or of Captain Pollard and the flights of his *White Heron,* or of Taunton and the evil doings there. He wanted to think of nothing beyond the carved walls of Queen Catherine's Room.

But the events of the day would not be so easily disposed of. He heard Rosalys tell gaily of the guests who had dined with Mark and Diana, of how she had refused to go down, as if she could now laugh at her foolish fears. John listened, answered her, but the stream of his own thoughts ran on. What an unfathomable mystery was life. No philosophy, no deep knowledge of seer or savant seemed to hold the key to it. It was so easy to condemn a human soul to death, yet what lay beyond, no one knew.

A log in the great fireplace broke apart, and bright flames leaped up, catching the deep undercutting of a carved panel in rosy light. John looked at it intently. In one light the paneling seemed but a formless riot of exquisitely carved trees and fruit and flower; in another, one could see the intricate and perfect design, each panel blending into the next, forming a clear picture of pomegranate trees in all the stages of their growth, from seedling to young tree, from flower to forming fruit, until in the two panels facing the fireplace the ripened fruit hung heavy from the slender boughs, and one pomegranate had fallen to the ground, the seeds ready to sink into the earth to begin the cycle again.

Was life like that? Could one, if one could get near enough to it, or far enough above it, see the perfect design there? John Locke, the philosopher, declared all nature shouted and sang that perfect design. Was it with reason that Dame Alice must die upon the block at tomorrow's sunrise? Was there some inexorable purpose, working toward their own good—toward the growth of their soul—that had driven West Country lads to the horror of the slave ships, and the even greater horror beyond?

Rosalys spoke softly, her eyes wide and dark with remembered fear.

"Perhaps some day I shall learn not to grieve when there is no need for grief, but this evening when you had gone and the sunset made all the valley red, I felt I was drowning in a sea of misery."

A sudden gust of rain beat on the circular window, as if to remind those within that all through the West Country tears were being shed tonight. Rosalys leaned forward and touched John's wrist with her fingertips. She smiled as if she would belittle the evening's anxiety as the fears of a foolish child.

John kept very still, as one would lest an exquisite butterfly that had alighted on one's hand might vanish; then he took both her hands in his and held them tightly. He saw that the smiling lips did not erase the look of haunting fear from her lovely eyes, fear that had returned as she remembered the hours of waiting.

Then, because it was intolerable that she should be unhappy, he did what he had not thought to do.

"Canst keep a secret, little one?" he asked.

A long shining curl fell upon his hand, and smiling eyes looked into his. "Should not a lady about to be married, who is no longer a child, be able to keep secrets?" she asked.

"Well, listen, I will whisper it. But not a word to anyone.

Giles is safe. Today he came in, and soon will be in France with Dick and Hal."

Rosalys rose up, her hands clasped together in joy; tears glittered on her long curling lashes.

"I knew it," she said. "This morning I told Sarah this was too happy a day for any grief, that soon we should hear that all was well with Giles. Oh, I am ashamed of myself. Instead of going down to sing and dance and help Mark and Diana entertain our guests, I moped and wept and worried poor Susan into a dither—more like a five-year-old child than a lady soon to be mistress of a great house—because you had to go again to Taunton for a little time. Tell me—I will keep the secret well— is Giles in Taunton? Is it to see him that you went there?"

John shook his head. "He is not there," he said. "He is nearer home, but that is enough for you to know."

John remembered the look of infinite relief that had passed over the faces of Rosalys' maid, Susan, and Mrs. Allison, the housekeeper, as they had stood in talk at the foot of the west staircase and had seen him enter the west hall upon his return. What was it that they feared?

Fear lay like a gray veil over all the land. People feared who knew not what they feared. He felt that he must break this nebulous thing apart to show its nothingness: when it was clothed in words, it would be seen as mere foolishness.

"Sir Samuel will feel cheated," he said, "for he dearly loves to see you dance. Silly little one, the evening would have passed more quickly had you gone down to dine. What was it that you feared?"

The girl's wide eyes darkened, and the small hands were held out toward him. "I kept thinking that Jeffreys would find cause to hold you there, that perhaps you might not come back, and how would I bear it if midnight came, and dawn, and sunrise, and still you did not come? I remembered that a gentleman from Winchester was held and tried and sentenced to transportation, without proven cause. Susan said that was but an idle tale, but I knew it was not, for Sarah told it to me."

"The trials have made us all nervous," John said gently, "but there is no cause for it. Jeffreys would need positive proof indeed to arrest Beausire of Sudbury. And that he will never get."

"Oh, I know that no harm could come to you, but the time passes so slowly when you are away," she replied.

It was easy to be brave and confident now. Perhaps now that Giles was safe, John would no longer ride abroad for hours, attended only by Frank, for though no one had dared to put it into words, they all knew it was because he hoped to find Giles and bring him to a safe hiding-place.

For the first time since that terrible July morning, when the defeated followers of Monmouth had fled after the battle of Sedgemoor and the first of the Sudbury men had sought shelter at the Court, John felt the cold breath of fear. That she should suffer, or have but the least shadow cast upon the brightness of her life, was a heavy price to pay.

But he reminded himself quickly that the worst was over now, that there was only joy to come. He leaned closer to her, saying, "Soon we shall not be separated at all. At night there will not be the gallery between us. Sometimes it seems to me that it is as long as the road from here to Taunton, and all the pictures ever painted in the world would not fill it."

Rosalys dropped her eyelids shyly: the long lashes lay like black silk fans against the porcelain smoothness of her cheeks, which were flushed with pure color, more lovely than the perfect peaches in the silver fruit bowl. Sometimes, in her own rooms, she, too, had thought the gallery unduly long. Soon she would come as a bride to live in the west wing that had always seemed the loveliest part of the house to her, and from her bedroom window she would be able to look down on her own little court.

She raised her eyes with the candor of a child and said, "I have wished that St. John could change places with St. Luke this year, for in three weeks it will be St. Luke's Day."

John laughed happily. He, too, had thought of that. It had long been a tradition that the feasts of the Evangelists were fortunate days for the Beausires, and whenever possible they were chosen for important events.

"Mark insisted that you should have turned fifteen," he said, "and you will not do so until November. I was too overjoyed to gain his consent for this year to parley further with him—lest he raise further objections."

Rosalys shrugged her shoulders with the little French gesture of her foreign childhood. "Diana will think of me as a child when I have gray hair and six children," she said. "She cannot forget that I am twenty years younger than Mark."

Now that all was settled, John could think kindly even of Diana.

"It is just as well we have to wait," he said. "The tenants will expect a great feast for our wedding. We could not have one with any real happiness until the trials are over."

Rosalys nodded. "John, tell me the truth. I am not a little girl to be saved from unhappy things. I am grown up, and must take my share in whatever comes. Do you really think they will be over soon?"

"I am sure they will," he said. "Then I shall ride to London to see the King and demand amnesty for the fugitives. Sir Francis and Lord Stawell will be with me. There will be nothing to fear. You will have so much to do preparing for our wedding that the time will not seem long. Two weeks, at most, I think. His Majesty will be in better humor when the matter is settled, and I do not doubt he will see how overzealous his men have been."

"Two weeks!" Rosalys exclaimed. It seemed so long a time. But had she not determined to behave as a great lady should? It would ill become the future Lady of Beausire to begrudge her Lord the time to visit his King.

"Well, two weeks will pass, however slowly. The milliners and dressmakers shall come, and my bride dress shall be finished."

John rang the silver bell upon the table. Then he stood up, and taking her hands raised her to her feet.

"It is late, but we will sit by the fire for a while," he said. "We can send word to your Susan to come and play duenna—from the far end of the library."

The time since his return had gone quickly. John dreaded the passing of this day and the coming of the morrow. Yet the passing of the morrow, and every day after it, brought nearer the day of St. John.

It was not a footman who came to take the supper dishes, but the steward, Thomas. He looked so glum that John asked him if all was well below stairs.

The man hesitated for a moment, looking anxiously to where Rosalys stood like a tall white lily against the paneling, her satin dress gleaming like pearls in the firelight.

John caught his meaning. Thomas would speak of Giles and the lad, but dared not.

"Mistress Rosalys knows the great good the day had brought," he said. "I had to tell her. Sarah is the only other soul to know it, though I had to exercise firm self-control not to run shrieking through the house that Giles was safe."

As he spoke John saw how heavily this time of anxiety had

weighed upon Thomas. His always thin body seemed stooped and old in its rich crimson livery. This morning when he had come upon Thomas in the stable yard he had noticed that the steward's hair was now as white as the curled wig without which he was seldom seen.

It was cruel to twit Thomas with reminders of danger. John added hastily, "I have just been telling Mistress Rosalys that this unhappy rebellion will soon be a thing of the past, and we shall all live in peace and joy again."

Thomas picked up a crystal wine flagon and put it on his silver tray. His gloomy face did not lighten. His eyes were fixed upon the two standing by the hearth. Children, they were, unable to grasp the full import of the danger they were in. Cruel, it might be, but something must be done. It was through the little lady he would make his Lordship observe more caution. If she could be made to understand, she might prevail upon him to do so as none other could.

"I trust your Lordship does not hope too much," he said. "For my part, it seems that peace and joy are far from us. Hast heard that Sir Archibald has been attainted, and will lose his lands and all civil rights and be dubbed outlaw and rebel? And he as good an Englishman and as kind a landlord as ever lived in Dorset. And what he did was less than"—Thomas hesitated, then faced the pair boldly—"less than what you have done, my Lord."

John saw the terror that leaped into the eyes of Rosalys. He would gladly have berated Thomas for a craven dolt, but to appear casual and unimpressed would more easily console her. Stepping to the tray which Thomas carried toward the door he took a nut from a dish there, cracked it, ate the meat and flung the shell into the fire before replying.

"Sir Archibald was careless," he said, "and had little wit.

The only place he could think of in which to hide two yokels was under his lady's bed, and she began to screech like a hoot owl the moment the King's men set foot in the house. You forget the secret room of Sudbury, Thomas."

John remembered then what he had disclosed. So Rosalys knew Giles was in the house now. Later, when they were alone, he would tell her how safe he was, and about the poor lad with him.

"I forget nothing, my Lord," Thomas replied, speaking with the freedom to which his years of service—and the service of his forefathers—entitled him. "I remember also that it is said someone in Sir Archibald's own household must have sent word to the King's men, so swiftly did they follow upon the fugitives. 'Tis said his sister—as sour an old maid as ever lived—never forgave him that years ago he would not let her wed where her heart was given, and has waited almost a lifetime to do him harm. She was in the house when the fugitives sought shelter, and they say when they were dragged out, and Sir Archibald with them, she laughed like a madwoman."

John smiled. "In times like these gossip flies fast," he said. "But comfort yourself that I have never done wrong to a soul. I have no enemies, and would trust my life gladly to any servant under my roof or on my lands."

"Any servant, yes." Thomas spoke softly, but he meant his words to be heard. Looking at them, rage and fear almost overpowered him. A better master and landlord never lived. Truly, he had no enemies. And the sweet lass, so soon to be a bride, who would harm her? Well, he for one would hazard a guess that there was one at least who would dare much to stop this marriage.

Thomas had visited the home farm during the evening. Sarah had added fuel to the flames of his worst fears. She, too, distrusted Mistress Diana. She, too, had seen that the sweet, gay girl who had come to Sudbury five years ago had departed and a bitter woman had taken her place, a woman who would stop at nothing to gain her ends.

But he could not say what was in his heart, though Sarah declared fear had driven her to it.

"Why fear, then?" John said smiling. "And there are but four who know that Giles lies here tonight. Now, send Susan to await Mistress Rosalys in the library."

Thomas closed the door softly and went to seek Susan. Only four knew. Sarah and himself were the only ones who could harm those two, and they would defend them with their lives. Thank God, the wind had changed and was set fair for France. Tomorrow night Giles and the lad would be on their way.

The rain beat against the window, the wind cried in the great chimney, but within the Queen's Room all was peace. As they sat before the fire, watching the sparks that flew upward like the escaping spirits of jewels, John felt all sadness and anxiety fall away. He did not want to think any more of those dark questions of life and death that had lately so concerned him; he would sit here, the soft weight of his little love against him, her hair shining gold against the dark silk of his coat, her hands in his, and forget there was grief in the world. Not far away, his good friend, John Locke, was at Sutton Court with their mutual friend, John Strachey, and no doubt hard at work upon his book, which was to be called *An Essay Concerning Human Understanding*. It would tell of many things John Locke had found upon the long road of his own search for truth. It could not tell a truer thing than this, that life and love and home were very good.

It was Rosalys who broke the long silence. Suddenly she

pulled away from him and turned that she might look into his face.

"Why do you take such risks?" she asked. "Is it true what Thomas said, that you have done more to help the rebels than did Sir Archibald and many others who have been condemned?"

John shook his head. "I have no enemies to betray me," he said. That he had not done more he could not say.

Then suddenly he knew that she must understand. He wondered if he could find words to express the thoughts that had come to him as he rode at sunset beneath the oaks, that strange flash of knowledge that the key to all things was at hand, so familiar that it was overlooked.

"I have but done what I must do," he said. "Long ago a Baron of Sudbury promised, for himself and his heirs forever, that the Faith should be kept. Not a faith of church or creed, but the greater faith of the law. Look, there it is, the reminder of that promise."

Standing, he raised his hand to the carved shield above the mantel. The four emblems stood out boldly, and the lettering of the motto beneath them.

"Fides Servanda Est." John repeated the words in Latin, as the Baron of long ago must have done, then in English: "The Faith is to be kept."

There was a strange dignity of absolute honesty about the girl as she answered, "I know. And the Faith means charity, mercy to the afflicted, helping the helpless, which you have done. But I am not brave. I cannot help being afraid. If you were taken from me I should die."

It was strange and horrible to John that she should speak of death. The sense of complete union with her, the assurance that neither life nor death could separate them for long, which he had had for some time now, left him, leaving in its place cold terror of separation. No promised heaven, if heaven there was, could match what they now held or spread a more shining road before them than the road their life would be.

"Hush, do not say such things. It is but the sadness all around us that makes you afraid. Forget what Thomas said. He is old, and the old have death always before them."

Rosalys tried to smile. She wiped the tears from her eyes with her little lace-edged kerchief. "I have forgotten it," she said. "Tomorrow it will seem an evil dream."

It was long past midnight when the sleepy Susan was roused to escort her mistress to the east wing. She straightened her cap and followed them into the gallery.

When the door leading to the rooms of Rosalys had closed, John turned quickly and walked down the gallery again to the west wing. He did not hear another door open, or see Diana standing at the door of her room, a candle in her hand, her dark hair hanging over her shoulders.

Diana watched him go. A sickening excitement shook her. There was something afoot, she thought. It was not for nothing that the girl who loved gaiety had refused to come down to meet the guests.

Slipping back into the withdrawing room off her bedroom Diana paced the floor restlessly. She could hear Mark's steady breathing. He slept soundly. Diana closed the door between the two rooms. She felt as though she would never sleep again.

Fury, searing as fire, swept her. For a long time she had despised John; now she hated him. "It is Mark who should be Lord Beausire," she thought. For sixteen years Mark had been the heir. It was a cruel trick of fate that had taken his heritage from him.

All the dreams she had allowed herself to dream rose up to

mock her in their dying. Mark, as a wealthy peer, would cut a great figure at Court; his name would shine in the history of England. The Duke of York, King now, had always liked his brother's handsome page. He would be a favorite of the King, and honors would be heaped upon him.

If only the things that were being whispered about John's aid to the rebels could be proved! Her own maid, Kitty, had told her it was common gossip that Jeffreys hated his Lordship and would dearly love to prove him disloyal to the King.

Diana came to a sudden resolve. She must know what it was that kept John and the girl up so late. If it were but a lover's meeting, Susan would not have been with them. Was Susan party to the plot? Susan was a niece of Sarah Giles, and would be greatly trusted.

Almost before she knew what was in her mind, Diana was walking quickly and quietly down the gallery. A footman came into it from the little staircase that twisted down into the buttery, and began to blow out the candles. Diana slid into the cedar room. It was dark and deathly still. She waited there until the man had gone, knowing now what she meant to do.

She would see whether John had gone to his bedchamber or was still in the library. If he was there, she would say her little dog, a King Charles spaniel, was missing, and she had come to look for him. Then she would try to trap John into an admission that he had hidden rebels, that he knew where Giles lay hiding.

John went back to the Queen's Room. For some time he stood before the dying fire, looking at the room as if he would impress every detail of it upon his mind forever: the gold brocade of a screen, the ruby glow of the velvet chair backs, the grace of an old carved chest. He was filled with a wild desire to run to the door of Rosalys, rouse her and beg her to come back to him, to stay with him until morning. He could tell her then that there was nothing in all the world but her, that all the beauty of the house, all the richness of the valley, were but a setting for her incomparable beauty, that without her all he loved and valued would be meaningless.

But it would startle her, turn her thoughts once more to fears. It would be better to try to sleep, to meet the morrow bravely, for in a few hours now he would have to set out for Taunton, to do that last service for Dame Alice.

John turned toward the door, hesitated, then went back across the room. He would see if Giles slept, and if not, say a word of cheer to him.

Quietly the panel slid back beneath his fingers. He ascended the little stone stairs. The lamp burned steadily at the top.

Giles was awake, looking at the waning moon that could be seen through the air slit under the eaves. The boy slept heavily.

A long line of moonlight lay like a silver sword across the uneven stone floor. A lamp burned on the narrow stone ledge with the crosses cut into it that had once served as an altar. The light fell upon the two pallets on the floor, the food on the rough table.

The fugitives had eaten prodigiously. John smiled. It was no wonder. For many weeks now they had lived upon apples and pears snatched after dark from garden and orchard, or upon wild berries and nuts. Their drink had been water from the streams they passed.

As he talked to Giles in whispers, John saw it was a senseless thing to keep the position of the room a secret from him. It was as safe with him as it would be with one in the grave. Moreover, should he himself be long detained, it was Giles who would have to get himself and the lad to Thomas in the buttery, to be taken on the next stage of the flight to freedom.

They had been talking of the little homely things of field and farm. There would be no harm in taking Giles down to the warm brightness of the Queen's Room for a glass of wine.

"Come, I shall show you how to open the panel if need be," John said. "If I do not come by midnight tomorrow, bind the lad's eyes and go down to the buttery. You will know the way."

Giles knew how greatly he was being trusted. He tried to say that the secret of the house would be safe with him, but he could not.

A night owl swooping near the eaves cried mournfully as they went down the steps. The silver sword of moonlight had slipped a little nearer to the altar of sacrifice. The boy still slept, his tow-colored hair struck to silver in the lamplight.

In the Queen's Room they drank canary wine together, as they had so often done in the past. John promised Giles a visit from Sarah. She would come to the Queen's Room before sunset on the morrow.

Diana had been sitting in the library for a long time, watching the closed door of the inner room. The chill of night and the storm made her shiver, in spite of the logs that still burned with a red glow. She crouched nearer to them, thinking that it was useless to wait longer: the fire would soon be out and the cold unbearable.

The door into the Queen's Room fascinated her. Slowly she went toward it, opened it gently, and looked into the room.

After the gloom of the darkened library the light dazzled her. Then she saw two figures standing beside the paneled wall, directly across the room from the fireplace. They were deep in talk. She could not hear what they said. She did not need to hear. For John Beausire bent down, the panel slid back, and Farmer Giles stepped into darkness, leaving John alone.

As the panel slid into place and John stood facing it, his fingers still on the carving, she slipped back, silent as a wraith, into the shadowy library.

Though her heart pounded until she could hardly draw her breath, Diana knew she must not pause there. John had not seen her: she was quite sure of that.

"I must think, I must think," she told herself, though she already knew what she was going to do.

The great length of the gallery stretched before her, lost in darkness. She knew she must not attempt to return to her own rooms now, for if he crossed to his own bedchamber, carrying a light, before she reached her door, he would see the glimmer of her white robe.

The dark brocade curtains of the oriel window caught her eye. Quickly she moved toward them and slipped into their heavy folds as John came out of the library door.

The light of the candle he carried cast a pale glow about his grave young face, burnished the dark red of his hair. As he crossed the wide space, terror seized her. What if he should come to the window and part the curtains to look down into the court below? Often she had seen him standing there on the way to his own room.

But he did not pause. She heard the door of his bedchamber close. With a gasp, Diana pressed her face to the mullioned windowpane. The lead pressed into it, but the coolness calmed her. She sat very still.

Images swept across her. She called upon them to strengthen her resolve.

There was that day of which Mark had told her. He had been sixteen then, the handsome and flattered heir to a great estate. He had been in attendance on the King, and the letter he had opened carelessly seemed but another of the jokes that had been tossed from one to another in the brightly lit little room where the King sat at cards. It was from his uncle, Lord Beausire, and told him that, after so many years, there was a direct heir at Sudbury.

Mark could have had his choice of heiresses, but the years had passed, while she, her childhood darkened by poverty, grew to womanhood in the desolate farmhouse that was all the Civil Wars had left of her father's heritage.

A rich marriage had seemed the only hope. A distant relative of her mother's seeing her beauty and grace, had taken her to London and obtained for her a position at the Court as one of the ladies of the unhappy Queen.

The rich marriage had been offered all too quickly, but within a few days of that betrothal, she had seen Mark Beausire ride out to the hunt, had prevailed upon an older woman to seek him out, and from that day, they had both known there could be but one end.

Slowly Diana walked up the gallery toward the dim glimmer of the lamp that burned all night above the main staircase. She lashed herself into a firm belief that John was a traitor, that a loyal subject of the King could do no less than inform the King's men of what was hidden behind the panels of the famous Queen's Room of Sudbury Court.

Other images rose up to fight feebly against her resolve. She remembered that day soon after her marriage, when, almost penniless—Mark pursued by creditors—they had waited at the inn on the road to Bath for the reply to Mark's letter to his young cousin, the fourteen-year-old boy who had just come into his inheritance.

Diana thrust from her as a dangerous thing the memory of the relief and joy the reply had brought them, of its prodigal generosity, and of the well-filled moneybag sent with it by a Sudbury man who had ridden hard.

Of the arrival at Sudbury she would not allow herself to think. She dared not remember that this traitor she was about to deliver to the most merciless judge in England's long history was none other than that eager boy who had stood upon the terrace watching for their coming, and had welcomed them royally, only counting himself fortunate that he had their company.

When she reached her own rooms the doors of her mind were closed to all happy memories. Coldly, with a calm cunning, she considered the best means to achieve her end.

A letter was too great a risk. It might fall into the wrong hands. So few could write, it would be easy to trace it to its source. There was no one she could trust to go upon this errand for her.

Diana entered the dressing room off her bedroom. Mark still slept. She did not pause beside the bed. He might wake before she could return, but risks had to be taken.

It was as if other hands dressed her, so fast did her cold hands fly in their task of collecting the garments she would need and fastening them upon her slender body. She thought grimly that five years ago she had never had the hands of a tire-woman about her.

The great hall seemed immensely vast and empty. Every nerve recoiled from the walk across the rain-drenched park to the inn at Sudbury St. Luke, where Captain Moffet, in command of the soldiers placed in the valley, lodged.

The catch of the French window in the small morning room was stiff, her fingers cold and numb, but at last it yielded, and Diana stepped out upon the terrace, a gust of rain spattering her face.

Fear leered at her from every darkened bush and tree. The eaves of the great house dripped fear, the shadowy outline of the gables seemed to waver before her as she turned, fighting the desperate desire to return to the house.

What if Moffet should no longer be at the inn? What if she should be recognized? More terrible than all, what if the discovery of the thing she was about to do cost her the love of Mark?

But as if beating in upon her from an outside source, a sea of hate and covetousness broke upon her. Biting her lips until a thin stream of blood trickled over her white chin, she stood for one more moment irresolute. Then a frenzy of determination seized her. If Mark should never be Lord of Sudbury, if all this richness be forfeit to the Crown because of what she would expose tonight, let it be. John Beausire and Rosalys should not have it.

Gathering her cloak about her she ran. Soon the stone of the terrace gave place beneath her feet to the gravel of the driveway, then the grass of the park, as she fled directly toward the gate that opened onto the Sudbury road near the inn.

The moon slipped from the clouds again. Diana stood, rooted to the spot, terror clutching her like merciless hands. An immense tower of darkness loomed up before her. It was as though a tangible barrier had been flung across her path.

"It's only the trees," she realized after a long moment, seeing that in her flight she had come to the first of the four great oaks of Sudbury. She went on swiftly, but something forced her to look back. Voices she could feel, not hear, were calling her. The immensity of those four trees seemed to blot out the whole world. For a moment she felt that every living thing in the valley, every bird and beast, every human creature, even the inanimate things, the earth and the stones and the river, the dark old tower, were calling her to go back.

But there was a stronger force dragging her on. The moon

shed a dim and eerie light on the splendid house high on its ter-races. It was a prize worth fighting for. In a moment she was running over the wet grass again.

The inn looked a house of the dead. It did not seem possi-ble that there had ever been or ever would be life in it. Diana seized the big brass knocker boldly. The sound of it seemed to boom and echo, then died away into a more deathly si-lence.

At last a window above opened. A head was thrust out, and a man's voice called out impatiently, "Who's there?"

It seemed to the woman upon the doorstep that someone else was speaking when she heard her own voice answer boldly in the Somerset drawl she often imitated to amuse her husband.

"A message for Captain Moffet. It is urgent. Send him quickly."

At last heavy steps could be heard descending the stairs. The door opened and a tall man stood there. It was too dark to see his dress, but she knew it was not the landlord or any man of the village.

"What do you want?" he asked gruffly. "Come in and show your face."

Diana stepped back, choking. This she had not reckoned with. She drew her hood more closely about her face, terrified that the whiteness of her hand would be noticed, and the rings she had not thought to remove.

"There is no need." Desperation made her voice firm. "I have word of rebels. Will you hear it?"

Captain Moffet, none too pleased at being wakened at this unearthly hour, stretched out a hand toward the hooded fig-ure. Her voice was soft. Perhaps she was a comely wench. She pulled from him and half-turned as if to fly.

"As you will," he said. There were many wenches. They were easier to come by than the good gold he would get for a fine haul of prisoners. In the six weeks he had been here to watch Sudbury Court his vigilance had yielded nothing, and the Judge was getting daily more acrimonious in his censure. Colonel Kirke was hinting at demotion and disgrace.

"Speak up. Where are they?" He spoke sharply.

In a voice, low and distinct, not slipping for a moment from that carefully imitated drawl, she said, "I am a servant at the Court, loyal to the King. I have watched for weeks. Only his Lordship knows. It is his doing, his only. His cousin knows nothing. Behind the library there is another room, called the Queen's Room, in which there is a secret hiding-place behind the panel facing the hearth. It is behind the thirteenth panel, counting from the door. Giles of St. Luke's Farm is hidden there tonight, and there may be others also."

"How long will he be kept there?" Moffet could scarcely credit the story. Beausire was young. This was perhaps some maid he had fooled with, mad with jealousy now he was to marry, trying to make trouble for him. But it was worth talking to her. Should it be true—should it be true! Bright visions of promotion, money, honors, flashed before him.

She would have gone then, but the Captain reached out and grabbed her. He was wide awake now. Of course it was true. How else had the Sudbury men got away? Beausire was at most of the trials. If he would part with the money he had paid in fines, would he not also take risks to help the escape of men who had no hope of getting off with a fine? He had said openly that when the first fury passed the King would be forced by public opinion to grant an amnesty.

"Listen," the Captain said roughly, his hand still on her arm. "I've half a mind to keep you here, under lock and key, until I prove your words. You said it was behind the thirteenth panel, counting from the door of the Queen's Room. There are many rooms there. How shall I know that room?"

"It is round, round as a ring, paneled in wood so dark it is black by candlelight." Diana gasped out the words, then with a convulsive movement broke from his grasp, and before he realized it, was running like a hunted deer down the path to the road.

The Captain did not attempt to follow her. Almost before she had covered the few yards to the gate he was at the foot of the stairs, shouting to the ostler who slept in the kitchen to get up and saddle a good horse. He ran up the stairs, thinking that he had failed to ask the wench how the panel opened. No matter: a few blows from the halberds of his troopers would settle that.

All he needed now was his men and a warrant to search the Court.

The clock in the tower of St. John's Church struck three as Diana cowered into the shadows to let a horseman pass her. He bent low over his horse's head, spurring it to an even greater speed. She knew it was Moffet, on his way to Taunton. The hoofbeats became fainter and fainter, the forms of horse and rider merged into blackness. Diana leaned against the gate, gathering strength to go on toward the safety of the house. She could feel neither hope nor fear, gladness nor sorrow. She knew only that now no power on earth could undo what she had done.

With every gust of wind elm leaves fluttered down. A hunting owl, also out for prey, hooted mournfully, as if it grieved with a bitter grief.

The curtains of the morning room had blown out through the open window and were wet and draggled. Diana did not notice them, nor did she shut the window when she had entered.

It seemed but a moment before she was in her room, in her night gear again, lying beside Mark. She felt quite sure none had seen her go or return.

She lay until daylight, sleepless, numb. Then she rose and went to the window and looked down on the terraces strewn with leaves, the borders and parterres filled with broken flowers whose glory of color had gone. It was the first day of autumn, that one day in the year when it is felt that summer is dead.

Chapter Four

✦ ✦ ✦ ✦

THE RHYTHMIC CLIP-CLOP OF HORSES' HOOFS BECAME louder and louder. Rosalys stirred, opened her eyes and saw the windows were filled with the gray light of early morning.

"Mark leaves early for the hunt," she thought drowsily as the hoofbeats broke into irregular sound. A shout of command seemed to ring through her room.

The pale silk curtains swayed gently. One by one the familiar objects in the room greeted her awakening. It seemed a long time before the thing she was unconsciously trying not to realize broke upon her mind.

She sat up suddenly, small and slender in the big bed of French gilt, with its elaborately carved tester and hangings of rose damask. There was no eluding the knowledge now, no slipping back into the peace of dreams.

"No huntsman ever shouted in such a manner," she thought, and as the words formed in her mind, there was a thunderous knocking below the window, and a hoarse voice cried, "Open, in the name of the King."

Again came the heavy sound of the great iron knocker, again the demand to open.

The girl leaped out of bed and ran to the open window, looking down at the wide space between the terrace and the front of the house. It was filled with mounted troopers, their horses moving restlessly, their faces indistinct in the half-light.

A chill wind blew upon her but she did not feel it. Fear that was physical anguish clutched her, making her unable to move or cry out, leaving her mind clear to grasp this awful thing, to realize that the King's men had come to the Court as they had come to so many lesser houses, to search from garret to cellar; that somewhere within the house Giles lay hidden, the boy with him; and that it was John who would be called to account for the sanctuary offered hunted rebels.

The massive front door of Sudbury Court had opened now. Leaning from the window, Rosalys caught a glimpse of the frightened face of a lackey, a boy in a long linen coat, the big cloth with which he had been waxing the floor of the hall still in his hand.

The troopers were streaming in, while others who had just ridden around the curve of the drive were spreading out as though according to a prearranged plan to ring the house with a mounted and armed guard, through which it would be impossible for the most desperate man to break.

Slowly she turned from the window. The tasseled bell pull beside the bed seemed very far away. The floor was no longer an expanse of deep rose carpet but an abyss of darkness that was rushing up toward her, a sea of darkness through which she must find her way to reach the bell and summon Susan.

Then suddenly Susan was beside her, her round freckled

face with its pert snub nose curiously white, the ends of her linen fichu not tucked in, her cap askew, the ribbons of her slippers unlaced.

"Get into your bed, mistress, you'll be catching your death of cold," the woman said, and putting a plump arm around the slender shoulders drew her to the bed, smoothed the pillows, and with a quick and determined movement lifted her and laid her on them as if she were a child again.

"Susan, they've come," Rosalys said, surprised at the sound of her own voice, low and normal, not rising to a scream.

Susan's reply was aggressively cheerful, though she hid her hands that could not stop trembling.

"And why not? I'll warrant that it's bread and meat they want, with as much good ale as Thomas will offer them thrown in. With all those good-for-nothing soldiers eating their heads off at the inn, it's small wonder if there is no provender there. Their Captain would know there is always food and drink for all comers at the Court."

Rosalys fixed her eyes upon the maid's face. Dear Susan, she was trying so hard to be brave! But it was no use to try to pretend. Men seeking hospitality would not come at daybreak, or pound upon the door, demanding it open in the name of the King.

"They have come to search the house, Susan," Rosalys said. "Bring me my clothes quickly, I must dress and go to his Lordship."

The ribbons in Susan's cap bobbed cheerfully. She was almost beginning to believe her own suggestions, in spite of the abject terror on the faces of the six boys who had been waxing the hall and the gray face of Thomas as he looked down from the gallery.

"Maybe they have followed some poor fool who used what

little wit he had to seek protection from his Lordship. If the King had sense it's to Bedlam he'd send these rebels instead of to death or prison. Only God knows what made men follow that ill-begotten brat of Lucy Walters and his late Majesty— though God also knows he was beautiful enough to make any woman who saw him want to follow him."

Susan rattled on as she dressed her young mistress in a flowered taffeta morning robe. The first hour of the day was usually a happy time, for his Lordship, who would have been up for a long time and already have ridden to one of the farms or talked with Giles, would visit his cousin, and plans for the day would be made.

Today there would be no visit. This would be a grim business, and there was little doubt it would be all his Lordship could do to prevent a hanging at the end of it.

As Susan combed her hair and tied up the curls with a white ribbon, Rosalys watched her own face in the mirror as though it were the face of a stranger. The pale lips were set and did not tremble. She had hopes her voice would behave as well.

At first it had been hard not to cry out that Giles was hidden in the house, hidden in the secret room of Sudbury Court, but now, with the overwhelming relief of a desperate and exhausted swimmer who feels at last the earth beneath his feet, she felt strength flow into her. She would behave as was seemly, with dignity and poise, not as a terrified child who was aware of the danger of this search and could not conceal fear.

"I will go to the west wing and seek his Lordship," she said calmly. "He is sure to be there, receiving the commander of the troopers in the library."

That it was his friends he liked to receive in the library flashed into her mind as she crossed the room. Susan was before her, to open the door, smiling bravely, her unruly hands hidden beneath her apron.

These men were not his friends. What were they then? Last night John had said he had no enemies.

"No enemies, no enemies." As she crossed the gallery Rosalys repeated the words under her breath as a talisman, a desperate effort to cling to that misty hope that good would be rewarded with good.

It was when she saw Diana that her composure threatened to desert her: she came perilously near shrieking to John to come.

Diana was standing by the balustrade of the gallery, looking down into the hall. Her face was a frozen mask, her eyes sunken black holes. Her hands, clasped on the carved rail, looked frozen, too, as if they were of marble, and would be a part of the carving forever.

"Diana." Rosalys spoke in a hoarse whisper, but Diana did not stir or answer. Rosalys was beside her now, seeing what she saw.

The hall below seemed full of troopers. They stood stiffly, waiting the word of command that would send them hunting through the lovely peaceful rooms like hounds upon the scent of prey.

Raising her eyes to the staircase, Rosalys saw John. He looked at her and smiled, as though he had sensed her presence as he walked calmly down the wide stairs. He passed the curve under the window, and the light caught his hair for a moment. Rosalys thought of the red leaves in the wood through which they had ridden—when was it, not yesterday, but the day before, or was it long, long ago that he had turned to smile at her before he jumped his horse over a gate, and she had seen the light catch his face and hair so? Today—tomorrow, perhaps, would they ride again through the autumn woods, sup together in the Queen's Room, with the firelight red upon the dark walls?

John was dressed in somber black, a silk so rich that it was as heavy as cloth. A great collar and cravat of dead-white starched Dutch lace made his slender face seem a deeper ivory. He wore deep cuffs of the same lace, carried heavily embroidered gloves. The jewels in his sword hilt gleamed as he moved. There was a splendid dignity about him that had no trace of arrogance.

The Captain of the troop held a parchment in his hands. As Lord Beausire stood upon the last step he unrolled it and read from it. Rosalys recognized the man's thin dark face with its hawk-like nose and pointed black beard. That was Captain Moffet. For weeks he had lodged at the inn, his men scouring the valley by day, prowling about the woods and fields by night. The innkeeper, an unwilling host, had pointed him out to her.

Mark burst out of his room. Rosalys turned when she heard the opening of a door, but Diana continued to look at the staircase.

Mark was not fully dressed. He was flushed with anger. He wore no wig, though he kept the fashion and seldom appeared without one. His own dark hair was hastily dressed.

"The fellow has a warrant." Mark leaned over the gallery, the words coming from him as though he were shocked or surprised. "The King will make amends for this insult before the year is much older. I declare they intend to search the house for fugitives."

Diana did not answer immediately. She looked as though she had not slept at all. She seemed intent on hearing what was being said below. She turned her burning eyes to Mark and said in a choked whisper, "What can they do?"

"Nothing," Mark replied sharply, with defiance in his tone. He was far from sure of what he said. "They will not find anyone, of course. John is not such a fool as that, though God knows he has given ground for suspicion. He and I must ride at once for London. The King must hear John before Jeffreys has time to make his excuses for this outrage."

The dark shadows beneath Diana's eyes made her face look as though it wore a sardonic smile.

"She is afraid for Mark," Rosalys thought, watching her. Diana was about to speak again, but the voice of the man reading the warrant ceased, and he turned and shouted a word of command, his voice raised and clear now.

Diana swayed as though she would faint. She recognized that voice. She would remember it until she died. It had once said roughly, "Come in and show your face. What do you want?"

Mark held her. "There's nought to fear," he said. "Come, we must finish dressing. We must appear before these louts with dignity. John was ready for them, but he always rises at cockcrow."

Mark turned to his sister and said gently, "Dress, child. This foolery will soon be over." He looked down again into the hall and said, "They go first to the west wing. It is known Lord Beausire has his private apartments there. Do they think he has rebels hidden under his bed?"

John still stood upon the last step of the stairs. The troopers were going through the doorway into the corridor leading to the west wing. When they had all passed through, John and the Captain followed them.

Diana tried to fight her way through the black mist that enveloped her as her maid, Kitty, fastened the dark red silk which she knew would accentuate her pallor. She had no will to ask Kitty for a lighter dress.

Through the awful night, while she had waited for the King's men, all her frenzy of hate and jealousy had burned out. She did not think now of anything save Mark. Her whole being was one agonized fear that Mark would be involved. Forgotten things had come to mind to torture her. Mark and James Scott, Duke of Monmouth, had been close boyhood friends. In age they were but a year apart. Mark would have all to gain from a new King, John nothing. It was well known that Monmouth had offered lands and peerages to more than one gentleman who had followed him. It was Mark who would be suspected. What if John should deny all knowledge of the fugitives?

Panic was rising now to that madness she had felt a scant half-hour before the troopers had come, when she had all but run to John, to warn him to get Giles and any others who might be hidden out of the house, tell him, if need be, what she had done. In the dusk of early morning they could have slipped away.

But she had not gone to John. Something had pulled her back, some return of last night's determination to see the thing through to the bitter end. Now it was too late for any warning.

Mistress Allison, the housekeeper, white-faced and trembling, came to the door. She told Kitty that the troopers were ascending the west staircase. When the girl returned to the dressing-table where her mistress sat and told what she had heard, Diana rose stiffly. She went out to the gallery. Mark and Rosalys standing there seemed shadows. They also knew, for without a word they turned toward the west wing.

As they passed the oriel window the light caught Mark's sword hilt. Diana thought of the flash of a falling ax. Someone, long ago, who had seen King Charles I, the martyr King, die upon the block, had told her of that sudden flash of the headsman's ax, the little splintering sound that follows the dull thud of its fall.

They entered the library. It was full of troopers. Diana knew she was going into deadly danger. Should she be forced to speak, her voice might be recognized. But she could not turn back. A horrible force drew her on. She had to see that panel broken down, to see the fulfillment of the thing she had done.

The cold courage of despair began to flow into her. If the worst came, she would ride night and day, fling herself at the feet of the King, confess what she had done, and why. She would save Mark—only that mattered in all the world, to save Mark. Desperately she began to think of those at Court who would help her obtain immediate audience with His Majesty. Oh, dear God, she thought, if it were but the late King— kindly good-humored Charles, who had so greatly admired her—with whom she would have to plead. She tried to thrust from her the memory of the hardness she had more than once seen upon the face of the man who was now King.

The door of the Queen's room was open, guarded by two troopers with drawn swords. Haughtily Mark walked past them, and Rosalys and Diana followed him.

There was an air of heavy gloom over the circular room. Never had the black paneling looked so somber. The fire was dead, gray ash where last night there had been warmth and light and color. The faint scent of the yellow roses was a poignant reminder of the happiness that now seemed so far away.

John stood before the fireplace, as he had stood when he talked to Thomas with such confidence that all would be well. Only four troopers were there with the Captain.

As Rosalys stepped to John's side, he was speaking to the Captain, who stood by the door as if uncertain how to proceed: "This room has no other entrance. Do you wish to search the chimney and the chests?"

Captain Moffet did not answer. He eyed the two chests, which were indeed large enough to conceal a man apiece, then turned sharply and began counting the panels, beginning from the door.

Though she was standing so close to him, Diana did not seem to see the man as he tapped panel after panel. She stared straight ahead, as if her whole mind were fixed on something she saw beyond the round window. Her hair and body seemed to have vanished into the panel before which she stood, leaving only a white mask of a face with two dark holes in it through which the black wood could be seen. Her hands were clasped behind her back.

When the Captain stood before the panel facing the hearth, Rosalys knew John was about to step forward. With an almost unconscious movement she gripped his wrist with cold fingers. He took her hand, and for an instant they stood there, hand in hand, knowing that something unbelievably awful was about to happen.

Captain Moffet raised his hand, pointing to the center panel. Two troopers advanced and raised their halberds, but John Beausire stepped forward, saying "Stop," in so firm and authoritative a voice that they drew back.

Then he spoke to the Captain. "This paneling was the gift of a Queen of England. We value it very highly. It is quite irreplaceable."

Mark crossed the room quickly, as if he would use force. His face was flushed with anger, his hand on his sword hilt. As he approached, the Captain gave a sharp command, the men raised their halberds again, and crashed them down against the delicately carved wood.

Thomas came running into the room, pushing past the troopers at the door. His hands were raised as if in anguished appeal. A great hole gaped in the panel: Captain Moffet thrust his hand through it and found the bolt he sought. The broken panel slid back.

Rosalys heard Mark exclaim, "Good God!" in a strangled voice. The Captain stepped through the opening, followed by the two soldiers, who had thrown their halberds to the polished floor and held pistols in their hands.

Several troopers came from the library with heavy tread. The doorway was completely blocked now. The steps of the men who had gone through the panel sounded loud as they descended the stone steps.

"I will save them yet," John said, so low that only the girl beside him heard. At that moment a wild cry, like the shriek of a hare when the hounds close in, rang through the room. It beat upon the window and seemed to echo around the dark circle of the panels.

No one spoke or moved. They seemed petrified, waiting for the end of this awful drama.

Heavy steps were heard again, and the boy Jerry, his straw-like hair a wild mop, his face the color of ash, was flung through the opening. Then came Giles, his face dead, as if despair had already seized him. The other trooper and the Captain followed.

Rosalys knew now. The secret room of Sudbury had been found. She did not flinch as Captain Moffet approached. He faced John and said in a loud voice, "Lord Beausire, you are under arrest. You will be tried for aiding rebels and enemies of the King to escape justice."

John released her hand. She felt separated from him by an immeasurable distance. His voice seemed to ring through the room, though he spoke quietly. "I am a Peer of England. I claim the right to answer for this to His Majesty the King, and to His Majesty only."

The pale, terrified eyes of the boy Jerry turned toward him, as if new hope had been kindled by the sound of his protector's voice. Thomas the steward approached the Captain with the firm step of one who knows what he is about. His thin voice was steady.

"Sir, I beg you will hear me out," he said, looking into the coarse face that was already flushed with triumph. "Sir, I alone am responsible for this. My father and my father's father were stewards of Sudbury Court before me. From the time of the Interdiction my forefathers had known the secret of this room, and it was passed on to me. Giles offered me money, land that I coveted more than money. His Lordship knew nothing. I beg you to believe this is true. I will go with you willingly, to answer for my crime."

A long look passed between the steward and Giles, who stood with a trooper on either side of him. As the farmer spoke, a light seemed to be shining on his weatherbeaten face: suddenly he had come to life.

"Tha-at is true—"

He would have gone on, but Moffet cut him short with an angry shout of command. The troopers grasped the prisoners and pushed them roughly toward the library door.

Quickly Moffet considered this new aspect of the matter. It might well be true. True or not, if he accepted what might have been a prearranged story, he could probably get for himself a considerable sum of money from Lord Beausire. He was about to decide what he could ask, how best to make his meaning clear, when he seemed to hear the voice that had yelled at him in the still dark courtyard of Taunton Castle as the troop gathered, only a couple of hours before.

"Arrest Beausire. He is responsible for the escape of dozens. Now I have him."

No. Jeffreys would not take a steward as sole victim, even after he had hanged the farmer and the boy.

The Captain realized that Lord Beausire was speaking to his steward, that tears were running down the old man's face.

"It is no good, Thomas," John Beausire said. "But I shall always remember what you tried to do. This is a matter to be settled between His Majesty and myself. Now, go and tell the servants that I ride tonight for London."

Then he turned to the Captain, saying coldly, "I am ready. There is no more to be said."

"I also shall ride to London," Mark broke in furiously. "The King's minions will learn that they overstepped their orders when they broke into Sudbury Court."

The Captain had a mind to arrest Mr. Beausire on the spot but decided upon the more cautious plan of obeying his orders literally. He would not even take the steward into custody. The rebels themselves would of course be condemned with the barest pretense of a trial. He was not at all sure that Jeffreys would dare imprison Lord Beausire, who might be able to convince him that he had the right to answer to the King. The Captain was beginning to think the whole business smelled of trouble, and to wish himself out of it. If the King did stand by Lord Beausire, it was quite possible he would himself receive blame rather than praise.

"There is no time to lose," he said sharply. Jeffreys had ordered this and would have to see the matter through. The prisoners were hustled into the library.

Diana had slipped from the room. When she saw Giles, with death already in his face, her courage had failed her.

Mark turned toward the door. When he saw his own body servant standing white-faced in the library, he shouted to him to prepare for a journey.

John stood beside Rosalys and turned to Captain Moffet, who appeared uncertain as to the next step. Indeed, the business was getting more difficult every moment. A man of the rank of Baron Beausire could not be dragged off to jail like the farmers and small shopkeepers who formed the bulk of the haul of prisoners.

"There can be no objection to my being alone with my cousin for a short time," John said. "I will follow you to the library." Thinking the Captain hesitated, he added, "There is no other door but the one your men guard. You need have no fear I shall escape."

"Five minutes—no more," Moffet replied curtly. It had occurred to him to question the servants. Should he hear the voice of the woman who had come to the inn he would recognize it. He was curious to see her, to find out what had prompted her action.

Terror rose up before John like a great black wave, threatening to engulf him as the door closed. In five minutes he must say to Rosalys all the things he would have said in perhaps fifty years. He knew now, with an awful foreknowledge, that separation, long and terrible, loomed before them. The broken panel seemed to be the door to illimitable darkness that he must enter alone; the darkness was drawing him with a ghastly and irresistible power; it was the evil he had not known until the first of the trials.

But at the sound of her voice the dark illusion vanished. "You will not be long in London?" she said, her voice shak-

ing a little in spite of her desperate effort to appear unafraid.

"In a week I shall be home," he replied. "I would refuse to
appear before Jeffreys, but a firm stand in Taunton is the only
hope for Giles and that poor lad. I will offer any amount he
likes to name as a fine for them."

He stopped speaking. How many minutes had gone? Why
was it so terrible to leave her, if in his heart he believed he
would come back?

For both of them he must show courage. One hint of fore-
boding from him and the hours—perhaps days or weeks—of
waiting would be unbearable for her. He took her in his arms
and smiled.

"My little love," he said, "there is no need for fear. I will
come back. We shall be happy in this house. All our hopes will
be fulfilled. Wait for me in peace and patience, remembering
only that we have tried to keep the Faith."

Desperately they clung together in a last kiss. There was a
heavy knocking on the door. John turned as it opened, and
said, "I am ready, Captain. We will go."

Together the three walked through the library, up the long
gallery. John was glad the Captain did not go down the west
staircase. He had an overwhelming longing to see the great
hall once more, to go out of its stately doors proudly, a Peer of
England, unafraid, knowing himself as loyal a subject as any
King ever had.

Rosalys knew that nothing mattered now but that she find
strength to smile. All the beauty of the past had been swept
away, as by a tidal wave of terror. All the future loomed an
abyss of darkness. There was only this moment, while she still
saw him, and she must not shadow it by showing the grief tearing her very soul.

Taking her hand, he kissed it, saying, "We shall meet again soon," and then he went on with the Captain.

She knew she must not follow. Slowly she went to the balustrade and looked down, her eyes following him as he descended into the hall.

Mark was with him, talking angrily. The hall was full of troopers again. They had bound the hands of Giles and the boy behind their backs.

When the great doors had opened and closed again she still stood there. Susan called her gently to come to her own rooms, but she did not seem to hear.

Suddenly she turned. Susan thought that never had she seen her look so lovely.

"Mistress Giles is coming here this morning," she said. "Send her to me at once. She will be in great distress. I must comfort and encourage her."

The cavalcade, with each of the bound prisoners riding between two troopers, was nearing the great gates. John Beausire they did not dare to bind. He rode his splendid Arab horse as proudly as ever.

The gates were closed, and the command to halt was given. A figure dashed from between the elms, hair flying, cloakless, in spite of the chill day and drizzling rain.

Pity tore at John when he recognized Sarah. If she could but have been spared this!

With desperate courage she threaded her way between the restless horses and stood by her husband's side, leaning against his horse, her face upturned to him.

Roughly a soldier pulled her away. For an instant she seemed about to struggle, but John had come up beside her.

He knew there was but one thing to do, to draw upon that well of love and service that was within Sarah. Leaning down to her, his hand on her shoulder, looking at her as if he must impress every line of her dear face upon his mind forever, he said, "Fear nothing, Sarah. The King cannot refuse a hearing to Beausire of Sudbury. Go to Mistress Rosalys, stay with her until I return. Promise me you will not leave her."

Sarah fought for words. She pulled down the hand that held the reins, kissed the heavy glove with all the love of her unhappy heart on her trembling lips. Her tears made little dark stains on the leather. The babe she had nursed, the boy who had loved her, the man, were all there, looking at her through those hazel eyes.

"I promise, my Lord," she said. "I will not leave her. I will care for her until you return."

The gates swung open. The word of command was given. There was no time to say more. Sarah did not return to them. She walked up the drive toward the Court.

❖   ❖   ❖   ❖

The clocks of Taunton's many church towers struck six. John stopped pacing the narrow room and looked up at the small barred window through which he could see a patch of darkening sky. The slow hours had dragged away, and with them had ebbed the hope that he would be allowed to attend the trial of Giles and the boy.

Soon after midday the door had opened and a jailer had thrust in a loaf of bread and a pitcher of water, vanishing before he could be questioned or even seen. Though John had not eaten since the previous night, the bread remained untouched. Now he took the pitcher and drank some of the brackish water.

Like the ceaselessly turning blades of the waterwheel of

Markscombe Mill, hopes and fears revolved in his mind. Desperately now he marshaled the hopes.

Mark would have done what John had asked in those moments when their horses came together on top of Sudbury Hill. He would have obtained the bag of gold pieces Master Hare, the Taunton attorney, kept for emergencies, and would be ready with them at the trial of Giles and the boy. The avarice of Jeffreys was well known, and few farmers had been able to pay the extortionate fines he asked.

For himself he had no fear. Jeffreys could give play to his cruelty by keeping him thus confined, ignorant of the fate of a man whom all knew to be dear to him. But he could not keep him indefinitely. Sir Francis, Stawell, Phelips and others had gathered in Taunton to escort the body of Dame Alice to her home. Mark would have burst into the room at the White Hart, with the news of the daybreak happenings at Sudbury Court. One or more of them were no doubt already far upon the road to London, to lay the matter before the King.

But the King might refuse to receive them. He had refused audience to many who came from the West Country on missions of mercy.

That might mean the Tower. They would not dare keep him for long. Mark could always get an audience with the Queen. It was but two days past that Mark said he had heard on excellent authority that Mary of Modena had sold pardons to several and had made a pretty penny. Mark, whom she liked, would know how to present the matter to her. The Queen was a shrewd woman. She would know how dangerous a thing it would be for the King to deal harshly with so highly placed a subject.

Then the fears crowded in. John tried to fight them off, but, deciding that it was hopeless, accepted them for close scrutiny.

He had known from the moment he had dismounted in the courtyard of Taunton Castle that Jeffreys was going to squeeze the last drop of satisfaction from this matter. The hate of the evil-faced Judge had seemed to drift about him like a fetid wind, though he had seen none but the troopers who searched the Court.

It had often seemed during the trials that the Judge was possessed by a demon of cruelty, by some force infinitely stronger than his puny self. Giles might even now be dead.

The thought of Giles brought the anguished face of Sarah before him. This second day of October would have been a day of bitter waiting at the Court. With all the strength of his will John tried to send his own confidence to those two who would be together. Rosalys and Sarah. He knew that, once the first shock had spent itself, Sarah would be strong and comfort the little maid.

The light was going fast. Surely a jailer would bring rush-light or candle. But another hour dragged, and it was quite dark now. Strange thoughts came to him.

The secret of the position of the room must have been known to some family on the estate since the time of the Interdiction. There must have been a background of truth in the thing Thomas had so bravely tried to say, but he would stake all his chances of life and freedom that it was not Thomas who had let the secret slip, even had he known it, which he had not.

Who was it then? Something deep within him recoiled from the matter. He knew he had not the courage to face the knowledge, should it be given him. He must, for his soul's peace, think that it was some stranger who had by chance known the secret. During the Interdiction many had heard Mass there. Perhaps some of them had left the valley and the estate, and, thinking no harm, had told the story to their children. Why, a descendent of one of those secret worshipers might even be among the troopers.

It was hours later when a heavy step sounded in the corridor. John sprang up eagerly. A key grated in the lock, and he found himself looking into the face of the warden who had escorted him to the cell of Dame Alice. The man's face was stolid and unrecognizing. Before John could speak he stepped aside. The light from his lantern threw about the doorway a circle of light, into which stepped a mean-featured little man John recognized as a clerk of the court, whose name was Harris. He had dealt with this man several times when paying fines for prisoners.

Harris bowed stiffly. "I have to inform your Lordship that the case of the stable boy, who declared he had no name but Jerry, has been heard. In view of the undoubted fact that he is half-witted, his Honor has been lenient enough to pardon him upon payment of a fine of three hundred guineas. This fine was paid by your Lordship's cousin, Mr. Beausire, who was present at the trial. The boy was freed immediately and left with his benefactor, who promised to stand sponsor for his good behavior."

The man ceased speaking. His shifty eyes took in every detail of the prisoner's attire and appearance. He knew that the fine had been preposterous, that the boy would hardly earn so much in a lifetime, and that it had been paid with the money of the man before him.

Though he loved money with almost the same greed as his master, it was not Lord Beausire's money or exalted position that caused the envy tearing him now. From the first day he had seen the young peer in court he had envied him his perfect body. Had his Lordship been born the fifth son of a poor apothecary, as he himself had been, life would have been good to him, the eyes of women would have turned toward him as they did in the crowded courtroom of Taunton Castle when he stood up for the defense.

A surge of relief swept over John. Mark had been right, and had played his part well. It was money Jeffreys wanted. He would ask five hundred guineas or more for Giles. Never would he be so welcome to money. For that life, no price was too high.

"Was not the fine for Farmer Giles also paid?" he asked. The thought that it might have been so high that Mark had to seek Master Hare again flashed through his mind. Giles might well be still in the Castle. The trials for the day were over hours ago.

"Of that matter I know nothing," the clerk replied.

As he spoke, the warden stepped from the corridor into the room, hesitated a moment, then said in a low strained voice, "My Lord, it is better that you should know. Farmer Giles was tried, convicted and hanged within an hour of your coming to the Castle. Mr. Beausire was very greatly angered when he was told of it. No opportunity had been given him to plead for the man."

John did not hear what the clerk said, but he saw the cold anger in the man's face. For some reason Jeffreys had not wished him to know of this.

He would have thanked the warden for telling him the truth, but they had gone. He was alone again, the key turning in the lock.

Anger shook him, a fury of rebellion at this insensate cruelty. Now it had indeed touched him. Giles was part of the very fabric of his life.

How awful was the dark mystery of death! At every turn of life, over all its brightness, that shadow lay. One could, like

John Locke, spend a lifetime studying all that humanity had ever learned or thought about it, and still know nothing. Was it possible that Giles had vanished, disintegrated as one of the bright leaves did after it drifted down from the flaming autumn tree that had given it life?

All the high courage, the pure goodness, that had been Dame Alice—had that gone, too, into a fathomless abyss of nothingness? Did such an abyss wait for the bright beauty of the little maid, for the love that was between them and seemed now an imperishable thing?

Night and rain came down over the West Country. The rain-lashed River Tone slid beneath the Castle Tower drearily. Rain pattered upon the rooftops and cobbled streets of the fear-haunted town. John knew it would be streaming down the windows of the Court. With all the strength of his being he longed to be with the watchers there.

It was nearly midnight when the key turned again in the lock. Judge Jeffreys had decided to send for Lord Beausire and try him secretly. This was no sudden impulse. All day he had been thinking of the matter, weighing the risks he would be taking if he gave him an open trial. There would be an outcry over all Somerset when it was known that he had been sentenced. The execution of the De Lisle woman had caused sullen mutterings in street and tavern. Dearly as the Judge would have loved to shout his sentence before a packed courtroom, he knew he dared not do it. Yet what was done must be done quickly. Mark Beausire and several of the most honored men in Somerset were already upon the road to Whitehall, seeking, demanding, audience of the King.

Moffet had gone to fetch the prisoner. Tonight he would break his proud spirit, see him cringe before the threat of block or stake. Tomorrow, before the trials commenced, he would summon a few witnesses, men who could be trusted, and condemn him to death.

The Judge twisted his long thin fingers together as if they closed about the neck of a hated enemy. He knew he would not dare to carry out the sentence—Beausire was no helpless and kinless old woman—but he thought with infinite pleasure of how the proud young fool would suffer while he lay in prison. With sufficient evidence—the Judge's eyes slid toward the clerk Harris, who sat writing in a corner of the small room where they sat—with conclusive evidence, the King might well be angered into keeping him in prison for a year or more.

Last night it had been John Beausire who had won the duel between them for the amelioration of the sentence of Dame Alice. It was not the first of such duels he had won. The curious twitching of the limbs that sometimes seized Jeffreys gripped him now. Fiercely he longed to kill John Beausire. Suddenly he knew he could not face him in this small room: he must look down on him from the Judge's bench in the great hall. He laughed aloud, wildly, violently, and saw the startled clerk leap up like a rabbit from its hole.

He shouted, "Give me my gown and Judge's wig. We try a peer of England for his life."

Harris robed the Judge, wondering what in God's name was coming now, and followed him into the great hall.

In the voice of an old and tired man, utterly weary with the cares of office but determined to do his duty to the end, Jeffreys said, as he seated himself in the high Judge's chair, "Harris, we have many letters written by his Lordship, have we not?"

"Many, your Worship," the clerk replied. Instantly he knew the thought crawling in that dark mind. His own talent for copying handwriting exactly was to be employed again. Incriminating documents would not be lacking when this matter came before the King.

"I think we should receive his Lordship in state, do you not, Harris?" the tired voice went on.

"Certainly, your Worship," Harris replied obsequiously, knowing that some bestiality was being planned. What was it? There could be no trial—not even the miserable pretense of one that had been accorded Dame Alice. There was no jury, there were no witnesses for the defense.

The Judge seemed deeply sunk in thought. "Tell the guard we receive Lord Beausire here," he said at last, but as the clerk hurried to do his bidding, he called him back.

"Captain Moffet has gone for the prisoner," he said, with a curious little smile upon his thin lips. "There are flares in the courtyard, are there not, Harris? I should not like so illustrious a young man to stumble in the darkness."

"Yes, your Worship. The court is brightly lit." Harris turned again toward the door. He knew now why he had been instructed to tell Lord Beausire that the boy had been freed. It was to raise his hopes for the farmer, Giles, whom he would see swinging from the gibbet as he crossed the courtyard. The shock would unnerve him. He would be less cool and collected when he stood before the Judge. A man who had been hanging for hours was not a pretty sight, particularly if the victim happened to be a loved and trusted servant and friend. As he gave his message to the guard at the door, the clerk hoped that the warden, who had had the courage to disobey orders and tell the truth, would have the wit to cover that distorted face.

When John Beausire entered the hall, surrounded by armed men, he felt curiously alone, surrounded by illimitable darkness. He looked up at the figure seated above him.

The Judge leaned forward, his sunken eyes narrow slits beneath gray brows. His old and weary voice had a tremor in it. "It is a sad thing to find a Baron of England a traitor to his King," he said sorrowfully.

John answered clearly, with the quiet dignity to which the old hall had many times been witness.

"I am no traitor. All knew where I stood when the son of King Charles would have seized the crown."

"Rebel!" The cold voice cut like a lash, then rose to a scream. "Son, you said! Loyal men say natural son."

"There are none in England who do not know the parentage of James Scott."

Back and forth question and answer went. There was not one of the guard who did not wish himself out of this, yet none thought for a moment that Jeffreys would dare do more than impose a heavy fine at tomorrow's legal trial.

"Why did you hide traitors if you are loyal to the King?" The Judge's voice had a ring of evil triumph in it.

Instantly the reply came. "I hid Giles because he was my friend. He sought only to bring in his hotheaded sons. He bitterly regretted their stand for the Protestant Duke. I was willing to answer to the King for him, to stand surety for his future loyalty. As for the boy, to condemn him to death for what he had done would have been as senseless as to have tortured and killed a dog which followed his master to the field of battle. It is beneath the dignity of His Majesty to show harshness to such as he."

The two looked at each other long and intently. Fury rose in Jeffreys because he had no proof this man had helped others to escape. He was filled with hate for John Beausire and at the same time feared him. The young peer would stand up just as boldly before the King, protesting the cruelty and injustice of the trials.

The word of Lord Beausire would not be treated lightly. Who better than he could make the King understand that the sums of money paid into the Treasury were but a small part of the amount collected? A thousand voices, high-pitched as the squeak of a bat, seemed to beat about his ears, crying, "Break him, break him, or he will break you."

If only he dared to do to this man what he had done to others of less exalted station for the same crime!

"What say you in your own defense?" he asked, waiting, hoping for one of those strange flashes of intuition to come to him and show him how he could safely dispose of the prisoner before him.

"That Giles was very dear to me, and I who knew him best knew him to be no rebel. He was the friend of my childhood, the helper and counselor of my manhood. As I have said, the boy was too pitiful a thing to punish. He is not able to understand what he is accused of."

The Judge looked down in contempt at the clear-cut ivory-pale face. A Baron speaking of a farmer as friend and counselor! The prisoner went on speaking.

"The King of England is named Defender of the Faith. England is a Christian country. The Faith of Christ demands that we forgive our enemies, deal mercifully with sinners, help all who are in need. Had these men been a danger to the realm or to the King, I would have given them over to a just Court."

Jeffreys knew now that at a public trial he would not dare condemn John Beausire. "Hang him, out of hand," the voices whispered. "Send forged letters to the King, proving him guilty of having conspired with Monmouth."

But if John Beausire were hanged, all Somerset would rise in fury. The King might well turn on his Judge in anger. It was not safe to do that.

"Make him suffer—make him suffer," the voices urged. Sweat rolled down Jeffreys' face, blinding him. He wiped his eyes. When he could see again, a small dark man in the garb of a seaman was standing behind Captain Moffet. He was looking at the strange scene in unconcealed astonishment.

Judge Jeffreys felt the cold flash of decision strike him. This was Hewitt, the master of the slave ship, the man who had shown him how to make a fortune out of the trials.

He beckoned to Harris. The clerk stood beside his chair, head bent to catch a whispered word of command.

"I would speak with Hewitt," the Judge said.

Before the shipmaster reached his side the whole thing was clear. He would send a letter to the King, telling him he had found Lord Beausire so clever and determined a plotter against His Majesty that he had felt it necessary for the safety of the Throne to get him out of England until the matter could be more fully considered. Should he be imprisoned in Somerset or even in the Tower there would be open rebellion throughout the West Country, so popular he was.

Jeffreys smiled. He knew how to touch the unpopular King, who above all things feared men that could draw people to them. It was the beauty and charm of James Scott that he had feared, not his birth or the reforms he promised.

Hewitt was beside him now. The Judge did not speak. He saw troopers looking sidelong at each other, trying no doubt to see if the same thought had struck them all. Judge Jeffreys went on thinking about his letter to the King. His eyes turned to where the clerk sat, his pen scratching upon parchment. He would say it was Beausire who had encouraged the Duke to make his wild venture, that there were proofs he had been promised rich rewards by the new King should the rebellion prove successful. Had not the Beausires received their lands and honors from a Conqueror, who was also of illegitimate birth? The King was curiously superstitious. He would note the circumstance.

The last glimmer of doubt flickered out. He turned to Hewitt.

There was a whispered conversation between them. The slave ship lay off Watchet. Hewitt said he must sail before dawn, or he would miss the tide. He had his own reasons for wanting to get clear of England without delay, but these he did not feel called upon to discuss with his patron. He merely made it clear that he could not wait for the prisoners who would be condemned to slavery at tomorrow's trials.

The warm feeling of invulnerable power that came over Judge Jeffreys when he was about to condemn a man took possession of him. He felt that he had placated something within him, that he was immensely strong, unassailable in his power. He leaned forward until he almost lay across the table before him. His words fell like hailstones.

"John Beausire, you are a traitor to His Majesty, James II, by the Grace of God, King of England. I condemn you to ten years' transportation to the West Indies."

"A death sentence," the Judge thought triumphantly. "He will not survive the voyage." Hardy laborers and soldiers died like flies in the hold of the slave ship.

There was a silence in the hall that made the breathing of the soldiers sound like rustling leaves. Why had he said ten years? He had a horrible feeling that he had not, that it had been said for him. Some force greater than himself was using him, twisting him as it would. He wanted to cry out against it but could not.

The sense of power passed. He felt weak, limp, utterly consumed with hatred for all who dared oppose his will or question his power.

"Take the prisoner away," he shouted.

John walked firmly, his head held high. He could think clearly. Mark would already be well on his way to London. If he had already been transported when Mark returned with the King's pardon—which was hardly likely—the pardon would follow. How swiftly would the *White Heron* fly upon that errand!

He felt a strange power, as if he were immeasurably stronger than the thing that had come upon him, and he knew a deep inner satisfaction that he had been called upon to stand for his beliefs and had not faltered. He knew he was willing to suffer whatever might come. There was only one thing he dared not do—think of his little love, waiting for him, perhaps in ignorance of his fate.

In the room in which he had waited all day he was stripped of his clothes, and made only a momentary protest when a trooper wrenched off his emerald seal ring. It was useless to expect courtesy or fair treatment. The ring was too valuable and rare a thing to disappear, and could be bought back. He was convinced he would again wear it.

The warden entered the room as the troopers left it. Anger rose in him when he saw Lord Beausire dressed in rough fustian, with peasant boots upon his feet. Outside in the corridor the soldiers stood waiting.

John stepped forward quickly, and in a low voice asked the question he had been waiting all day to ask.

"Dame Alice?" he inquired, with a last hope, though there was nothing to hope upon, that her sentence had been commuted.

The warden leaned close. "She died at eight of the clock,"

he said, "calm as if she had been setting out for church. One stroke and, as she had said, it was all over. Several gentlemen, Sir Francis de la Warre, Lord Stawell and others, claimed her body and took it to her home. As your Lordship entered by the west door, the cortege was leaving by the east."

There were more steps in the corridor, not the firm tread of soldiers but the shuffling of hurried feet. The warden raised his hands as if in horror, took a small object from the wide sleeve of his coat and thrust it toward John. Hurriedly he whispered, "I got this from her. She blessed you for the loan of it. That I return it to you was the one request she made of me."

John seized the little book of the Gospels. As he slipped it into his rough coat he thought of his name written in it. John Beausire, Sudbury Court, Somerset. This was a tangible link with reality.

Four husky bearded men in seamen's jackets stood in the doorway. The warden vanished. John felt a rough cloth thrown around his face; his hands were seized and tied behind his back with cords which cut into the flesh. He was pushed into the corridor, on and out into the dark courtyard, where the wind tossed the flame and smoke of torches around a gibbet. The warden might have spared his trouble and the risk of dangerous censure. John Beausire, gagged and blindfolded, did not see the swinging figure with its carefully covered face.

The smell of the sea, clean and fresh, was getting stronger. John felt that he would wake soon from the awful dream of lying in dank and dirty straw on the bottom of a jogging cart.

The journey seemed to have been going on for hours. At last the cart stopped. He was dragged from it and rushed forward between two men, he knew not where. He heard the sound of sea water lapping against a ship's sides.

Someone tore the bandage from his eyes. He looked into the

face of the seaman who had entered the Castle Hall as he stood before Jeffreys.

"That's him. Heave anchor," the man said, and as he spoke two sailors thrust their latest prisoner down a narrow ladder into darkness.

The dimly lit hold was full of wild-faced, desperate men, who crowded to the foot of the ladder as the hatch opened and closed again. They were of all ages and classes. A cry went up from an old man in a far corner when he recognized the newcomer.

"So that spawn of Satan has got Lord Beausire, too," he shouted. "God damn his accursed soul in hell!"

Almost immediately the creak of ropes and whine of winches, the movement beneath them, told the prisoners that the slave ship was putting out to sea. A muffled howl rose and was flung back by the low roof; then it subsided into a shuddering groan.

John felt for his book. It was safe. He knew that while he had it he would not lose courage. "I am John Beausire, of Sudbury Court, in the County of Somerset," he repeated.

Again he had that sense of power. He knew that whatever came, he would find strength to meet it. He would live, for he could not die. The things that had seemed so dark in the nightlong talks with John Locke, in his own musings during the bitter days of the trials, were now crystal clear.

He knew he was a living immortal soul, invulnerable even in death, for death was but as a passing shadow.

Time had no reality. He would return. When seemed of little consequence. Rosalys would be there waiting for him, for she too was an immortal soul, bound to him by a tie no power could break.

He lay on the floor of the hold, looking up at the one lantern that swayed with the rocking of the ship. How foolish to talk of death as a dark and awful mystery. Death did not exist: it was a shadow created by men's minds.

A numbness crept over him, as though he had stepped unknowing into the waters of Lethe.

◆　◆　◆　◆

As he slept, deeply, peacefully, Captain Pollard on the bridge of the *White Heron* watched the slave ship beating out to sea in the gray light of dawn. He raised his hand and made a vow that, on the very day the King granted the amnesty that a furious people would force from him, he himself would sail to bring back those slaves, sold to enrich Jeffreys and his hangers-on. The mate, coming up behind him, muttered a curse as he also recognized the ship. They stood wondering whom the black Judge had sold now and how long it would be before justice overtook Hewitt.

Eastward, over the land, the sky was faintly flushed with red. The slaver was a dot that dissolved into the western sea.

Chapter Five

✦   ✦   ✦   ✦

MARK HAD RIDDEN HARD ALL THE GRAY NOVEMBER day. With every mile his dread of this homecoming grew greater. When at last he stood before the blazing logs in the hall, he could think only that he had not known how terrible it would be.

Thomas, standing at the door with upraised hands, mutely imploring some word of hope, had been brushed aside with a curt, "I could not see his Lordship."

It had been a momentary relief that Diana was alone by the hearth. At least for a few moments more he would be spared the sight of that ivory mask of a face, framed in red gold, with deep eyes like storm-darkened sea water, that had watched him mount six weeks ago for his ride to London.

It was still believed at the Court that John was in the Tower, awaiting trial or the King's pardon. Mark stepped forward and kicked a log until the fire seemed to blaze in Diana's tortured eyes.

She knew something awful had happened. Mark had

barely touched with his lips the hand she held out to him. Not once had his eyes met hers.

"He knows," she thought. "John saw me at the door of the Queen's Room. They know who betrayed him."

Still Mark did not speak. She said, her voice hoarse with her effort to keep it steady, "What word of John?"

Surely Mark had seen him. Monmouth, condemned to death in the Tower, had been allowed to see his wife and a few friends. A prisoner of John's rank would not be accorded less courtesy.

It was a stranger who turned slowly toward her. As they stared at each other Diana knew that if John were dead, the man she had loved, gay, careless, happy Mark, was dead also.

He did not look at her as he spoke. He turned again to the fire.

"He was convicted of treason, of plotting to kill the King. He has been attainted, deprived of his lands and titles."

Again Mark kicked a log with his mud-splashed boot. Diana felt the whole world one vast roaring flame. She had ruined them, she thought wildly; she had dragged Mark and their children down as well as John. Mark's words came to her from a great distance as he said, "As next of kin, I inherit. The King is no thief."

Gasping, Diana sank into a chair. "Mark inherits. Mark is Lord Beausire." She repeated the words silently, as if she could not quite grasp their meaning. She tried to realize that all she had snatched at was hers. Mark was Baron Beausire of Sudbury, one of the richest peers in England. The splendid old house, the great estates, were his. They would belong to his son after him.

But no realization came. She felt that if she turned her head she would see John walking down the great staircase with calm dignity, as he had gone down to meet his doom. There was no sense of triumph, only an intolerable fear that Mark knew, or would one day know, what she had done.

Of course John was dead, beheaded in the grim Tower of London, but she had to hear Mark say it.

"And John?" she asked at last.

The reply, spoken harshly, curtly, as though Mark loathed the words he said, struck her like a blow. She had not thought of this.

"He was sent to the Indies. Ten years' transportation. The slave ship. For him, that is death."

"Yes, death," she said. "John is already dead."

She had to know more. Every word was a horrible effort, but the effort had to be made. "Did you—see him?"

Mark turned to her. His face was flushed with the intense heat of the fire. It looked haggard, old. There was a new quality of bitterness and fear in his voice.

"No. He was not sent to London at all. I tried all the means I had to get an audience with the King, but was told he would see none from the West Country. At last—three days ago—her Majesty consented to see me. Lady Allingham had begged the favor on her knees. The Queen was cold at first, but she softened when she spoke your name. She told me that Judge Jeffreys had sent to the King letters written by John to Ferguson, one from Monmouth to him, and a letter from Grey to Ferguson, naming John as their great hope in the West Country. Her Majesty showed me that John's guilt was undeniable, but promised to do her utmost to obtain an audience for me. This she did, late that same night. His Majesty was greatly distressed. He has become old, hard and bitter. He is no longer the man we knew as Duke of York."

Mark stopped speaking. For one moment he was on the

point of telling Diana the whole truth, of the cringing clerk he had visited in response to a queerly worded message, and the story he had heard from the fever-devoured man who had forged those letters, of the written confession so eagerly offered him.

That strange scene in a squalid lodging rose up before him: the dying man, burning with the jail fever he contracted in performing his duties, the triumphant screech of his voice as he begged, holding his confession in shaking hands.

"Take it to the King. Save as fine a gentleman as ever lived with it. Say Harris the clerk is beyond the power of Jeffreys now, so he dares to write truth."

A flash of green fire, cold and brilliant, had dropped from the folded paper to the floor. Stooping to the grimy wood, Mark had picked up the ring with which the forged letter to Ferguson had been sealed.

He had barely regained his lodging when the King's messenger summoned him to Whitehall. As he dressed hurriedly for that audience, he had tried to think. Tonight a man sent by the King might speak with Harris. Tomorrow no man would: he would be silent forever.

The confession and the ring had been in the pocket of his gold satin coat. He had not withdrawn them. . . . Diana spoke, but he did not hear her. He heard the voice of the King, conferring on him the titles and lands of his attainted cousin. He had known then, as those words were spoken, that he would not offer the evidence of that confession to His Majesty, that he would count the hours until the dregs of the wretched clerk's life dripped away. Twelve hours, the apothecary had said, twelve hours at most, and probably it would be less.

Diana repeated her question fearfully. Was it the fatigue of the long ride that made Mark so strange?

"But he was gracious to you, was he not?"

Mark stirred then, but he did not look at her as he spoke. "Yes. He spoke of my long service to his late Majesty, of his own conviction of my loyalty, saying but for that he would have sequestrated the estates. Jeffreys had acted upon his own responsibility, so clear was the evidence. He had unlimited power to deal with rebels. John must have—" Again Mark paused, but the words had to be said. He knew now he would never tell Diana. "He must have left England the day he was taken. Certainly it was not later than the following day."

It was a relief to have told part of the story. Mark fingered the dark-brown curls of his wig, touched the rich braid on the sleeve of his Saxe-blue riding coat.

Diana thought dully, "Ferguson. Who was Ferguson?" Then she remembered. He was the Scottish minister who had been with Monmouth, the man who had written the Duke's "Declaration," which had been publicly read and posted over all the West Country. Ferguson and another Scot, Fletcher, had come to the Court to see John, who refused to receive them. Grey was another active supporter of the Duke's cause.

Something even more terrible than her own guilt was seeping into her mind. She could no longer feel she was alone in guilt. Her voice was sharp with the horror rising within her. "Did you not protest to His Majesty that John was innocent of these charges?" If only Mark would say that he had.

Mark replied sullenly. "How could I? Had I not seen rebels taken here, known of the great sums he paid in fines, of his constant endeavors to help fugitives escape justice?"

As if she had been present when the King of England received Mark Beausire, she knew he had not protested. He had not tried to defend John, though he knew the bitter injustice being done. She stared at him as though her eyes would read his mind. She saw the stranger again, and knew that hence-forth the only bond between them would be their unconfessed guilt.

"Did you not think the letters might have been forged?"

Mark turned to her angrily, as if he could not bear more, but he had not the strength to leave her. "Jeffreys believed them genuine. He obtained them, probably from the same source as he obtained the knowledge of the secret room. Ferguson, Grey and Fletcher were beheaded weeks ago, a few days after Monmouth, as were nearly all the adherents of the cause. The evidence will stand. There are none to gainsay it."

Terror drew Diana on to probe still further into his mind. "Who could it have been? Who knew the position of the room, or that its very existence was more than legend?"

"At the time of the Interdiction many must have known of it. Hundreds heard Mass there. The secret was passed down in some family."

Perhaps he did not know. Diana was certain that there was only one thing to do now, only one alternative to madness. Mark must believe, she must herself believe, all the valley must believe, that John was guilty. Every small happening that implied it must be magnified. There had been strange comings and goings at the Court since Sedgemoor. Twice John had spent the night at the Plume of Feathers at Minehead. On returning from a voyage, Captain Pollard had ridden to the Court even before going to his home. Sir Francis and others had warned John that Jeffreys hated him with a bitter personal hatred.

He had never shown interest in courts or kings. It was but natural that he should have thrown in his lot with the simple people who had risen for the Duke. He was bitterly opposed to many of the new taxes, and no more than a week before the Rebellion burst upon the West Country, had spoken of raising a deputation of gentlemen to ride to London and protest to the King against the Hearth Tax, that two shillings exacted each year for every hearth in a house. He had paid it himself for his own people and had been angry when he saw houses built with only one hearth because the dwellers there would be too poor to pay for more.

The mist about her began to lift. She felt sure now that Mark did not suspect her. It was true that many knew of the room at the time of the Interdiction. Soon all would believe that John had been attainted justly, as she was beginning to believe it.

"Mark," she said, forcing her voice to the right note of pity, regret and firmness. "Mark—"

But before she could say what was in her mind there was a cry from the staircase, a rush of light flying feet, a flash of pale silk against dark wood, and Rosalys was running across the hall to her brother.

Diana saw Mark turn and then draw back as if he cringed before the girl. She knew that she must be strong now—or break Mark's will to take what had been offered him.

It was Diana who told the story, not daring to look into the pearl-white face but thankful that there was no outcry.

She spoke quickly in her effort to be calm, knowing that here was one who would never believe John guilty. She was also aware that here was no frightened girl, but a woman, strong with a courage that bordered on despair.

Choosing her words carefully, Diana tried to break the final horror gently. "There was no possible doubt about the evidence. John has been—transported—for ten years. He has been attainted by the King."

Still there was no sound. Mark sat still, his face shielded by his hands, his broad shoulders hunched in utter despondency.

Without a word Rosalys moved to his side. She grasped his

hands, and their eyes met. The still whiteness of his sister's face was more terrible to him than any wild outburst of grief. She spoke as if it was only from him that she would accept this thing as true.

"You mean that John has been sold as a slave," she said. Her voice was high and clear, and pierced Mark like the point of a dagger. He nodded: he could not speak.

"He has been robbed of all his lands, of his rank, of all that was dear to him, because he tried to shield a man he has known all his life, and a weak-minded child, from the cruelty and injustice of Judge Jeffreys."

Mark did not reply. So she knew about the slave ship. Why should she not know? All the West Country spoke of it in whispers of horror and loathing.

"The King does not see it so," Diana said. She meant to make her voice bitter and regretful, but it rang with the stony hardness that was beginning to freeze her very soul. "He sees John only as a dangerous rebel, able and anxious to stir up others against the throne."

Diana looked away from the clear eyes that were turned upon her.

"John was no rebel. The evidence, if such there was, was forged. Why, I do not know. Some day it will be known."

After Rosalys had spoken, a violent trembling seized her. Her voice strangled in her throat when she tried to speak again. Watching, Diana thought she would break now, but a moment later she turned to Mark again with a controlled urgency.

"We must get Sir Francis here, and Lord Stawell, Sir Samuel, and others. The gentlemen of Somerset must protest this wicked thing. Sir Edward Phelips will stand with us. Mark, send for them now. Frank must ride at once with a letter to Hestercombe. Write, Mark, write now, bid Sir Francis come to us before dawn. There is no time to lose."

Rosalys stepped forward to grasp the heavy bell with which servants were summoned. Quickly Diana put her own hand upon it and drew the girl away. She knew this courage was being dragged up from the depths of a tortured being, and it frightened her. The child loved John so much that she could forget her own despair in the need to fight for him. Diana did not know whether it was shame or wonder that she herself felt at the sight. Or was it fear?

Rosalys was still speaking to Mark. "Will you be able to draw upon John's money while he is away?" she asked. It infuriated Diana that she spoke only to Mark. Did she know or suspect anything? That fear would always be present. Her determination to fight the sentence must be met now. Mark might be weak, but she herself would never be. Rosalys should be made to understand what attainder meant.

"Rosalys," she said, "you do not understand. Mark is now Lord Beausire. The King was generous enough not to sequestrate the estate, but to allow it to pass to John's legal heir, as it would have done had he died."

"As—it—would—have—done—" Rosalys gasped as if she could not force herself to repeat those last words. She turned her great eyes to her brother, to Diana, then back to Mark, as if desperately seeking hope or comfort from him. Silence hung like a heavy veil over the hall. Even the fire seemed to be dying. With a sigh, as if the words were torn from her, she went on: "had—he—died."

Then, with a bitter cry, she flung herself down beside Mark, her green silk skirts shimmering, her shining head bent down on the dark brocade of the chair arm. For some minutes she lay there, as if mortally wounded. Diana wanted to go to her, but she dared not.

Then Rosalys lifted her head. There were great dark shadows beneath her eyes. With what appeared to be a great effort she stood up and looked at Mark steadily.

"So you accepted the inheritance," she said, "knowing John to be innocent, as loyal a subject as ever a king had." There was more wonder than anger in her voice.

Mark turned to her furiously. "What would you have had me do?" he shouted. "The evidence was absolute, I tell you. Should I—after six hundred years—have let the name die out, the lands be seized by the Crown and broken up? No fight or protest could save John from the consequences of his deeds."

Rosalys did not reply. She was looking out across the shadowy spaces of the hall. When she spoke it was not to them.

"John is innocent," she said. "There must be a way of proving it. He is strong. He will live; he will come back. Love is stronger than death. He loves this place—and me—too much not to come back."

Then, without looking again at the two by the hearth, she walked slowly across the hall.

It was hours later when Sarah Giles entered the room where Mark and Diana sat. She knew what news he had brought. It had been told her in gasping sobs.

Diana half rose. "Mistress Giles," she said, turning her eyes from the widow's face.

Sarah asked that the thing she had heard be repeated. It was Diana who again briefly told the story.

Sarah looked at her unflinchingly.

"That is all, Mistress Giles," Diana said, in a tone of curt dismissal.

The reply was sharp and clear, "It is not all, Mistress

Beausire. I have no belief in saints. They went from England long before I came into it. But I believe in the gospels a Lord of Beausire promised long ago to honor. I believe that because that promise has been kept, there has been luck and happiness here for long years. And if Lord Beausire was betrayed by anyone of this house, there will be a black curse upon it, bringing death untimely, sorrow and loss, until the wrong is righted."

Diana tried to speak with calm gentleness, to appear unafraid. "You speak wildly," she said. "Betrayal is a foolish word. No one believes in curses now."

Straight and tall the country woman stood before them. "I believe in curses," she said, "upon whosoever sent Lord Beausire to his death, sent his little love to death also, for the child will die if he does not return shortly. Something within me tells me murder has been committed, and that he will not return."

Diana was aware that though the woman might never be able to prove who had betrayed John Beausire, she knew it was the wife of his cousin, the new Lady Beausire. They stood face to face, and fear and loathing stood between them.

"I am going to care for the little maid," Sarah said. "Susan cannot do enough for her now. While she lives, I will be with her."

There was no asking permission to stay—just a simple statement. They knew that they would not dare deny her hospitality at the Court, though Diana shuddered at the thought of seeing that ravaged face daily. Sarah left the room without a curtsy.

Long after Diana had gone to her room Mark rose. He did not follow her, but went to another room in the east wing. He had no will to ring for his man, for candles and necessities for the night. He could not stand the thought of a familiar face. Better to lie down on the unsheeted bed and try to sleep.

With a vague idea of seeking lamp or candle he went to the gallery. There, huddled against a door, he saw a dark figure. He started violently.

The figure rose and seemed about to run. Mark recognized the boy Jerry, whose fine he had paid and whom he had brought with him from Taunton. He remembered telling Thomas to find him occupation in the house.

"Here, lad," he said. "Find me candles."

Jerry scuttled down the gallery. He returned with candles. Like a faithful dog he followed Mark into the room.

"Take off my boots," Mark said, seating himself in a chair.

The boy obeyed. He looked up at his defender adoringly. This was the one who had poured gold coins on a table, who had taken him from that awful place. The memory of the other, with the flamelike hair, was dim and misty now. This Lord was a reality, to be served and worshiped.

Jerry obeyed. He fetched hot water, soap. He obtained from Mark's own man the things asked for.

An odd thought struck Mark. Here was one who could be trained into a tolerable body servant. He had not known John. There would not be a silent reproach forever in those pale eyes.

"Jerry," he said, "you shall be my man."

Jerry smiled. He felt the heavens had opened. This mighty Lord was being gracious to him.

"I will serve you faithfully, my Lord," he said. He did not need to add, "I will love you, too."

Mark saw that in his eyes. It pleased him. He knew the time was coming when he would need that love, and all the devotion Jerry could give.

Chapter Six

❖ ❖ ❖ ❖

MISTRESS ALLISON STOOD AT THE HEAD OF THE NARROW staircase that twisted up from the buttery to the gallery. She leaned against the door to steady herself, taking a firmer grip on the silver tray she carried. On the tray was a heavily chased lidded cup, containing the warm posset she had prepared with her own hands.

Tears slid down her lined old cheeks. As she watched the little maid walk slowly down the darkening gallery, she knew that all her possets and strengthening foods, all Sarah's ceaseless care, were quite useless.

With a sense of blinding shock—though they had been saying it in the servants' hall for a year now—she knew that the girl was marked for death.

The red-gold hair looked redder now against the marble whiteness of the face, which was so thin that the lovely modeling of the bones stood out sharply, and the eyes were unfathomable pools of grief, dark and shadowed.

"God of mercy," the woman murmured, as the sound of the

faltering steps died away and the glimmer of the white figure disappeared into the shadows, "for a thousand nights, more than a thousand, she has gone at dusk to the west wing to sit for a while in his Lordship's rooms."

Sarah Giles, her hair snow-white now, followed quickly, almost running, as if she feared to leave her charge alone in those memory-haunted rooms.

In the library the fire burned brightly, all the lamps and many tall candles were alight, but they could not chase away the heavy gloom. The tick of the clock, the crackle of burning wood, the wind in the chimney seemed to be murmuring the words that still rang in the ears of the girl who listened.

"Three years—three years."

Desperately she tried to fan the last flicker of hope to life again. At first it had burned brightly. The King would hear the true story, he would grant a pardon, John would come home. The wedding gear had been made ready, laid away in folds of fine linen in a great chest.

Then it became evident there would be no wedding on the day of St. John. Well, St. Mark's day was in April: it would be then.

At the turn of the year another hope died. Sir Francis de la Warre, waiting in London for an audience, was curtly ordered to return to Somerset, there to collect the fines imposed by Judge Jeffreys. Sir Francis refused to have any part in such injustice. He returned, not having seen the King, and was in disfavor at Court.

Hope flickered then, but soon the spring came, with its primrose-starred lanes, daffodils blowing their gold, buds bursting on the trees, the first filmy veil of green on hedge and branch. On a day when all the world was vibrant with new life, Sir Edward Phelips pulled up his panting horse at the great doors of the Court. He shouted in his joy as he waved a paper, and hope flared with a brilliance that lit the world as he read and explained the amnesty signed by the King two days past, the pardon for all prisoners and fugitives of the Monmouth Rebellion.

The *White Heron* put out to sea, flying toward the western horizon with incredible speed.

Diana had explained that the attainder would not be annulled, that should John return, he would be landless, penniless, without civil rights. What did that matter? They would live in some cottage, they would farm Combe St. Philip for Mark.

Spring slipped into summer. Many fugitives returned. Dick and Hal came back from France, but for many days their mother would not see them. Sarah wept, saying their lives had cost too dear, but at last love was the stronger, and it was they who wept at the sight of the white-haired old woman who had been so beautiful on the day when they rode out against her will.

Autumn had returned in all its glory, the earth had sunk again into winter sleep, when word from Captain Pollard was brought at last by a homebound ship that carried many fugitives. He had found no trace of John Beausire, though he had sent home several who sailed in the slave ship with him. They had said that on that dreadful voyage his courage and kindness had been their only light in the darkness.

Hope had flickered then, almost glimmered out, like the flame of a lamp whose oil is spent.

With an effort Rosalys raised the heavy cup and drank. It pleased Sarah and Mistress Allison, she knew. How could they understand that the shadows were closing about her, that nothing they could do would hold her back?

Did one know when hope died, she wondered, or just know one day that it was dead, had been dead for a long time?

Slowly she rose and went toward the door of the Queen's Room. Sarah, sitting at a distance, sprang up as if to stop her. Yet when Rosalys asked for lights, without a word she brought a bronze lamp and set it on the floor inside that heavy door.

The panel was restored. Flemish carvers, who had come to do it, said that when the soldiers hacked it down they had not injured the mechanism. The carven pomegranate still lay beneath its tree. Touched by one who knew the secret, it would still open the panel, disclosing the hidden room.

The Queen's Room was not used now. The two whose lives had been laid in ashes here stared into the deep shadows outside the little circle of the lamp's light.

"Come, my darling, it is cold for you here," Sarah said, her heart breaking with pity. She had herself almost broken under the weight of her grief, saved only by her determination to fulfill that promise made upon the rain-wet drive of the Court three years ago. This child had been robbed of all before she had really lived: she did not have twenty years of happiness to look back upon: she did not have sons and daughters to carry on the life of her beloved.

As they went back to the east wing Sarah told herself that she was not self-deceived: for days now she had felt a peculiar tension. There had been visitors at strange hours, and Mark Beausire had ridden out at dawn, returning after dark, on more than one occasion. What did it mean? Could it be that word had come from the Indies, that the new Lord Beausire had secret tidings of the cousin he had supplanted?

Mark Beausire seldom rode abroad now. He had sunk into heavy gloom, sitting late into the night drinking canary laced with brandy, gambling heavily with men who came from neighboring houses or from Bristol and London. Several of the outlying farms had been sold to meet his debts.

Lady Beausire had aged beyond belief. Her stone-hard face was lined with bitterness. She took little interest in her daughter, or in the second son who had been born within the year. All her hope seemed centered on her first-born, Mark, now a handsome lad of seven.

Sarah caught the sound of horses' hoofs upon the gravel. Taking the girl's arms she drew her hurriedly toward her rooms, for the sound of a horse, of carriage wheels, could make her start up in an agony of hope, leaving her weak and spent when the hope died.

Sarah was too late. The trampling of many horses, the loud voices of many men, came in with the wind and rain. Rosalys, transfixed with tension, stood like a white carved statue staring down into the hall.

Thomas crossed the hall, quickly followed by two footmen. The great doors were opened, and men in riding gear entered quickly.

These were not soldiers. As if through a veil, Rosalys saw the familiar faces, tense and stern. There was Sir Francis de la Warre, in a black coat, Sir Edward Phelips, Sir Samuel, Mr. Venner, many others.

It was when Mark came from the gunroom that she gasped, "They bring news of John," and gathering her long white wrapper about her, ran and was lost in the vastness of the staircase.

Sarah turned toward the gallery. She would go down the buttery staircase, watch by the west wing door, be ready when the child needed her. Sarah had no hope at all, for it had died long ago.

Up the narrow stairs a form shot past her, taut with fear.

"Jerry," she called, as she recognized the lad. He turned, came close, his clawlike hands grasping the skirt of her dress.

"Soldiers," he moaned. "Soldiers." The old dark fears beat about him.

"Nonsense, lad. They be gentlemen of Somerset, coming no doubt to play at cards." Sarah tried to comfort him. She had grown fond of the boy for whom her husband had done so much.

Jerry had improved vastly in three years. His wits were so much sharper that many thought of him as normal. His devotion to his master was an absorbing passion. If Mark Beausire played at the White Hart in Taunton until daybreak, Jerry was there, waiting with the groom. When he stumbled to his room after a night of heavy drinking, Jerry followed, to serve him with a clumsy skill. When he rode recklessly, Jerry's horse was never far behind. The one real skill the lad had was with horses. It served him now. It was to Jerry that Mark Beausire talked, telling him of losses at the card tables which the boy was not able to comprehend. He could not understand that this almighty being could need money. Had he not poured endless golden guineas from a leather bag to save the life of a worthless stable boy?

Rosalys, running down the stairs, was radiant. Color flushed her cheeks, her eyes were shining stars, her hair a nimbus of fiery gold. She was vibrant, strong, a lamp through which the white flame of joy blazed.

All the countless times she had visualized this homecoming seemed with her now; every hour of waiting and hoping was condensed into these moments on the staircase. Had these gentlemen ridden from the sea with John? From Bristol, even from London?

The hall was in uproar: boys ran with tapers, lighting lamps and candles; doors banked; a footman shouted an order. Mark stood in the center of a group, where Sir Edward was talking in a low grave voice. Diana, somber in black velvet, stood at the door of the small drawing room, her face as white as paper.

Because she was nearest, Rosalys turned to her. "Diana, John has come home!" The words rang out above the murmur of talk, heads turned, eyes filled with pity.

"Where is John? Surely they have come with John?"

Diana spoke harshly. "What makes you think such foolishness?" she said. Her nerves were about to snap. This mad girl was more than she could stand.

Mark was beside them now. He understood what had happened.

"John is not here," he said. "It is the King, my dear, of whom we have news. These gentlemen have brought grave news about the King."

"John is not here." The words rang up to the high ceiling, seemed to wail about the paneled hall. All the brightness of the lights guttered out into darkness. Dimly aware of many eyes upon her, Rosalys drew her hand across her brow in a gesture of despair. The door of the west wing was open. She stumbled toward it, and fell into Sarah's outstretched arms.

It was quiet in her own rooms, where they carried her. Below the great house seethed in confusion.

Diana stood in a little room off the hall and stared at the window through which she had gone three years ago to give the word that had sent John Beausire to his death. He was dead, though that silly girl would not believe it. He was dead.

Her eyes were heavy with sleepless nights. She fingered her ropes of pearls and tried to brace herself to face what might come now. What she had heard in the great hall filled her with sickening terror. Mark must have no part in this thing. Mark must be loyal to the King.

Mark came into the room and closed the door. They looked long at each other. Every line of his ravaged face burned itself upon her. Heavy, gross, his splendid looks all gone, Mark was an old man now, though he was not yet forty. Before he spoke, Diana knew she had lost. He would ride with the others to Exeter, to proclaim a new King.

"You will go?" she asked quietly, knowing that a hysterical burst of tears would avail her nothing.

"Yes. I ride with them. Prince William of Orange has landed at Torbay in Devon, with a small force. The meeting place is Exeter. He will be proclaimed there."

She nodded. Better to remain calm, poised, and then point out the flaws in the venture. "What chance of success, think you?"

Mark was eager, more vividly alive than he had been for a long time. He had not been drinking, though usually at this hour he was stupefied with wine and brandy.

"Good," he said. "The King is hated. Prince William's wife, as eldest daughter of the deposed King, will be made Queen, co-equal with her husband. They will reign together. We are tired of the vagaries of James."

Cold fear lapped about Diana, but her face was composed. A little smile played about her lips. "A dangerous venture, my love," she said. "Think you the English will accept a Dutchman as their King? What if the army remains loyal to his Majesty? Would it not be better to wait a day or two, see how Exeter responds to this Prince of Orange?"

Mark stepped nearer. There was a look on his face she had not seen before. It was crafty, vicious.

"There have been whispers that the famed luck of the

Beausires was over," he said, "that with the going of my cousin John it ended. I think that is not so. Last night I heard that something known to me for three years had come to the knowledge of my Lord Stawell, who rushed with the tidings to Sir Francis. Together they rode to London, where Stawell had audience with the King. His Majesty was considering recalling John for a public trial that could only have ended in acquittal. To return to the luck of the Beausires, fair lady—tonight I hear that by tomorrow's sunset, James II may no longer sit upon the throne. William will not forget those who stood for him from the first, who took the risk of ruin. Mary, as Queen, will think kindly of her friends. They will not wish to entangle themselves in brawls over long past actions of a court of justice."

"What were these momentous tidings?" Diana asked. Before Mark answered, she knew.

"Merely that the letters upon which John was condemned were forgeries. The miserable clerk who wrote them told me his story before I saw the King, three years ago. When his Majesty dubbed me Baron Beausire of Sudbury, the confession and John's seal ring, returned with it, were on my person. I entered the palace meaning to lay them before the King, but as he spoke, I thought otherwise. It is no small thing, for me or for my children, to be Baron of Sudbury."

Diana sat down, for she could no longer stand. There was a hard, cold gleam to the gold satin of the window curtain. Had it been the same curtain, that night three years ago? If so, there were no marks of rain upon it now. Their guilt would not be so easily erased.

"So it is a new King, or we stand to lose all?" she said.

Mark nodded and smiled until his strong teeth gleamed wolfishly. "You have summed up neatly, my love. You were always a clever woman. Our luck is indeed prodigious. The clerk also confessed to his father, an apothecary past eighty years old, wringing from the dotard the promise to seek Lord Stawell and tell him all. The old man's wife—his second—had a shrewder wit. She bade him not mix himself in such matters. But his conscience nagged him so, at last he set out for Cothelstone, arriving half dead to blab his story. Had the wife been a little less determined, his conscience a little swifter, or traveling less difficult for the old and the poor, we would be in a sorry case, my dear. Do you wonder that I speak of luck? Unfolded to the public gaze, not to speak of his Majesty's, it would not be a pretty story. In taverns it is whispered that Moffet, well primed with liquor, is wont to say that the maidservant who brought word to him of the secret room had a passing white hand for one of her station."

So Mark knew. It did not hurt him, for now he had sunk to her level. She stared at him, but no words came. Mark went on talking, with that awful forced lightness.

"It is, of course, a gamble. I often gamble, and though I lose with distressing frequency, I sometimes win. Good night, my love. News will come to you from Exeter. I think in three days we shall know if we have won or lost."

The door closed, and Diana was alone again. Three days to wait. Three years ago she had waited nearly six weeks. She thought of all the bitter words she had heard lately about the King, weighed the chances of deposing him and putting his daughter and son-in-law upon the throne in his stead. Of the girl who had been shocked into agonized hope by the late visitors, and now lay on her bed in a deathlike swoon, she did not think at all.

It was in the still hour when human vitality sinks lowest that sleepy-eyed Susan came to tell Sarah that Dick and Hal, her sons, were below, for they were off to join the standard of the new King, and asked her blessing.

Straight and tall Sarah stood up, glanced at the still form in the bed. She would not stop them now, even if it were in her power to do so. This time they rose against a King who had given power to the most evil man who ever darkened the earth. She would speed them on their way.

"She sleeps, Susan," Sarah whispered. "She woke and talked a little. Her mind is clear. Watch her well. I shall return very quickly."

Rosalys seemed to sleep so deeply that Susan thought she would lie so for hours. Her fear and curiosity overcame her. She slipped out of the room, crossed the gallery and stood looking down at the throng in the hall below. How gallant his Lordship looked, more like the happy man he had been three years ago.

More riders came. The minutes slid away.

Susan had barely gone when Rosalys opened her eyes. The room was in darkness, but through the open door of her drawing room she could see candles burning steadily in their tall silver holders. As she watched the steady flames she remembered the Tenebrae candles in the Convent chapel on Holy Thursday. There had been an awful fascination in watching the candles going out, one by one, symbols of the lights going out on the dolorous way to Calvary.

That was how it had been for her. One by one the lights had gone out, one hope after another had died. Now, tonight, the hand had been stretched out for the last time, putting out the last little candle.

Did all who passed through great sorrow know that sense of being utterly alone, abandoned by God and man? How could one believe in the mercy of God when desperate prayers for mercy were met by silence, nothingness?

The dark waves broke over her. Her eyes were wide and dry, even the mercy of tears denied her now.

Then, far off, as a light seen through the darkness of an immense tunnel, a hope glimmered. It was misty at first, almost without form, and then it became clear.

John was alive. Because she lived, somewhere he lived also. The *White Heron* was but one small ship. The new King would command many ships. She would go to Mark, beg him to let her ride with him to Exeter. Sarah had said William of Orange was a good and just man. He would send ships, many ships, to search for John. Only she could make him understand the awful injustice that had been done.

Better still, he would let her go also. As they sailed among those islands, her heart would tell her where John was. He might be ill, dying, but she would find him, and once they were together, all would be well.

She rose quickly, flung the white wrapper around her. In a moment she was in the gallery. Sarah hurried up the buttery stairs, but the girl drew back into the shadows. Not even Sarah must know what she meant to do. Mark was good at heart, Mark would let her have her way.

The gallery was empty. Rosalys went quickly down the west wing staircase. The west hall was empty too.

A voice heard through a half-opened door said, "They are off now. They are gathered at the head of the west drive. His Lordship went by a few moments past."

Rosalys tried to run. With a gasp of relief she saw that the west door was open. She forgot her bare feet, the thin silk wrapper that covered her night shift, and went out into the rain and darkness.

She knew she had to cross her little court and run down the

path between the lilac trees, out into the lime-bordered west drive.

The cold cut her like whips, rain drenched her. The darkness swirled about her for a time, then dragged her down into itself.

It was a gardener coming early to his work who found her, unconscious beneath the heavy shadow of an ilex tree. He picked her up and carried her to the house, where for hours the frantic search had been going on. Sarah wrung her hands when she saw what the man bore in his arms. Relief was lost in terror.

Sarah's worst fears were realized. By evening the little maid raved in fever. Sarah wept, and with Susan did all that the doctors summoned from Bath ordered.

The children's nurse came in to watch. She was hopeful.

"Youth dies hard," she said. "Even when the heart breaks, and the spirit longs to go, the body fights for life."

It was weeks before they knew the nurse had been right. Weak, racked with coughing, the little maid came slowly back to life.

They told her when she was strong enough to hear it that William and Mary were firmly established on the throne of England, that James II had fled without a fight.

❖   ❖   ❖   ❖

The summer of 1690 was an exceptionally lovely one. September came in with the golden warmth of July. The court of St. Francis was bright with flowers. The yellowed bricks of the west wing shimmered as if the house were built of fairy gold.

Rosalys lay very still, an unearthly peace wrapped around her. She felt she had been wandering endlessly in some strange dark place, alone, going deeper and deeper into darkness, as one by one the doors of life closed upon her.

There had been nothing there but darkness and the racked torment of her body, the gasping struggle for breath, the coughing that seemed to wrench her frame apart, the burning fever, the half-world of delirium. But that was all over now. Her body no longer had power over her. It was as if she existed apart from it, yet never had she been so vividly aware of life.

There was an exquisite cadence in the thrush's song she had not heard before. Color was so lovely that it was almost unbearable. Two white doves, perched upon a great bush of scarlet roses at the foot of her couch, were as lovely as those white birds must be who fly about the courts of heaven.

When the birds had gone Rosalys saw the roses as if she had until now seen flowers—all the world—through a dark veil. The scarlet of their petals seemed vibrant, alive; their golden centers were minute golden flames, and their scent drifted toward her like incense swung from an unseen thurible.

She knew that she was dying, and it was because she was beyond hope that the doctors had said she might be indulged in her whim of being carried out into the court. It would make no difference now.

How strange to talk of death! It was life, vibrant, immortal life, that had swept her into itself. With it had come a sense of oneness, unity with all things. The beauty of the flowers, the song of the birds, the sleek grace of a little rabbit that peered at her from beneath tall spires of blue delphinium whose color was a song, were all part of that unity of life.

Now, enclosed in radiance, she could look back over the long dark road by which she had reached it. How small were the things that had loomed like mountains of sorrow and loss upon that road, mountains over which she had had to climb, slowly and painfully, feeling that she had been lost in an eternity of darkness.

It did not matter now that John had been betrayed. The years of separation were but an infinitesimal shadow in the circle of Eternity, that radiant living light that was the fulfillment of all things.

How poor and gray were the little joys she had relinquished with such bitter grief, in comparison with the joy that swept about her now! How needless had been her fear of death, and its power to separate them, when the reality was this sense of invulnerable life, of being with him beyond the reach of sorrow or separation!

Sarah, sitting on one of the carved stone benches, her sewing untouched beside her, thought she slept. The sun was sinking, and soon the evening breeze would chill the air, but it was good to see her rest so peacefully. Sarah dreaded to wake her, lest the awful coughing return, and the fever with it.

A few minutes more, she thought, until the church clock strikes the hour. But she did not wait so long.

The hands that were as white as the silk coverlet fluttered for a moment like birds escaping from a cage. In an instant Sarah was beside the small carved bed the footmen had carried down that morning.

For a moment Sarah was only aware of the beauty of the dark lashes lying on the modeled cheeks. Then they fluttered, rose as if with an effort, and the girl's eyes, shining like stars, alight with some tremendous revelation of joy and wonder, looked not at her but beyond her.

For a moment Sarah fought off the knowledge that pressed upon her.

"We must go in, dear," she said softly. "Soon the dew will be falling."

She slipped to her knees beside the bed. Rosalys gave one long deep sigh, that had contentment, not weariness, in it. Sarah slid a hand beneath the pillow to raise it. As she did so the lovely head fell sidewise lying like a flower snapped from its stem.

A blackbird on the fountain edge burst into song. Sarah seized the slender blue-veined hands that were almost transparent now and covered them with kisses, as if with her own life she would warm them again.

They were so still. With a cry Sarah let them drop to the coverlet.

Diana, dismounting by the west door, heard that cry. She turned toward the court, her full pearl-gray riding skirt gathered up in her hand, the white plume of her hat ruffled by the breeze.

Directly she looked down at the pillow she knew it was all over. A sense of relief seeped through her. Coldly she drew off her elaborate gloves and flung them to the ground. Bending down, she lifted the petal-like lids, slid her fingers beneath the lace of the girl's gown.

Then Diana stood up. "Mistress Rosalys is dead," she said. "Send the doctor here. Also ask his Lordship to come to my morning room."

Sarah did not appear to hear her. Her white head was close to the pillows, her hands smoothed the red-gold hair that lay over them.

Diana herself went to the house to seek the doctor. There was a curious smile upon his face as he descended the stairs. He thought Lady Beausire the hardest woman he had ever had the misfortune to meet, and the man that had told him of the gay and generous girl, who had thrown over a splendid match to elope with penniless Mark Beausire, sadly lacking in discernment of character.

Within the hour the sweet clear bell of the Church of the Evangelists was tolling, answered by the deeper tone of the bell of St. John's across the valley. Those who heard them knew then that the little maid of the Court was dead.

Late that night Sarah stood in the candlelit room, looking at the still form upon the carved bed. She held in her hands the little cap of rare lace that was to have been worn by a bride. For nearly five years it had lain, wrapped in linen, in the great chest in a corner of the room, with the gown of ivory brocade that had been so hopefully put there with it.

She did not hear a step behind her, and it was only when a small, slight man—with dark eyes that were shining now as if at the sight of a marvelous peace and beauty—turned his face toward her and spoke that she recognized Monsieur Dupuis, the Frenchman who had given hospitality to her sons when they fled from England.

"Madame, she is at peace," he said softly. "How beautiful she is!"

Then he left the room, as swiftly and silently as he had entered.

Weeping bitterly, Sarah pressed the little cap gently over the still head, laid long curls over the brocade clad shoulders. Four candles in tall silver candlesticks burned at the corners of the bed. Sarah knelt at its foot to keep her night-long vigil.

When she heard a step she did not turn her head. A moment later she realized with a feeling of revulsion and anger the articles that Monsieur had brought into the room and was carefully arranging beside the bed. There was a great bowl of steaming hot water, a mass of soft wax, white linen laid upon a board.

"A death mask," she whispered. "No, no. It is an outrage."

Amadis Dupuis stood beside her. There was an infinite pity in his gentle voice as he told her that kings had tried to buy his skill, and could not, but that because he had greatly loved John Beausire and the little maid, he wished now to make such a tomb for her that all who saw it would look on it with wonder and with pity for her beauty and the sorrow which had cut short her radiant life, a tomb that would keep alive her memory as long as the chapel of the Beausires lasted.

Sarah stood up and faced him. Her face had hardened until it might well have been a death mask also.

"Sir," she said, "you are right. Let her be remembered, and the sin which murdered her also. She promised me that I should dress her for her wedding. I have put her wedding gear upon her. It is the last time that I shall tend her—"

The voice broke into sobs. Quietly, quickly, Amadis Dupuis went on with his preparations, searching in his mind for words, simple words, in the English tongue, that would convey to this unhappy woman that the little maid had only passed for a time into a light too bright for mortal eyes to see but would surely return again to earthly love and beauty.

Sarah was beside him now, holding the silver bowl steady as he worked the wax to the right softness. The sobs ceased, and she went on, "You were my dear Lord's good friend. If he should return when I am gone, tell him that I did . . . the best I could . . . to keep my promise to him, to care for her."

The sculptor laid back the heavy curls gently, that he might model the perfect line of the jaw and neck, the small, shell-like ears.

Ah, if he could only speak in French, he thought, surely then he could tell her what all the East knew, what the Church had once known, but he would have to do what he could with the unfamiliar words.

"Mistress," he said, "some day John Beausire will know. That I do not doubt. Some day you will dress her for her wedding, for they will come back. Oh, be sure of that, for God does not leave unfinished lovely things, they will come back, and they will be happy here."

There was no comprehension in the ravaged face before him, and then, when he took the wax in his hand and turned to the bed, Sarah Giles fled from the room.

On the day of the burial Diana took the big pencil sketch for an alabaster tomb to Mark.

Mark looked at it. His face was quite expressionless. "Dupuis is a great artist," he said. "He might have had fame, had he striven for it."

Almost hysterically, Diana pleaded that this thing could not be done, that there was already too much talk of John Beausire and his little maid, that pity and grief would soon lead many to question how this thing had come about. They would become a legend that would keep the story fresh in men's minds.

"I have given my word," Mark said. "When the tomb is ready, it shall be placed over the spot where she lies, beneath the floor of the Lady Chapel."

Diana knew she must accept this thing. The little maid might be dead, but her image, in purest alabaster, would lie before the gaze of all who entered the chapel of the Beausires.

Diana began to think of Amadis Dupuis with hatred. He had come to stay at the Inn. Why, no one knew. There could be little companionship between this brilliant cultured man of the world, this great sculptor, and the farm lads he had sheltered. It was not for them he had come, and John Beausire was no longer here.

Between Dupuis and John there had been a deep friendship. He had helped and advised the boy in enriching and beautifying the house and gardens. Many of the statues and fountains were his work.

She hoped with an intensity that frightened her that Dupuis would go now, that he had merely waited to make the death mask, knowing that the time was not far off when it could be done. The Frenchman seemed to look into one's very soul with those strange eyes of his, to read the secrets there. John had said that he had traveled much in the East, delving into the ancient wisdom which the West once possessed also but had forgotten long ago, that it was because of his search for hidden knowledge that he neglected his art. The sense of being pitied by him was intolerable to her, but she could not overcome it. He seemed to know what she had done, to be appalled by the punishment that must come to her.

She struggled to dominate her own mind. Five years had lapsed and there had been no word of John. Captain Pollard had failed in his eager search. Sir Francis de la Warre had not been well received when he appealed to the new King and Queen to command an investigation of the case. The attainder stood.

Rosalys was dead. Sarah would leave the Court tonight, to return to the Home Farm: her sons wanted her there. Susan would marry and live in Bristol. Thomas would die soon, even if she could not persuade Mark to send him away now.

The harvest had been bad. Disease had broken out among the cattle. Mark's debts were piling up again to a staggering total, and Diana knew land must be sold to pay them. The thought tortured her, but she forced herself to entertain it coldly.

Mark had refused to go to London and appear at Court. He took no interest in the estate, but was drinking heavily, finding his only pleasure in gambling and wild rides over the countryside with Jerry in attendance.

Suddenly Diana laid her hopes for Mark down, faced what

for a long time she had known to be true. Mark would never be other than he now was, a drunkard and wastrel. He was not strong enough to bear the burden of their guilt.

Resolutely she turned to the figures before her. She would save the estate from ruin, supervising every detail herself. Mark, her son, not her husband, would be the great Lord Beausire, the shining light in the long history of the house. He was nine years old now, with all the grace and charm his father had once had. When he came into his heritage he would find that his mother had saved it for him. From now on there would be no mismanagement of the estates. What John and Farmer Giles had done, she would do. Prosperity should return. Diana felt her will strong enough to compel it.

Chapter Seven

✦ ✦ ✦ ✦

FEW GUESTS CAME TO SUDBURY COURT AT THE CLOSE OF the seventeenth century. The neighboring gentry avoided it. One jovial squire who had been a frequent guest in other days was heard to say that, when he was forced to go there upon a matter of business, the chill had clung about him for many days. He had come upon a bright day in June.

Thomas was no longer at the Court: his place had been filled by a stranger from London. It had taken Diana four years to persuade Mark to replace him. In 1694 she accomplished it.

Sarah had died—from shock it was said—in the autumn of 1691. Soon after the harvest a disastrous fire had broken out in the kitchen of the home farm. The house had gone up like tinder; sparks carried by a high wind had set the great barns alight, and by morning blackened ruins were all that remained of the richest of the farms.

The loss had been very great. Diana, counting upon that year's good harvest, had been stunned by it. Yet through her misery, like a bright thread, had crept a sense of overwhelming relief that she would not have to see Sarah Giles again.

Sarah Giles was curiously in Diana's mind as she stood by the oriel window of the gallery on this early January day. She seldom came to the west wing now, but today something seemed to draw her there.

The stirring branches of the trees meant that the wind was rising. That might bring rain and the breaking of the frost. Diana watched anxiously. The cattle were dying in the cold. It was becoming increasingly difficult to get water for the farm needs: even the mill pool at Markscombe was frozen fast, every stream and river locked in ice.

It was Sarah who had put the idea of a curse into the minds of the credulous peasantry, Diana thought bitterly. Now it was accepted as a fact, and sometimes she felt as if she were surrounded by watching ghouls who waited gleefully for the next blow to fall.

It had been in the spring of 1696 that Captain Pollard returned from the west. She remembered the terror of the day he had ridden at breakneck speed from Bristol, knocked at dusk upon the door until the hall rang with the sound, and when the startled lackey opened to him, pushed past him, and without awaiting permission or announcement, burst into the gunroom with the awful tidings that John Beausire was alive.

Slowly, forcing herself to conceal the shock which had almost made her cry aloud that it could not be true, she pieced together the sailor's excited story.

In 1695, John had escaped from the Indies, where he had heard nothing of the amnesty. He passed from island to island until he found a friendly captain who gave him passage to the new colony of Maryland, telling him of the amnesty granted in 1686 and advising him to seek the hospitality and help of a certain James Campbell of Campbelltown, Maryland, a Cavalier who had received a grant of land in the new country. Mr. Campbell would help and advise him, the skipper said. On arrival at Baltimore he escorted his passenger—whom he believed to be dying—to Campbelltown, where he was received gladly.

Pollard had spared them nothing of the horror of that ten years, of the terrible journey hidden in the hold of a ship leaving the island. He had had it from the skipper, whom he had met by chance in Baltimore the day before he was to have sailed home in despair of news of John Beausire.

From that night, the story was the Captain's own. He told how he had obtained a horse and ridden the twenty miles to Campbelltown without a stop, of the rage and pity that had torn him when he saw what had been done to the man he had sought for so many years.

But the will to live had been there. The dark red hair was streaked with white, the slender hands scarred and bruised, the body almost broken, but an unconquerable spirit looked from those hazel eyes.

"I saw that spirit die. It was I who had to give him the news he could not bear. His first words were to ask news of Mistress Rosalys," the Captain said, his black eyes shining with tears.

Diana walked slowly toward the library. Those two rooms could not terrify her more than her memories. She threw up her head with an unconscious gesture of defiance. She knew it was said that she avoided those rooms, that she had her own reasons for being afraid of them.

Deliberately she remembered the following days of fear and tension. She had told herself then that if all was well when the century died she would have nothing more to fear. Well, today was the third of January, 1700.

How well she understood what had passed in John's mind when he had come to his decision! The little maid was dead; his cousin had immediately entered into the inheritance. Perhaps he knew who it was that had betrayed him. He knew the attainder stood. He had no will to fight. There would be no one who loved him waiting for him now. Even Sarah was gone. He decided to spend the remaining years of his life in Maryland, with the new friends who had been so kind to him in his need. He asked that one of the outlying farms be sold and the money sent to him, as he wished to buy land.

There was bitter discussion. Ten years of Mark's gambling had left little but the entailed estate. After a night of fear and misery, Combe St. Philip was offered to the man who farmed it and who had wanted to buy it for some time. The money was sent to John.

Mark wished to go at once to London, to come to an understanding with William of Orange. Mary, daughter of James II, was dead now. He would have to deal with the dour Dutchman, whom he did not understand and who had no memories of Mark Beausire as a young man.

Diana had persuaded him not to go, to wait, to see if further word came from John.

The weeks had slipped into months, the months into years, and no word came. Gradually the agony of fear that she felt when a carriage or a horseman approached the house died away. Pollard returned from Maryland again in 1698. He said that John Beausire had not long to live. Through the black years his spirit had sustained his ill-used body, and he had lived on hope of seeing his little love again. Now there was no hope.

The next year passed with no further word, and Diana told herself that she was safe.

Almost unconsciously she opened the door of the Queen's

Room. The late afternoon sunlight streamed through the window. It struck her with a sense of shock. For days there had been no sunshine.

She looked up, and the strange thing that the Frenchman, Amadis Dupuis, had painted was caught in the pale winter sunlight.

It was after he had finished the alabaster tomb, which had been almost terrifying in its beauty, that he asked Mark's permission to paint the ceiling of the Queen's Room. Indifferently, Mark agreed. Diana remembered now that her only thought had been of how it would keep the man longer about the Court. Now she stared up at the thing he had done. The message of that painting was as clear as the sunlight striking it.

Planets whirled in space. There was an awful symmetry about them. The flawless order of the Universe seemed to sing from those rushing spheres. There was a suggestion of a terrible and celestial light about them—all save one, and that was darkly shadowed.

"There it is—this earth of ours," Amadis Dupuis had said, pointing to the dark star. "How sad that it will not learn the lesson of inviolable law, that evil begets evil, as surely as good returns good. There is Infinite Justice over and through all things. An evil deed will return again and again, a curse upon the doer, until it is repented and expiated. It seems that only through eons of suffering will humanity learn this simple lesson, though the enlightened ones of all ages and all races have taught it. 'As you sow, so you shall reap,' is a true saying. The One who told us that knew—all things."

Then he had gone to the great circular window, and standing with his paint-stained hands on the deep embrasure, had looked out over the terraces and treetops to where the four oaks towered in the meadow. When he turned again, his face was infinitely sad.

"When I first came here and heard the legend of the Four Evangelists, I thought it a lovely thing, a legend of true poetry, great because it is true. In essence the thing is true. The law has been broken: the curse upon the House will be as plain to see as was the blessing when the faith was kept."

He had spoken as if he knew. Diana felt now, as she had then, that he did know. That night he had left the Valley. They had not seen him again, and a year later word came that he had perished in a storm at sea as he journeyed again to the east. She had counted his death as another break with the past.

A great cloud covered the sun, and the ceiling was but a darkened blur. Diana left the room, closing the door carefully.

That night a great storm lashed the land. Tall trees tossed wildly, as if they must break before it. Branches were flung about the lawns and drives as though they were twigs. The wind screamed among the chimneys. The valley seemed filled with diabolic voices, too wild for grief, that screamed in hate and fury.

Diana moved about her little drawing room restlessly. The storm depressed her. She felt she could not bear to be alone. Mark had sent word, as he so often did now, that he would not sup with her. She knew that he would drink far into the night, attended only by Jerry, and that he would resent any attempt on her part to enter his apartments.

But she could not keep away. In all the great house she had not a friend. Her elder son was in London, by her own wish. The younger slept the sleep of a healthy child.

If only Mark would talk to her! If they could but speak openly of the thing they had done, face its burden together! Perhaps the time had come to ascertain if John still lived. If he had died, as was almost certain, there would be no further need to fear the future. They could build a new life, if not for themselves, for their sons.

As she went toward the Cedar Room she thought for the first time in many months of her little daughter, who had died in 1692. The servants and villagers had whispered of the curse then. How foolish—so many children died. It was strange, but now she could not recall if she had grieved or not. One day the child had been playing happily, the next lying still and white in her bedchamber. Had she lived she would have been sixteen now. Diana tried to imagine her, a tall young woman, but she could not. The little Diana was as though she had never been.

Standing in the doorway of Mark's rooms, Diana stared at the scene before her. All hope that Mark would ever again help her bear their burden died. The candlelight flickered dimly on the cedar paneling, the details of the familiar room penetrated her mind, before she admitted into it the knowledge that the disheveled figure, with its torn coat, wine-stained ruffles, flushed and bloated face and ungainly body, was Mark, the Mark she had once so loved.

Mark had cast aside his wig, and his graying hair fell about his face. Slowly her eyes sought the head of the table, fixed themselves upon the figure seated there. At first it seemed an awful caricature of Mark. Then she recognized Jerry.

He wore Mark's wig, which almost obliterated his narrow face. His thin form was lost in a laced and embroidered coat of cherry satin, and his pale eyes were fixed on Mark, watching, alive and aware.

"Look at him," Mark shouted. "Look well. Is it not seemly that he should be honored, finely clothed and housed? His life was bought at the price of the life of a Baron of Sudbury."

Seizing a crystal flagon of wine, Mark cried, "Drink to him, the stable lad who lives, while the Baron was hounded to an awful death."

Then he burst into laughter. Diana felt icy fingers moving up and down her spine. She could not speak or move.

The wine Mark poured spilled in a red stream over the damask cloth, staining it as if with blood. With a sweep of his hand he knocked over one of the gilt candlesticks. Diana watched a small pale flame creep down the laces that fell to the floor, but still she did not move.

Jerry slid out of the heavy coat and came forward in his coarse shirt. In a moment he had extinguished the flame, mopped up the dripping wine with a napkin. Methodically he put the candles out of Mark's reach, took the flagon still clutched in his shaking hand.

Then he came toward the door and Diana. The eyes that looked into her own were alight with intelligence. "Go, my lady," he said softly, "go."

And Diana went, knowing that it was only Jerry who could help Mark now. The creature whose very face filled her with horrible memories had become a necessity to her.

Returning to her own rooms she told the waiting footman that she would not sup tonight. Usually she forced herself to eat, lest it be said that she was haunted by remorse. Tonight food would have choked her.

"Whatever comes now, I must meet alone," she said, and then was startled by the sound of her own voice. She bit her lips sharply. Should a servant hear her speak aloud to herself, rumor would soon have it that she was going mad.

She rang for a maid to set up her embroidery frame. For hours she drew the brilliant colored threads through the heavy silk, listening to the little tearing sound they made, and the stupendous clatter of the storm.

At dawn the storm dropped as suddenly as it had risen. Diana rose early. Standing by a window, she looked over the ravaged gardens.

As she stood there, a carriage with four horses, one ridden by a postilion, and a coachman and footman upon the box, drove slowly around the curve of the terrace.

Every muscle tense, Diana watched, and the words she had said last night flashed into her mind. She knew she had been right: whatever came, she would have to meet it alone.

She rang for her maid and dressed carefully in somber black silk. Her face might have been carved in stone, and her eyes looked as dead and dark as her robe.

She was ready when word was brought to her that a lady from Maryland wished to see Lord Beausire upon a matter of great importance.

Looking into the face of the pale fair girl who had brought proof that she was Henrietta, widow of John Beausire, Diana felt for the first time that her fifteen years' fight had been useless. There was a terrible strength about this daughter of James Campbell.

There was no doubt that the story was true. The calm clear voice went on. "I was nineteen when John came to Campbelltown. From the first I loved him with a love that was born of pity. One I loved had died, and I thought I should not love again. Sorrow drew us together as he slipped ever closer to death."

Diana could see the white-pillared house Captain Pollard had described, the gracious gardens and dignified charm of it. What a haven it must have been for the tortured man who had so loved beauty and graciousness!

"You say you have a son?" Diana felt she must hear again those words that had already been spoken.

A shadow passed over the girl's fair face. Diana watched her closely. Her long eyes were ice-blue, her hair so fine and pale that it looked in some lights like spun silver.

"My son was born two months after his father's death. The day John died I promised him that, should the child be a boy, I would return to England and claim the inheritance for him."

"Do you not know about the attainder?" Diana spoke softly; there seemed a gentle pity in her voice.

As the blue eyes regarded her steadily, the patrician face with its chiseled, faintly pink lips bespoke a courage and determination that would not be easily crushed.

"Yes, but I believe the King is just. Captain Pollard told me where to go, to a certain house in London, where a clerk named Harris died fifteen years ago, and ask to speak with the man's stepmother, who would have much to tell me."

"You will go?"

The answer came without a moment's hesitation. "Yes. Then to the King. I have friends in London who will help me."

"It would be a great joy, an overwhelming relief to us if John could be proved innocent," Diana said sadly, as if she had but little hope.

"I have no fear. It will be proved," Henrietta responded.

Diana now saw that the widow of John Beausire was bravely fighting an unutterable weakness and weariness. "You must rest, my dear," she said. "I will take you to your room. In a few days you will be refreshed and can think of continuing your journey."

Through the day Diana gathered much information. The parents of Henrietta had been bitterly opposed to her journey. It appeared that Mr. Campbell, the Cavalier, had little faith in the justice of kings. He had besought his daughter to bring up her child in Maryland, where he would be heir to his grandfather's not inconsiderable property. He had tried to make her see that it was but seeking trouble to take him back to claim the estates of a father who had been attainted, though he himself had not a shadow of doubt that John Beausire had been innocent.

Diana left her at last and sought Mark. He was dressing to ride. When he heard this new turn in the tragedy of John Beausire he burst into laughter.

"The ways of fate are strange," he said. "Last night, so tangled in debt and difficulties am I, I felt I did not know which way to turn. Now it appears that I am to be turned out."

Fury rose in Diana. Her pale face flushed a dark red.

"Only a coward and a weakling would be turned out," she stormed. "If you have no pride for yourself, think, pray, of your sons."

Mark shrugged his shoulders. "You are more astute than I," he said. "You must decide what we are to do. I grant you it will not be a pretty story, if aired in a court of law, or in the House of Lords. Our sons would no doubt be thankful to hide their heads in the colonies. Perhaps they might be granted a holding upon the land John purchased with the price of Combe St. Philip."

To be mocked was more than she could bear. Without another word, Diana left him. She was alone, alone. Today she alone must decide what she was going to do.

The long day dragged. At sundown the unexpected guest sent word that she felt rested and much stronger, that she would like to dress and see something of the house.

There was no doubt at all that John had talked much about the house. His widow knew its history. She spoke of the oaks, of how she looked forward to seeing them.

Mark did not appear. Smoothly Diana made excuses. Lord

Beausire was much occupied with county affairs. He would return tomorrow.

As they supped, Diana thought of the papers that had been shown her. This was no simple country wench who could be thrust aside, but the aristocratic daughter of an honored family. Many men of standing in the colony had known John Beausire during the last years of his life, and knew of the marriage and the birth of the child who had been left with his grandparents in Maryland, to await the King's decision.

It had slowly dawned upon Diana that here was a woman with a single purpose. She knew the power of such people. This woman would not give up easily. She had youth, beauty and wealth. She would stay in London until she had achieved her purpose.

"I would like to see the library and the Queen's Room," Henrietta said, when they had returned to the small drawing room off the hall.

As they mounted the staircase Diana wondered if she knew how John had come down it fifteen years ago, if he had ever told her in detail of that awful morning.

Henrietta stood very still beside the curtained window of the library. Her face suddenly went haggard with grief. Her voice shook as she parted the curtains and looked down into the darkness. "The little court is down there," she said.

Diana, listening, knew that the tragedy that had become a part of her own life touched this woman to the depths of her soul.

They were in the Queen's Room when Henrietta spoke again. She had been standing for some time by the fireplace, staring at that central panel now so perfectly repaired. There was no doubt that she knew everything. When she saw Jerry, she would recognize him.

Her pale hair seemed white, like a nun's coif, and her long narrow hands were clasped together on her breasts as if she would still the beating of her heart.

"I would that I could make you understand something of what John Beausire suffered," she said. Diana did not know if it was hate or tortured memory that made her voice so low and bitter. "Even those who watched him welcome death so eagerly could not really understand. Of that poor child he so greatly loved I do not dare to think."

Diana knew that she had struck the source of Henrietta's strength. There was no bitterness here, no jealousy. She made it clear that John had given her only friendship and affection. She did not resent this: her whole being was consumed in pity and the determination to see justice done.

"I would so gladly have given my life could it have bought them but a few days of happiness," Henrietta said, her mind wandering back over the past.

"John Beausire tempted fate. He rebelled against the King." Diana said the words in desperation. This pale girl was lashing her as no one else, not even Mark in his drunken remorse, had the power to do.

"That is a lie. He was betrayed. I will find his betrayer, if it takes all my life and every penny of my fortune. And it is not only I who will hunt the murderer down. I am a Scot. I believe in curses. I tell you that unless justice is done, there will be a curse upon this house."

"Justice has been done." Diana spoke coldly, all her strength exerted in the effort not to show her fear. Again the talk of a curse, of punishment to come. She thought of Mark, as she had seen him last night. Was that not punishment enough? She went on speaking, for she felt now that she was fighting a duel to the death. "No pleas would move the late King when he had

seen the letters, written by John to the rebel Monmouth's ad-
viser Ferguson, by Monmouth himself, and replies written by
John, sealed with his seal."

The eyes of Henrietta never wavered. They were blue
flames, burning steadily. "I will find the person who forged
those letters," she said. "Captain Pollard, who loved John, has
told me where to seek. God finds strange means to help those
who seek that help with a clear conscience. I do not think it was
by chance that the last words of an old apothecary were heard
by one who wrote them in a letter that reached its destination
after more than ten years had gone by."

Terror stifled Diana. This girl was an implacable enemy.
The gentlemen of Somerset had abandoned the cause as hopeless. She never would.

With an effort, Diana spoke calmly. "You must be very
tired. Tomorrow you will see things more clearly. Would you
not like to go to your room now?"

Henrietta nodded. She had not thought it possible for anyone to feel so tired—or so cold. Tomorrow she would make
the journey to London.

"Yes," she said, "I am very tired, and tomorrow I must
travel again."

"I did right to keep her here," Diana thought. As they
crossed the gallery, Diana saw that the oriel window was open.
Strange, it had been closed when they had passed it half an
hour past. She went toward it to close it.

Henrietta had gone on to the west staircase. Her breath had
been coming in gasps, and her steps dragged painfully. As
Diana saw her lean against the wall with closed eyes, she realized the weakness of her unwelcome guest. It was understandable. Her babe had been but three weeks old when she started
upon her long journey.

All the fear that had haunted Diana since she betrayed John Beausire seemed condensed into stifling terror now. It was as if she saw clearly for the first time the enormity of the thing she had done and felt there would be no forgiveness. What had it brought but shame and loss? She had lost Mark in a way that was more terrible than death. She had dragged him down, because he had been weak, into guilt as deadly as her own.

But there was no going back. The taunt he had flung at her regarding their sons pained her anew. She saw them, exiles in a strange land, unable to face the shame of what their parents had done.

It was through this woman leaning against the paneled wall of the gallery that shame would come to them. Diana could see those clear blue eyes fixed upon the eyes of the King. Oh, the King would see her. He was deeply interested in what was going on in the new world. Mark had found out that William knew nothing of John Beausire. Soon he would know too much.

It would all be discovered. Ghastly pictures flashed before her. She seemed to see Captain Moffet pointing at her accusingly, saying, "That is the woman. Look at her white hands. She came to the Inn to tell me where the fugitives were hidden."

Henrietta had stepped nearer to the stairhead. She stood on the top step, as if she meant to descend. Perhaps she wanted to see the west hall. It was of the west wing John would have talked most freely. He loved it, and his happy boyhood had been spent in it.

Diana thought again of her sons. Mark was nineteen now, a man ready to take his place in the world. Everything about her seemed to dissolve in a red mist of hate and rage. Out of the mist loomed the slender black-clad shoulders, the long white line of Henrietta's bent neck, so white that even the silvery hair looked yellow against it.

"Now, now," Diana thought wildly. "Now, or it will be too late." Almost before she was conscious of the thing she meant to do, she moved forward with one quick step, raised her hands and placed them with merciless force on Henrietta's shoulders. Then with all her strength she flung the widow of John Beausire down into the darkness.

There was one muffled cry, a dull thud, then silence.

"We are safe now," Diana thought wearily as she walked slowly up the gallery. She must not run, for servants might be about. She must walk, as if she had come from the library alone, with nothing to distress or startle her on her way to her own rooms.

It was hours before they found Henrietta. She was lying at the curve of the staircase, her slender neck broken.

"She missed her footing and fell," they said. "She did not know the house, and mistook the staircase for another corridor."

As the black-clad body was carried past them Mark gave Diana a long look. She met it steadily, but she knew that Mark understood everything and that he loathed her with a deadly loathing. With all his heart he envied Henrietta the peace she had found.

It was after they had buried Henrietta, widow of John Beausire, in the vault of the little church that Mark dropped something at Diana's feet as they stood alone together.

"Your kerchief, my lady," he said. "It was found two nights since at the head of the west staircase. It is well for you that it was Jerry who found it."

Then, with no further word, he left her. She stooped and

picked up the lace-edged linen kerchief. Jerry would not betray her, for that would mean betraying Mark also.

It was nearly evening when she heard running steps in the gallery outside her room, then a sharp knock upon the door. The steward stood there when her maid opened it, but he seemed unable to speak.

It was Mistress Allison who at last made her understand the story that the groom, Frank, had gasped out in the steward's pantry.

Mark had ridden wildly. Frank was far behind, but Jerry, mounted on a better horse, kept near him. When they were on the top of Sudbury Hill, his Lordship pulled up and stared for some time at the valley below. As Frank came up to within about ten paces, he heard his Lordship shout something about jumping Markscombe Mill, and in bewilderment looked down the sheer side of the combe, to where the mill lay in the deep hollow.

With spur and whip, Lord Beausire put his horse to the gallop. Frank saw Jerry make one desperate effort to overtake him. He stretched out his hand to grasp the bridle of the other horse and turned it violently at the last moment. But Jerry was too late to save Mark Beausire, or to save himself. His own horse could not check its gallop in time and followed the other in its crashing fall down sheer rock to the deep pool below.

Frank told how the wind had carried away his terrified shouts, but the screaming of the dying horses brought Markscombe men running out into the dusk. On gates torn from their hinges they carried the mangled bodies of master and man home to Sudbury Court.

Diana sat alone by the open window in her room, muffled in a hooded cloak. It was only so that she could breathe.

It had begun to snow. Faster and faster came the flakes, and the whole universe seemed filled with whirring whiteness, glimmering in the fast falling shadows.

When gray dawn broke, Diana was still seated by her window. Every tree, every house and barn, was folded in whiteness. Cottages and byres were obliterated, the trees on the terrace were white watching figures, the house itself a vast thing crouching in its loneliness, lost in a white world where there was only the silence of death.

Diana tried to think of her son, who was Lord Beausire now and who would soon be traveling with all speed from London. But she could not think at all: the whiteness and silence of the snow seemed to have gathered her to itself, to lie like a death-cold hand upon her.

❖   ❖   ❖   ❖

The June sunshine fell warmly on the sunken Dutch garden where Diana walked alone. With a sense of having won a bitter battle, she realized that she had achieved a certain peace.

A week past, the letter for which she had waited in such tense anxiety came from Maryland. Even her grief for Mark had been over-shadowed by her fear of what that letter might contain. But the news was better than she had dared to hope.

James Campbell had written curtly. He accepted the story he had been told of his daughter's death and made it quite clear that he did not intend to make any claim for her son.

Sometimes, if she woke suddenly in the night, or if some word or sight brought back too vividly memories of the first happy years she spent at the Court, she saw the thing as it was, and for hours, days even, felt herself tottering upon the brink of madness. But those moments of insight had been fewer lately, and she was almost always able to make herself believe what she wished to believe. It was the story she had told to her son when he had returned from London to take up his position as Lord Beausire.

John had been guilty. Nothing could have saved him from exposure and ruin. Rosalys had grieved, of course, but was well on the way to consolation when a violent chill caused by her own foolishness ended in a serious lung fever from which she died. She had been born and brought up for the first years of her life in the warmth and sunshine of Provence, and was not able to stand the cold dampness of England.

The talk of a curse was an absurdity. True, there had been two violent deaths and a disastrous fire, but in the history of any great house one would find such things. The luck of the Beausires had been legend, to keep the myth alive; the evil that befell them had not been recorded. Eagerly she reminded young Mark of the great fire in 1497, when the old Castle had been destroyed.

In a few years the tragic close of the seventeenth century would be forgotten, and the family would rise to new heights of honor and prosperity.

The energy of Lady Beausire amazed all who knew her. There was no detail of the estate she did not supervise. Already she had made a good beginning toward recouping the losses of the past years.

The Dutch Garden was one of the glories of Sudbury. The ornately carved seats, the many statues and great marble vases, were the work of Amadis Dupuis. He had stayed for months at the Court in the summer of 1684 to complete it.

Thinking of him, feeling that in some way she had triumphed over him, Diana went to the sundial in the center of the garden. As she bent over it, the motto seemed like a voice from the grave. It was as if the strange sculptor had cried out to her from the shadowy darkness where he lay, fathoms deep beneath the sea.

He had chosen that motto after long discussion. He had told John there was a hidden meaning, occult wisdom, in those words taken from the Psalms.

"In memoria aeterna erit justus," she read, translating the Latin into English. "The just shall be in everlasting remembrance."

Diana hurried from the garden. Fool, fool that she was, to think there could be forgetfulness or peace. It was only in work that she would find peace.

Bending over the steward's books, she fought off the hounds of memory, but they gained upon her. Mistress Allison's wrinkled old face came between Diana's eyes and the figures. She had got rid of the old housekeeper two months ago, but she could not so easily get rid of the words she had said as Mark's body, crushed beyond recognition, was carried to the vault two days after the burial of Henrietta.

"Twice the vault has opened. Two deaths by violence. There will be a third one."

Henrietta's pale face seemed to look intently into her own. Where was that fiery determination, that passionate seeking after justice, that selfless love and pity for the two to whom life had once been so beautiful? Could that singleness of purpose, that love of Henrietta, have vanished into nothingness?

John Locke would not believe so. The philosopher had said many times that he believed the human soul lived on, bearing its earthly loves, hates, desires.

It was an awful thought. Did Mark hate her still, Diana wondered? Was he wandering in some dark and awful place, knowing that it was she who had turned his steps to ruin?

She could not stay alone. She must see faces, hear voices,

talk of simple things, the crops and herds, the haying that would commence this week.

The dusk had fallen quickly; in the hall it was almost dark. Diana saw the great black clouds of a gathering storm. She wished Mark and Matthew would return from Taunton, where they had gone to attend a horse fair.

No one replied to the summons when she rang the bell. Fear, forever crouching behind her, sidled nearer. She went to the door of the west wing. There was no one in the little room near it where the footmen usually sat. Panic-stricken now, Diana went on. She entered the bailiff's room. From the window there she saw that the great yard facing the stables was in uproar. Hoarse shouts mingled with the scream of trapped horses; black clouds of smoke billowed out; the entire stables and coachhouses were on fire.

With cold courage she joined the servants. Men from the cottages and farms were coming now, running or on horseback, summoned by the frantic ringing of the church bell and the towering column of smoke.

Choked with smoke, her eyes inflamed and tear-filled, Diana shouted orders. The clouds were black as ink, thunder muttered and rumbled around the valley, a vivid flash of lightning lit the scene, but still the rain did not come.

Handing buckets herself until the skin of her palms was broken and bleeding, Diana hardly noticed a horseman dismount and push his way into the crowd of men nearest the blazing building.

A hoarse cry of horror rose from the men, rising above the awful sound of horses screaming in terror and agony. Diana saw several men push forward as though they would enter the main stable, but a great belch of flame drove them back. A second later the roof collapsed. A column of flame shot into the air, higher than the tallest elm, lighting all the house and out-buildings, all the trees in the glory of their summer leafage, with a red, ghastly glare.

A low groaning broke from the watchers; the last shuddering scream of a horse rose above the roar of the fire; then there was no more screaming.

Diana thought it was because it was all over that a woman, the hard-faced housekeeper who had replaced Mistress Allison, pulled her toward the house.

It was the housekeeper, almost a stranger, who told her at last that the figure she had seen dash into the stables was her eldest son, trying to save his favorite horse, and that he had perished when the roof fell.

Over and over again Diana repeated the words of Mistress Allison: "Twice the vault has been opened. It will be opened again."

Weeks later she sent for her younger son. Matthew was tall for his thirteen years. There was nothing of the Beausires about his thin dark face and narrow black eyes that already had a look of cold arrogance in them.

To her horror she saw that the boy was wearing the emerald ring which had been taken from John and returned by the dying clerk, who had sealed his perjury with it.

"Take off that ring!" she exclaimed. "Burn it, throw it away."

Matthew looked at her with a level stare.

"Why?" he asked. "I am Lord Beausire now."

His satisfaction stung her to frenzy. In those dark eyes she saw the reflection of herself. Not what she had been, but what she had become. Mark, the boy who had had all the kindliness and charm, all the splendid mien of that other Mark she had loved in her youth and happiness, was dead. The son for whom she had obtained the heritage at such an awful cost was her own evil, incarnate in human flesh.

"Conceived in hate and fear, why should he not be evil?" she thought bitterly.

Diana sent her son from her. She was too tired to talk more of his many plans. She could only think of the price that must be paid for her greed. Matthew Beausire, the third Baron since the thirteenth century who had not been named John, would hold fast all that that greed had brought him.

In the face of the third Baron since the going of John Beausire, Diana had seen all the dark years that were to be. Somewhere far off, unattainable, were the courage and determination of Henrietta, the shining love that had been between John Beausire and his little maid. Would they be strong enough to triumph, even if it took centuries to do so?

Mark, in his desolation and ruin, had been loved, if only by a stable boy. Sarah's love and service had gone with Rosalys to the grave. Someone had said, long ago, that love was stronger than death, that there was no evil it could not conquer. Would it be able to conquer the curse on the House of Beausire?

PART

· · · ·

TWO

Chapter One

❖ ❖ ❖ ❖

🌿 A FEW HOURS AFTER LANDING AT SOUTHAMPTON, JOHN Boser stopped his car on the ridge of the Quantock Hills and looked across the panorama of the West Country spread before him. The wind sang through the green fronds of the bracken covering the hilltop. Sunlight touched great patches of yellow gorse to flaming gold. His eyes followed the road, which below the hilltop entered a wood that sloped steeply to the valley below; then he turned again to look at the towers of Taunton.

Hills and valleys lay peaceful in the May sunlight. The many hedges gave the fields the look of a patchwork quilt. The steeples of churches, the smoke rising in straight lines into the clear air, the clustered rooftops of town and villages told of human habitation, yet John was possessed with the sense of being absolutely alone.

With every day of the journey from New York his excitement had risen, until now its intensity was akin to terror. For the first time he acknowledged to himself what it was that he feared—that he would not find here the thing he sought.

It was no longer possible—on this wind-swept hilltop—to delude himself into believing that he was seeking no more than the place from which a remote ancestor had set out to seek a new life in Maryland nearly two hundred and fifty years ago. He was seeking things that had been woven into his dreams as far back as he could remember.

The stop at Taunton for lunch and directions how to find the village of Sudbury St. Luke had been the only break in the journey from the dock. John recalled now this unreasonable annoyance at the delay while his car was put ashore. He had tried to think of the thing rationally, but could not: every moment seemed precious, so great was his desire to be on his way.

John thought now of the stifling excitement that had filled him that day three weeks ago when he received a reply to his cable to the Town Clerk of Taunton. The answer to his inquiry read, "Sudbury Court, Sudbury St. Luke, Somersetshire. Seat of Baron Beausire. House a magnificent example of early Tudor architecture. Not open to the public."

A lark soared up out of the bracken, pouring out a torrent of song. John watched its flight until it merged into the shimmering air. Great silvery clouds drifted slowly past: the strange shape of one of them made him think of a great white galleon under full sail.

The idea gripped him, and he could not shake it off. A white ship, not sailing, but flying. A white ship, a white bird. It must be the subconscious memory of some poem or story. Yes, that was it, for he had a dim memory now of a tall, black-bearded man pleading with someone to return home after a long absence.

He knew that behind all this beauty was the feeling—growing clearer as he had sped through town and village, through twisting country roads with high hedges, past wide orchards of pink and white blossom—that he was coming home.

This sense of homecoming, of utter familiarity with all around him, had taken the sting from those words, "not open to the public." Only today did he realize how bitterly he had resented them. He was not the public. Though his name had become corrupted somewhere along the way, he was the direct descendant of the John Beausire who had left Sudbury Court for America two hundred and fifty years ago, and now, in 1938, he was going to find out from what sort of place his fore-bear had come.

At the edge of the wood—which the clerk had informed him was the beginning of Lord Beausire's property—stood a thick hedge of hawthorn, white with blossom. John got out of the car and stood breathing in the freshness of the wind, as if he could not draw enough of it. He thought of men in fetid places of stifling heat, and what a breath of this sea- and thyme-scented coolness would mean to them.

He walked slowly toward the wood. Tall and slender, his broad shoulders gave him an air of strength. His thin face had the ivory tint that often goes with red hair. The high forehead, firmly molded chin, finely cut nose with its narrow nostrils, and the straight line of the mouth gave his face a sculptured look, above which the thick reddish chestnut hair looked strangely alive.

It was not a happy face, yet it was not sad. Rather, it looked incapable of expressing feeling. The deep-set greenish hazel eyes were the eyes of a man who had learned to live—probably in great bitterness—within himself.

It was very still in the wood. John sat down just inside the hedge. With his arms clasped around his knees, his eyes on a patch of bluebells, John felt that he had been in this wood before. He was certain he knew it in all its aspects, through all the changing seasons of the year. The explanations that came so readily to mind did not satisfy him. It was not enough to think that certain vistas in all woods looked alike, that every exhibition in the picture galleries showed scenes of English woods, painted in all the seasons of the year.

It was a deeper thing than that. The wood had the quality of a beginning. It was the doorway to something unutterably beautiful. Now, on entering it, John felt that his life had reality and meaning.

He thought of that day, only three weeks before, when he had been sitting in the library of his grandfather's New York house. He had just returned from the funeral of the old man whom he had always known as "the Boss." He had thought of the new made grave in the North Woods and had almost envied the one who lay there.

His own life had seemed utterly meaningless. The Boss had done just what he set out to do, gloried in every day of his long fight, and died, suddenly as he would have wished, with his hands still at the controls of the vast lumber business he had built up.

The Boss had known from the beginning what he wanted—a free life, close to nature, a chance to escape forever from squalor. And he had wanted to marry the flaxen-haired blue-eyed daughter of the owner of the lumber company for which he worked.

The Boss had succeeded. Step by step. He had bought land, and before he was twenty-one he had begun the vast enterprise that brought nothing but good to himself and others. At twenty-two he had married his love. He had been a just employer, and a true woodsman. The misuse or pillage of forests maddened him, for to him trees were mysterious living things, to be used for intelligent purposes only.

John knew that in comparison his own life had been empty. Such love as he had known had been but a poor make-believe, snatched at because nothing better offered. At twenty-nine he did not seem to be really living at all—or had not, until today. The will, the great fortune left to him, had been a surprise—he had not known there was so much. But it had brought no sense of elation.

Now, sitting in the quiet wood which had all the beauty of a familiar place of many memories, he tried to face squarely what the dreams that had run through his life like a golden thread meant to him.

Going as far back as memory would take him, he could not recall a time when that thread had not been there. But what, really, was it?

Dreams, not in deep sleep but in that dim borderland between sleeping and waking, of a love that was wholly true and satisfying, of a sense of companionship, of a lovely laughing girl whose face and form he could never quite see, but whose personality was more real to him than anything he knew in actual life.

At first, in early childhood, it had been only a sense of companionship. A lonely child, he had felt there was always someone to whom he could tell his thoughts, someone he knew would understand and sympathize.

Later, when he was older, there had been a sense of fulfillment. He knew in those dreams that he was in his right place, supremely happy, doing just what he had come into the world to do.

There had been a house there, too, a lovely and familiar house. Often, during his schooldays, he had awakened with so vivid an impression of it that he had tried to draw it, but had always failed miserably. Yet, he knew that should he ever come upon the house he would recognize it instantly.

It was at college that he had first encountered the theory of reincarnation. He remembered vividly the thin bespectacled face of the young man who expounded it to him, who recommended the books he had read so avidly. There was a possible explanation there, but also the despairing thought that those things which made the dreams so beautiful were gone forever, sunk in the well of the irrecoverable past.

The Boss had said that you could achieve anything you wanted to, provided you wanted it enough. Yet how could you obtain what was no longer in the material world?

The years had gone quickly. He had taken his place in the business and found the work absorbing. But always there had been the feeling that his real life was elsewhere, that he had still to find the way to happiness. At each of his grandfather's four houses, which he knew he would one day inherit, he had felt himself a guest, a stranger.

As the years went by, the dreams became fewer, less distinct, and it was only rarely that he could recapture the old excitement and joy of them.

John knew that all his life he would remember that night, after the funeral of the Boss, when he sat in the old man's study, trying to decide what to do. His present life seemed futile. The work he was doing could be as competently done by another man, who needed the job and had long hoped for it.

Wishing he had talked more to the Boss, learned something of his philosophy, John stretched out his hand to take the small object a secretary had brought into the room, saying it had been found in one of the safes. The man wished to know if it should be forced open, since there did not appear to be a key.

John remembered now the curious thrill that shot through him as he told the man to force the lock. The opened box was laid upon the table beside him. It seemed to be filled with folds of yellowing silk. John unwrapped it carefully, vaguely expecting to find a fading miniature or an antique jewel.

In the silk there was a small book. John took the book from his pocket now, carefully covered in the soft leather case he had had made to fit it. Holding it in the palm of his hand, John looked at it, as he had done countless times in the last weeks. It was a very small book of the Four Gospels.

At first that had seemed odd. It was not a New Testament, only the Gospels. He could not, then or now, recall having seen anything like it.

The leather cover, worn so that the gold tooling was almost gone, was faded brown, the thin pages darkened with age. Inside the front cover was a crest, in whose quarterings were four trees and the symbols of the Evangelists. John looked at them now, as if he would force from them their meaning. There were the angel of St. Matthew, the lion of St. Mark, the ox of St. Luke and the eagle of St. John. At the foot of the crest was a scroll on which was the motto—so dim now as to be almost unreadable—*Fides Servanda Est.* "The Faith is to be kept," he had translated. He said it over and over again. The Latin words exercised a strange spell over him. What Faith was it that must be kept? What was the oath implied here? Had it been kept?

Then he turned the pages to the back of the book. There was a thin sheet of paper there, neatly folded. John spread it out on his knees, shielding it carefully from the wind. Every mark and stain was familiar to him. On it was written, in various handwritings and shades of faded ink:

John Beausire, of Sudbury Court, in the County of Somerset, England. m. Henrietta, d. of James Campbell of Campbelltown, 1699.

John Beausire, b. Oct. 18th, 1699, m. Jean, d. of Robert Campbell.

John Beausire, b. July 5th, 1728, m. Mary, d. of Hugh Murray.

John Beausire, b. Nov. 20th, 1760, m. Anne, d. of Henry Robertson.

John Beausire, b. May 2nd, 1795, m. Jane, d. of Ronald Sinclair.

John Beausire, b. July 7th, 1835, m. Mary, d. of George Beaton.

John Beausire, b. Oct. 1st, 1880, m. Isabel, d. of Robert McClaren.

John Beausire, b. Oct. 25th, 1909

It was the last entry, the record of his own birth, that had riveted his attention when he first saw it. The difference in the spelling was a matter of no importance: he knew he was the John Beausire whose birth was recorded here. His mother had been Isabel, only child of Robert McClaren, "the Boss," who had brought up his orphaned grandson.

It was Hallet, for thirty years secretary to the Boss, who told John things he had not known before. The old man had bitterly resented his daughter's marriage. She had been engaged, almost from childhood, to a man he approved of, and had eloped with John Boser, who showed no disposition whatever to enter the business and be trained to carry on in place of the son the Boss had so greatly desired.

There had been a quarrel, and the stubborn old man had not seen his only child again until she was widowed, and was within a few weeks of her death. He stayed with her until the end, then returned from Baltimore with her four-year-old son.

Hallet suggested that the Town Clerk of Taunton, the capital town of Somerset, would know if Sudbury Court still stood. With the exact location known to them, it would not be difficult to trace the family history of the Beausires.

The decision to go to Somerset was made the day the reply came. A week later John was at sea.

Three deep notes of a church bell rose from the valley. John realized he had been sitting in the wood for an hour. He got up to continue his journey. As he passed the hedge, he noticed a granite stone, half buried in spring grasses. On it—the deeply graven letters almost obliterated by time—he read "Sudbury St. Luke—III miles. Sudbury St. Matthew—IV miles. Sudbury St. Mark—V miles. Sudbury St. John—VI miles."

John read the names of the four villages with a shock of delighted surprise. They were the names of the Four Evangelists, whose symbols were carried in the crest of the House of Beausire. Again he had the sense of being on the threshold of something unbelievably beautiful and joyous, like one who returns at last to a dearly loved home after long and desolate wandering.

Then, as if it would no longer be pushed into the realm of the subconscious, John knew what had been in his mind since that day he had found the book of the Gospels. He had hoped, with a hope that was almost terrible in its longing, that Sudbury Court, in the County of Somerset, was the house of his dreams.

If it was, it might even lead him to the greater discovery, the finding of that shadowy companion of his childhood, the little girl who had later made of all offered love no more than colored glass beside rare gems.

John jumped into the car and slammed the door. The road went over a solidly built bridge of gray stone. The clear water rippled over mossy stones. John paused, looking at the exquisite freshness of the hazel and willow scrub. The marshy ground on either side was a blaze of brilliant yellow kingcups.

A little beyond the road the stream widened into a pool, across which a moorhen, followed by three chicks, swam and disappeared into the willow scrub.

John drove very slowly, afraid to miss the smallest detail of his surroundings. Great beeches almost met overhead, making a green tunnel of the road. He knew he could not be far from the Inn, the Beausire Arms, that he had been told he would find in Sudbury St. Luke. He decided to take a room there, park the car and explore the village on foot.

Before he reached the village he came to great wrought-iron gates, beside which stood a gabled lodge house with mullioned windows, almost hidden by laburnam trees whose yellow tassels were bursting into bloom.

The stone pillars on either side of the gates were chipped and lichen covered; the lodge appeared deserted. John drove the car close, and stopped. He saw a long driveway, choked with weeds, bordered by two rows of superb elms.

Then he saw the crest on the gates. It was the same crest as the one in the little book. He sat petrified, staring at those closed gates behind which was Sudbury Court, the house from which his ancestor had gone about 1690.

For a fleeting instant, 1690 did not seem to be in the dim and distant past. Time had no reality: it was an illusion. That going was the reality, and when it had taken place did not matter. He wanted to know, as he had never before wanted to know anything, why that other John Beausire had gone so far away.

John leaned forward as one gate creaked open slowly. An old man with white hair crossed the driveway and with an obvious effort opened the other gate.

John wanted to speak to him, but could not. The whole scene had the quality of a dream which the dreamer knows is a dream, yet in which he avidly scrutinizes every detail before him, seeking the key to some hidden meaning.

The man was gone, plodding through a wood opposite the lodge. John was alone again, outside the opened gates of Sudbury Court.

Looking up the tangled driveway an almost tangible force urged him to enter. He drove through the gates and stopped the car beside the lodge with a vague idea that he would have to ask permission here to go farther. He had quite forgotten those stern words, "Not open to the public."

The lodge, at close quarters, appeared even more abandoned. When he knocked on the door the sound seemed to echo through empty rooms. Receiving no answer, John walked around to the back. A few chickens were scratching there, and washing hung on a line strung across a tangled garden. Smoke rose from a small thatched cottage in a hollow below the garden. Perhaps that was where the old man lived. John considered going there to inquire.

Suddenly he decided to go on toward the house without permission. With any luck he would find a caretaker or somebody who—for a good tip—would at least let him walk round the outside of it. He had been told at Taunton that Lord Beausire was not in residence.

Leaving the car he began to walk up the drive. The desolation and neglect oppressed him: he felt strangely responsible for it, as if he must set to work at once to put things in order. The rooks in the elms cawed loudly, skimming through the air in short flights, wheeling and dipping, returning to their trees. With an almost involuntary gesture John lifted his hands toward them. Their clatter seemed friendly and welcoming.

Suddenly, above the cawing of the rooks, came the sound of a waterfall. John quickened his pace. He knew that in a moment now he would see the house. Before he turned the curve he was certain where the bridge was and how the water fell from a broad lake down rocky falls to the stream.

Above the bridge of sculptured stone the ground began to slope gently up to two terraces. John stood still, staring at the house. His first thought was that he had not remembered how beautiful it was.

As he walked toward it the details became clear. The great oriel windows at the east end flashed in the sunlight. John visualized the huge room behind them. There were immense beams from which lamps hung. In the morning the sunlight streamed through those windows, chasing the dark shadows from among the beams of the ceiling.

He was at the foot of the first terrace now. The elm avenue ended; the drive swept round the terrace in a broad curve. Not all the reasoning in the world would have convinced him that he had not seen this place before. It was the house he had seen countless times in dreams.

It was a very large house, but its perfect symmetry gave it a look of compactness. Every line was perfect. The yellow sandstone had been mellowed by the centuries to a pearly softness. A forest of twisted chimneys with ornamental finials rose above the gabled roofs. The many mullioned windows reflected the sunlight.

Then, standing there, staring as if he could not take his eyes from it, John decided to go no farther. He could not bear to be turned away from that door as a stranger. He would find someone in authority, present his credentials and show the little book, and ask to be allowed to go through the house.

But he could not leave the sight of it yet. He wanted to see it from other angles. Leaving the driveway, he struck out across the park from the foot of the terrace.

To the west of the house was a copse of trees, standing alone in a wide expanse of grassland. John made for it with a feeling of curiosity and excitement and found four great oak trees. He stood amazed at the immensity of their girths. Looking up into their branches, fresh with young leaves, he thought he had never seen such trees, not even one alone. Four of them was incredible.

They must have stood there for more than five centuries. The grass beneath them was as green as unflawed emerald. As he stood, touching one of the huge trunks as far up as he could reach, he was again overwhelmed with the feeling that he had stood here many times before, touching these trees in exactly the same way.

Not far from the oaks was the ivy covered ruin of a tower, and a stream twisting its way through the meadow a little way beyond it. This he knew was the remnant of a Norman building, centuries older than the Court. An uneven flagged path, with the remains of stone columns on either side, ran for about fifty feet to a low stone wall, beyond which was a small gray church.

Stepping over the broken wall, John saw the ground was filled with the sunken mounds of ancient graves. The whole churchyard was a mass of waving white narcissi. As the flowers bent before a sudden breeze they looked like white waves breaking gently against the sides of an old gray ship.

There were worm-eaten benches on each side of the small church porch. John sat down. The sunshine fell warmly on his bare head. Then he saw an enormous iron ring hanging from the handle of the thick oak door. He got up and touched it, and was surprised at its great weight. The handle turned easily, and almost before he knew it, John was inside the church.

What light there was came through splendid old stained-glass windows. When his eyes became accustomed to the gloom, he saw great beams from which hung tattered banners whose color had long departed.

The altar was obscured by the great tomb which lay before it. As John went toward it he became conscious that every foot of space, on wall and floors, was covered with memorial tablets. Tombs with reclining figures, their feet toward the altar, stood in the window niches, between pews, under the organ loft, in every possible spot. There were knights in armor and ladies in quaint high headdresses, their hands clasped in prayer.

But the whole church seemed dominated by the tomb before the altar. John stood looking down at the figures sculptured there, so old that the faces were almost featureless. They represented a knight in full armor and his lady.

The knight's mailed hands, clasped on his breast, held a sword, the hilt, in the form of a cross, touching his chin. His crossed feet indicated that he had fought in the Holy Land. His lady lay meekly beside him, in a long robe with a heavily jeweled belt. A veil, the stone folds of which fell over the tomb's edge, hung from her high pointed headdress. The feet of the couple rested on hounds which lay as if on eternal guard.

John bent down to read the Latin inscription at the foot of the tomb. The stone tablet must have been of a later date than the tomb itself, for it was readable. He murmured the Latin words:

Orate pro anima
GEOFFREY DE BEAUSIRE
qui, postquam in Terra Santa, contra infideles militasset,
obiit in hac patria sua, anno 1220.
Requiescat in pace.

The words seemed poignantly beautiful. "Pray for the soul of Geoffrey de Beausire, who fought in the Holy Land against the infidels. Died in his own country, in the year 1220. Rest in peace."

It was the words, "died in his own country," that appealed most to John. Had this Crusader of old, after years of perils and hardships, come riding down the hillside on his clanking charger to his home in the valley, just as he had himself done today in his twentieth-century car?

On the lectern a book whose crimson and purple silk markers made a vivid splash of color had "Church of the Four Evangelists" lettered in gold upon its cover.

He was about to turn back toward the organ loft, to look at the carving there, when his eye was caught by a white glimmer behind a richly wrought iron screen at the side of the chancel: six yellow wax candles were held by prickets in the door which formed the center of the screen; the iron-work was an intricate design of twined roses and lilies.

Pushing open the unlatched door, John entered a chapel so small that it was almost filled by the one tomb there. John bent to look at it in the gloom. On the tomb was the figure of a very young woman, little more than a child. Her clasped hands held a few flowers—also roses and lilies. They were so exquisitely carved that the petals seemed alive.

The clear alabaster was ivory-tinted. The long dress almost covered the feet. The soft hair escaped from a little lace cap and fell to the waist in heavy curls. There was an extraordinarily life-like look about the figure. On the still face was a look of heartbreaking sorrow.

John struck a match for light and read the worn black letters of the inscription.

Here lies Rosalys,
daughter of Mark Beausire,
sister of Mark, Baron Beausire.
She died of grief, in the twentieth year of her age.
A.D. *1690*

Beneath the inscription were the lines of a verse.

Four great Angels round my bed,
Two at the foot, two at the head,
Matthew, Mark, Luke and John,
Guard the bed that I lie on.

As John read the words of the child's evening prayer his eyes misted with sudden tears. The sorrow that was graven on that alabaster face folded him in its shadow. Her grief was his. His whole being seemed to reach out to find her, to comfort her, to tell her that on the other side of sorrow there was joy, that death was but a shadow with no reality.

His fingers touched the sculptured curls lightly. Their coldness startled him. He knew that this was what he had come to find, that all the strange sense of familiarity was because of her, all the beauty of the house and valley lit with memories of her. She was a living reality to him, more real than all else in his life. He knew that the knowledge of her had always been with him. Now, in sculptured beauty, he could see her face.

This, then, was the end of that half-realized search, that reaching out for something that was wholly beautiful and true. A white tomb in an ancient church held all of life for him. It was this that he had sought and found. All beauty, all joy had vanished long ago.

But he would not admit that it was the end. It was only the beginning. She had lived. The nearly two hundred and fifty years between them were nothing, for time was nothing but a dream. He would seek her still, though their meeting could only be beyond the veil of death.

Still kneeling in the semi-darkness beside the inscription, he said her name aloud.

"Rosalys!"

He was surprised at the sound of his own voice echoing in the empty church. It died away, but he stood up, listening intently, for what he did not know.

There was the sound of a step. A figure was standing by the screened entrance to the little chapel. In the dusk John saw only a white face. He stood absolutely still, fearing that if he stirred it might vanish.

Then the figure moved, and spoke. There was anger and a note of fear in the voice.

"Will you please tell me who you are, and what you are doing here?" the voice said in cold clipped accents.

John stepped forward. A tall girl stood with her hand on the half-open door of the screen. He sensed that she was very frightened.

"The door of the church was open, so I came in," he said simply.

He heard her draw in her breath with a little gasp. He smiled, wondering if she had thought he was a ghost. Until she spoke he had been quite certain she was one.

She hesitated for a moment, then said, "I am going to lock the church now," and turned and walked down the aisle.

John followed her to the porch. She stooped and picked up sheets of music that lay on one of the benches there.

"You are lucky," she said coldly. "You might have been locked in. Then you would have been here until tomorrow evening."

"I must apologize," John said. "It was really unpardonable

of me. One trespass led to another. I came into the park. Then, seeing the church, came to have a look at it and tried the door. It was open, so I went in."

He wanted to keep her talking, to make her naturalness dispel the eerie realization that had struck him with the force of a blow as she stepped out to the sunlit porch. Furiously he told himself that this was a lovely girl, obviously an aristocrat, who had some connection with the family or the church—a parishioner, perhaps—but the likeness, almost shattering in its exactness, to the figure on the tomb, was but his own imagination.

She seemed nervous, or really angry and making an effort to conceal it. Going again to the door she looked into the church.

"Isn't there someone else there?" she asked.

"I don't think so," John replied. "I came alone and didn't see or hear anyone else there, until you came."

As she turned again he knew there was no doubt about the likeness. She was young, not more than eighteen. Her slenderness made her look taller than she was. Her ivory-white face was set now in stern lines, as though finding a stranger in the church had really distressed her. She pushed a red-gold curl impatiently up under her green hat. Her simple suit was of the same soft green. Her long hands were lovely, with the pink nails unlacquered. For all her dignity there was something fresh and childlike about her.

It was when he looked into her eyes that John knew he had seen this living face before. They were as green and cold now as a winter sea, but he knew they could change strangely, sometimes looking almost black, according to her mood.

She took a large key from her coat pocket and fitted it into the lock.

"I'll shut the door, then," she said.

"I hope you forgive me," John said. "I am an American. I

only docked today. I was looking for the Beausire Arms. When I saw the park gates open I couldn't resist its beauty."

Her face did not soften. He sensed that she was trying not to look into his face. For the first time the similarity of their coloring struck him, though the copper brightness of her hair was shades lighter than his.

"The best way to the village is through the park by a path I will show you," she said, and led the way to an old lich gate at the back of the church.

They walked down the path in silence. The covered gate looked very old. The symbols of the Evangelists were carved at the four corners of the roof, under which innumerable coffins must have passed. As she stretched out her hand to the gate John wondered if the coffin of the girl who lay beneath that white tomb had rested here as it was carried from the Court.

"This way," the girl said, indicating a path that cut across an expanse of grassland to a small wood, in the opposite direction from the one in which he had come.

"This path strikes the main road a few yards below the Beausire Arms," she said. "You can see the sign from the gate at the end of it. I must go now. Good afternoon."

With a little nod she left him, walking quickly over the grass. When she reached the tower she turned and went toward the house. John stood watching her until she disappeared among the trees.

The sun was sinking toward the west, and the rooks made more noise than ever. John stood watching them wheel and dip, reluctant to move, trying to separate in his mind the girl who had died so long ago and the modern young woman who seemed to resent his presence so deeply. He could not do it. They merged into that one personality which he had known in dreams.

Remembering his car, he started to walk slowly toward the drive. It was not imagination that she was like the sculptured figure, he told himself. She must be a Beausire. How else could she have acquired that short straight nose, broad low brow, and soft fullness of the mouth, with its still childish line? Even those long lovely hands were the same.

The clerk in Taunton had assured him that the house was closed, with only a caretaker and his wife living in it. Lord Beausire was unmarried, and an only child.

Excitement and a joy in life he had never felt before swept over him. It would not be difficult to trace her. A girl like that would be well known in the village. He would find her and show her his little book, which would explain why he had come to this place. She would forgive him then, and be friendly. Suddenly it occurred to him that she might have been as startled at the sight of him as he was when she appeared at the screen. Perhaps he looked like a Beausire and that had puzzled her, as she could not place him.

The car was there. The lodge still gave no sign of life within it. John knew he would stay here, for weeks if necessary, until he had found her.

As he drove out of the gates, he thought of a lecture he had once heard on the powers of the subconscious mind. He remembered vividly the moment when Hallet had come into the room with the black tin box in his hands. Why had he himself at that moment felt in his subconscious mind that, with the opening of that box, he was moving at last toward his destiny?

That night he had thought he had no chance because he did not know what he wanted. He knew now. He wanted to have the house that stood so proudly on its terraces. He wanted to put the great derelict gardens about it in perfect order, and more than that, more than he had ever thought it possible to want anything, he wanted the girl who seemed to have slipped out of a marble tomb to appear before him when he called her name.

◆   ◆   ◆   ◆

A hundred yards or so above the gates of the Court the road curved into a village street. Thatched white cottages stood on either side of it, set back in gardens gay with spring flowers. The place seemed as deserted as the lodge had been, though at one gate an old hound lying in the sun looked up lazily as the intruder passed, then went to sleep again. John did not know that this was the sacred hour of tea and all the inhabitants were within.

And the inhabitants of the four Sudbury villages did not know that they were in for the biggest sensation experienced here for two hundred and fifty-three years. Wars and rumors of wars might come and go. Famine and pestilence, good times and bad, deaths of Kings and the accession of new ones, rise and fall of governments and cabinets occurred with dull regularity, but all these things were history, while the affairs of the Beausires were strictly personal to every soul in the valley. What was about to happen concerned them all closely.

Mrs. Meggs, coming to the door of her cottage beside the forge, saw a gray car stop at the inn. She knew nothing whatever about cars, but an inner sense told her when they were expensive. This one, being new to the valley, warranted investigation. She decided to pop up to the Arms after she'd washed up the tea things, ask Ellen Hobbs for those carnation plants, and find out whether it was merely a passing car stopping or whether it carried folk who would stay a few days or more. She hoped it was the latter. Since the Court had been closed—with his Lordship in India—things had been quite dull.

Small, spare, with a prim neatness which those who knew her felt that even the crack of doom would not disturb, Matilda Meggs went inside again. She poured another cup of almost black tea, helped herself liberally to sugar and reached for the milk jug.

Meggs, the local carter, did not look up from the Taunton paper he borrowed daily from Mr. Parret of the forge.

" 'Oo was it?" he asked, knowing perfectly well his wife had gone out because she heard the horn of a car.

"Strange car. Good un, too. Stopped at th' Arms. Reminds me I 'as to see Ellen 'bout them plants for out front."

There was silence for a while. Both applied themselves to the serious business of tea. Then Matilda spoke thoughtfully.

"I was sayin' to th' girl up to Combe St. Philip's t'other day, when I went for nine penn'orth o' cream, that nothing ever 'appens 'ere any more. Why, there ain't even been a Beausire tragedy, 'count o' th' curse, for, let's see"—with deep concentration and her fingers she counted up—"forty-one years."

Meggs stuffed tobacco into his clay pipe with a mournful air. "Better touch wood," he said. "Don't never do to speak too soon. If there was a wind a bit stronger than ornery I'd 'ate to think o' where the roof o' the west wing 'ud land. Wants reparin' summat crewel, it do."

"Ain't no chance," his wife replied. "If there's war, taxes'll go up again sure as eggs is eggs. An' we all knows the fam'ly can't stand no more o' that."

She got up and had the things put to rights in record time. That car had intrigued her. It was not for nothing that her best friends admitted—with a grudging admiration—that Matilda Meggs had a nose for gossip. Seemed as though she just smelt it out, they said.

Chapter Two

✦   ✦   ✦   ✦

A FADED SIGN HUNG FROM THE SHARPLY GABLED STONE-and-timber house that was flanked on one side by a splendid old apple tree heavily laden with blossom, and on the other by a neatly kept garden bright with scarlet and yellow tulips. The crest on the sign was almost obliterated by wind and weather, the lettering barely decipherable, but the Beausire Arms needed no identification. There were few such houses left in England.

Looking at the inn, John thought—with a sense of triumph over the now familiar feeling that he had seen each new scene in the valley many times before—that the picture postcards of the Sudbury St. Luke Inn offered for sale in Taunton did not do it justice, though they accounted for his knowledge of its façade.

He also knew what the back of it looked like. A clear picture formed in his mind of a great cobble yard, connected on one side by a long galleried building with the stables and coach houses that faced the back of the inn. There was a mounting block near the back door and ringed hitching posts outside the stables. The yard was big enough to accommodate several coaches.

Odd how these old places made one think of horses and coaches, he mused. A car seemed curiously out of place. His eyes turned to the garden, seeking the coach entrance he knew was there, and he saw a man, walking with a bad limp, come toward him.

Advancing to open the car door, the man raised a hand to his forelock in what was evidently a mechanical attempt at a military salute. Then the hand dropped heavily. John saw a pair of pale eyes looking with an expression of utter astonishment into his face.

"I would like to take a room here," John said.

The man nodded, but did not speak. John felt the tension between them as if it were a tangible thing. He sensed that the bewilderment his coming had caused would rise at any moment to panic, and then this groom or whoever he was would break away and bolt.

The situation was so ridiculous that he knew he must himself do or say something to force a reply.

The man was about forty, possibly older. His sandy hair was getting somewhat thin, and his narrow face had a curious expression that John suddenly realized was caused by a livid scar that ran from the outer corner of the right eye to the mouth. He wore a tweed shooting jacket several sizes too large for him, corduroy breeches, boots and leather leggings. John thought of him as connected with horses.

Opening the car door himself, John got out. The action seemed to break the spell of astonishment that gripped the man, for he said at once, "A room, sir? I ain't sure about that. You see, sir, it's early in the year, we don't 'ave the summer staff in yet. Maybe you'd be better served in Taunton. There's a right good hotel there. Listed by the A.A. it is, and very well run."

There was something pathetic in the obvious reluctance to take in a guest who might demand more than the place could offer. Then, remembering what the Taunton man had said about the Beausire Arms, John knew that this was not the reason why the man did not want to give him a room. He was conscious of anger and a determination to stay.

The inn was a center for stag hunters. It was well known to antiquarians. The inside of the house had been fitted with modern conveniences at considerable expense, and the food was in its way famous. They need not hesitate to take in anyone here.

"I like simple places," John said firmly, "and I will take any room you have. A house like this makes up for a lot of inconveniences."

As if he did not know what else to do or say, the man took two bags from the car.

"If you like old places, sir," he said. "Some do, some don't."

"I do," John replied. They started towards the open front door.

It was without surprise that he saw the now familiar symbols carved amid oak leaves in the spandrils of the superb entrance archway. The patter of the clerk who had said he stopped here sometimes on his day off came back to John.

"I'll fetch my mother, sir. She sees to the rooms."

"Your name is Hobbs, isn't it?" John asked. The man in Taunton had referred to "old Horace" in a way that had made John expect to see an elderly man. Perhaps this was the son.

"Yes, sir. I'm 'Orace 'Obbs, sir, at your service. My mother an' me runs this place, sir. She sees to the inside, I does everything else and 'tend to the taproom. Business is slack now, but come June, we're right busy on Sundays an' 'alf 'olidays. Folk come from as far as Bristol, they do."

"No wonder," John said as he looked round the long low room, black with ancient oak. "It's worth coming for." He wanted this man Hobbs to go on talking until he put himself into a friendlier frame of mind. He sensed that he was going to shift onto his mother the unpleasant job of refusing accommodation.

"Your family has been here some time, I understand?" he said, thinking how absurd convention was. Why could he not tell this man with the strangely familiar and frightened eyes that he was no ordinary tripper, that it meant more than any words could say to him to stay in this village tonight?

One did not say those things, not in England. However, the ice seemed to be melting, for so genial a smile spread over the thin face of Hobbs that it overcame the grotesque effect of the scar.

"To some way of thinkin'," he replied. "The story goes as the first 'Obbs to 'ave this inn was a sailor on the same ship as the son of Lord Beausire, when they went out after the Armada. Come on bad times, 'e did, when that show was over. Bein' broke—as we puts it—an' no place to go, William 'Obbs comes down from Bristol with a travelin' players show. When he sees those carvings over the doorway, he knows this is Beausire property, an' the captain of his ship wouldn't be far off. They got together some'ow, for William 'Obbs got a lease o' the Arms, seven-year lease, same as I gets now, in the spring of 1589. We've bin 'ere ever since, sir. 'Is Lordship renewed the lease just before 'e went out to India two years ago. I'll find Ma, sir. The bar opens in ten minutes, so I 'as to get back." He went out of the room quickly.

John sat down on the deep oak window seat, tense with excitement. He remembered the words of Horace Hobbs: "A seven-year lease. Same as I gets now." A seven-year lease of the Court, which had been shut up for years! What a lot he could do in seven years to stem the tide of neglect and ruin that seemed to be creeping like a slow and deadly tide through the gardens and park and would soon be lapping about the old walls of the house itself! It was a shining goal. Already he saw men working on those neglected driveways and gardens, the best architects in England advising repairs for safeguarding the house. Old buildings could be preserved indefinitely if enough money was spent on them.

The long lists in English papers of ancient and storied country places for sale and rent came back to him. Surely Lord Beausire, with his regiment in India for several years more, would see the advantage of such an offer.

Reason did not enter into this: it was too deep and mysterious a thing. John knew he would spend a fortune on the place, and then, if need be, leave it, asking nothing more than to know he had saved its beauty for a little longer. How strange it was! Yesterday he would not have understood how a man could love a place. Now he knew, because he loved an old Tudor house he had not even entered.

He began to think of long cables to India. Mentally he began to compose a cable; then he became conscious of a low urgent voice outside the window.

"I've bin 'untin' everywhere for you, Ma," Horace Hobbs' voice said. "Come in, quick. A bloke's 'ere, from America. Anyway, there's American labels on 'is bags. Ma, you could've knocked me down with a feather when I laid eyes on 'im. One of the family, 'e is."

A curious exultation seized John. So that was it! It was not antagonism, but surprise, that had made Hobbs so inhospitable. He would tell him about that John Beausire who had gone to Maryland. There must be a record of him. Two hundred and fifty years would not seem so long to a man whose people had been in this house, running the inn, since 1589.

He could not hear the reply. A woman said something in a low voice. Hobbs answered with fear and exasperation ringing in every word.

"But I tell you 'e is. I knows a Beausire when I sees one. Ma, we've got to get 'im out o' 'ere. I tell you it means trouble."

Soon there were steps in the corridor. John stood up. He expected a sharp-faced old woman and was prepared to stand firm. They would let him stay or give a damned good reason for their refusal. What sort of trouble could they expect? It had not been the extra work caused by the demands of a fussy guest that Hobbs had been thinking of when he spoke.

Hobbs returned. He had a white linen apron on now, and as he took up his place behind the bar, he said, "Ma will be in right away, sir. She was gardenin'."

Now for the harridan. If she refused to open her rooms until June, nothing could force her to. But this was a public house: he would come here every day, have all his meals here, see every yard of the valley, make friends with some of the people.

A tall woman in a blue dress came into the room. Her hair was white but her fresh face almost unlined. John found himself looking into deep blue eyes that regarded him steadfastly, yet without a hint of impertinence. A feeling of utter well-being, of friendliness, came to him. He said, very simply, "Mrs. Hobbs, I have come a long way to find this inn. I want very much to stay here for a short time."

A smile, full of sweetness, spread over the woman's face, lighting her eyes. As a girl she must have been very pretty.

"And you shall, sir," she said. "There's no one else here, and we have but one maid, but if you'll put up with things till we get going for the summer, we'll do the best we can for you."

"Thank you," John said. "I'll take any room you have ready. A suite if you have one."

Horace banged three pewter mugs down on the bar with unnecessary force. His mother gave him a sharp look. Three farm laborers came in and went up to the bar.

John felt strangely shaken by the depths of his relief. Perhaps it was nothing more than a snobbish pride in being connected with so ancient a family—and the spring beauty of the land—that had made this matter one of such importance. When one saw a thing of great beauty, it was not difficult to imagine one had always known it.

He followed Mrs. Hobbs to a desk in the narrow paneled hall. She opened a big, leather-bound volume saying, "Perhaps you'll register, sir. I'll call the Boots to take up your bags."

John watched her as she went down the hall. The friendliness she showed was genuine. It was like a warm fire on a cold night. He knew he could tell her, perhaps not now, but soon, that he was no stranger here. He could ask her help in finding the gold-haired girl.

John bent down and signed, "John Beausire, New York City." He knew he would never sign his name again in any other way.

It was only his grandfather who had adopted the simpler spelling—Hallet had found that out. He would have the matter done legally, if it should be necessary, but from now on he was John Beausire.

Mrs. Hobbs came back, followed by a boy who took up the bags Hobbs had left in the hall. She looked down at the signature.

It seemed a long time before she raised her eyes. When she

did they seemed to be shining with unshed tears. She pointed with a work-worn finger to the words "New York City."

"Your people came from Maryland, did they not, sir?" she asked.

All that Hallet had dug up on his hurried trip to look up old Maryland records flashed into John's mind at once as he answered, "Yes. My ancestor settled there about 1695." His hand moved toward the pocket of his coat, but he did not take out the book. He would not show it to her now.

It did not seem strange that she knew something of his family history. Nothing that could happen here would seem strange, unless it disproved his right to be here and to feel that he had come home.

"Some folks hereabouts still speak of him as the Lord who disappeared," she said gently. "I'll show you our rooms now, sir."

There was a huge old fourposter bed in the bedroom. The floors were a little uneven, the ceilings low. There was a homeyness about these rooms he had never known before, John thought.

One window looked out on the apple tree and to deep meadows beyond it, the other on the village street. John suddenly thought of the courtyard as he had imagined it, and was filled with curiosity. He was quite sure now he had not seen a picture of the back of the house.

He found a window on the landing of the back stairs and looked out. There was no courtyard there. A neat vegetable garden sloped down to the meadow on one side; on the other there were flowers, with an orchard beyond. Opposite the house was a modern garage with space for several other cars.

John went back to his rooms. Some picture of an old inn courtyard he had seen and forgotten, and then subconsciously tacked on to the Beausire Arms, he thought. Funny how the mind worked.

The sky over the treetops of the park was flushed with red. Through a break in the trees, John watched its fiery glow deepen. Then, etched against it, came four herons, flying low, their necks arched, their long legs stretched out behind them. Again that strange sense of homecoming wrapped around him. He thought of the birds, seeking the shelter of the wooded valley after a day of hunting food in the marshes beyond the hills. A line from Virgil came to his memory: *"In alveo optato."* He recalled how pleased he had been with his boyish translation of it, years ago: "In the haven where they fain would be." That was what he felt now.

❖   ❖   ❖   ❖

When Ellen Hobbs came into the hall her son was standing by the door of the taproom. She knew he was waiting for her. She also knew she could tell him nothing about that desire to serve and please that she felt only for the family—and not even all of them—and that had come to her when she saw their new guest.

"Ma, you 'aven't gone an' let 'im 'ave rooms?" There was an accusing note in the voice of Horace, who knew perfectly well—having been told by Sidney, the Boots—that she had.

"Why, of course. Mighty lucky we are to let the best suite so early. I know troublemakers at once, spot them on sight. Mr. Beausire'll make no trouble. Not that he'll need to, he'll be well looked after."

Horace's pale eyes appeared to start from his head. He lunged forward, his voice rising to a wail. "Mr. Who?" he almost screamed.

Ellen stood on the last step. Her head was lifted with a triumphant tilt. "Mr. John Beausire," she said, "from Maryland. A direct descendant of the Lord who disappeared. Remember I always did say that the end hadn't been heard of that story. Miss Anne declared so, to her dying day."

Ellen went to the kitchen. Tonight dinner must be as good as humanly possible.

Horace leaned against the door of the taproom and stared into space, trying to sum up this extraordinary event. Mrs. Meggs bustled in, asking him where his Ma might be found and saying something about carnation plants. Horace jerked a thumb dumbly in the direction of the kitchen. Mrs. Meggs moved toward the back of the house, and her eyes gleamed. She sensed excitement.

Behind the bar, Horace drew himself a swig of brandy. Without looking at the label on the bottle he took the best, an extravagance of which he was seldom guilty. He tossed it down and felt somewhat better, but informed Sidney that he could tend bar—he might as well learn how, against brisk trade in the summer.

Then he sat down on a stool, to keep an eye on Sidney and to try to think.

"John Beausire!" he murmured. "Direct descendant of the Lord 'oo disappeared! What'n 'ell's goin' to 'appen now?"

The worst part of it was he couldn't for the life of him understand what it was he feared. Supposing what Ma had said was true? His Lordship was Lord Beausire, and that was that.

Dinner had to be served. Now the American had been taken in, he had to be looked after decently.

"Carry on Sidney," Horace said glumly, and went to the kitchen.

"I tell you what, Ma," he said, gloom exuding from him.

"It's the curse stirrin' again. Bin quiet too long, it 'as. Now somethin' 'orrible's goin' to 'appen. Mark me words."

There was still a radiance about Ellen's face. "Fiddlesticks," she said; then, not knowing why she spoke, added, "I know more about the curse than you do, Horace, and I tell you this may mean the end of it."

Horace muttered something about rich Americans splashing money around like water and making trouble; then he went out to see to the table.

Ellen prepared dinner carefully. She tried to concentrate on doing the very best she could with what she had in the house, not to give in to her wild desire to drop her work and run over the fields by the short-cut to the Vicarage, to find Miss Rosalys and cry out to her that John Beausire had come from America and was at the inn.

She thought of Miss Anne, that Beausire she had loved more than any of them, more than her own children, she sometimes thought, but not more than Miss Anne's daughter, the little Rosalys who had been given into her care as a motherless babe. She knew she could not wait until morning, that she must go to Miss Rosalys as soon as dinner was served.

Mrs. Meggs burst into the kitchen. "Ellen," she gasped, "I thought I'd just let you know. Miss Rosalys has gone off to London on the night mail train. She just stopped by the forge to give Mr. Parret a message about shoeing her horse tomorrow. She said she'd be back in a few days. Queer, ain't it, with Vicar away till end of the week. I've just seen the American. My, ain't 'e 'andsome? Makes me think of some of the portraits in the gallery up to the Court. Strange 'e's American, ain't it? Just as well. If 'is Ma came from 'ereabouts, people 'ud be thinkin' things."

A black wave of disappointment broke over Ellen. Why

had Miss Rosalys gone away, now? There would be no one to tell tonight. She thought of finding out from Emily, the Vicarage parlormaid, where she was staying, and telephoning her tonight. But no. That would be no good. She wanted to see her face when she heard it.

As he served dinner Horace Hobbs seemed to have recovered his self-possession. John knew that the man had accepted the situation, whatever he made of it. His own feeling toward him was tinged with pity for which there seemed no obvious reason, except perhaps those traces of terrible wounds. He determined on another effort towards friendliness.

"Have you stayed here all your life?" he asked.

"All me born days, sir, 'cept for the war."

"You were wounded, weren't you?" John asked. If only he could get Hobbs to talk, it might break down that barrier of reserve and distrust.

Horace handed the silver dish of pastry. John knew nothing about the sharp exchange of words in the kitchen when Horace found his mother using the silver service reserved for the Beausire family and their friends. He merely thought that the appointments of the inn were quite exceptional.

"Yes, sir. Twice. Last time was the worst. It was me face and leg then."

John knew he had struck the right note. Here was an old soldier who could not resist talking about the war.

"You must have been very young," he said. That too made a good impression, for Horace smiled broadly.

"Just twenty-one, sir, I was, when the war started. Up at the Court in trainin' under the butler. Ma thought as 'ow that 'ud 'elp me in runnin' the inn when it came to my turn. Six of us enlisted the first week, and by the end o' the year I was the only one left."

"You were lucky to get through," John said.

"That I was, sir. Seems as if them 'Uns couldn't kill me, though they came pretty near it that last October."

"Tell me about it," John said. He was on the right track now. Soon he and Horace would be friends.

"Not that them wounds trouble me now," Horace said, quick to disclaim the pity he sensed. "Get about spry as a lad, I do. It was like this, sir. I was just leavin' me dugout to see a pal near by, when I thinks of Master Mark, but I 'ad no call to go to his dugout then. But when I sees a man boilin' some coffee on a stove, and thinks 'ow Master Mark would like a nice 'ot cup o' coffee, I 'ung round till I saw me chance and the bird as 'ad it wasn't lookin', then grabs the can and makes off to Master Mark. When I found 'im 'e was lookin' that down-in-the-mouth I was glad I'd done it."

Hobbs paused. John did not have to be told that Master Mark was a Beausire. Mark, Baron Beausire, was listed in Burke's Peerage as having been born in 1900 and succeeded to the title in 1918. "Go on," he said.

"Well, sir, that was a day, that was. Master Mark drank the coffee. 'That was good, 'Orace,' 'e said. I could 'ear the 'owls of the blighter as made it by that time, but I don't bat an eyelid. I knelt down and tried to get some of the mud off of Master Mark's boots, when sudden like, 'e says, 'We ain't goin' to get out o' this, 'Orace, an' I'm the last of the Beausires.'"

Did they not then consider him a Beausire, John wondered. Mrs. Hobbs had known of the John Beausire who settled in Maryland, so surely Mark Beausire knew of him, and Horace, too.

Horace resumed, warming up to his story now. "'We ain't dead yet,' says I, tryin' to be cheerful, like. I says, 'If Kaiser Bill was to do for you, 'is Lordship would marry again, an' 'e'd 'ave a son, maybe two or three of 'em. 'E's only fifty-five, come March.' "

"Not a very cheerful thought for Master Mark," John said. He could not help smiling, yet he liked to think of this man kneeling in a muddy trench, trying with all his love and loyalty to cheer the disconsolate boy who was the last of the Beausires.

Horace nodded gloomily. "It was the best I could do," he said. "Master Mark gave a queer sort o' laugh, then says, 'It's a good idea, 'Orace, but it won't work,' an' without another word 'e pulls a telegram from 'is pocket an' gives it to me. Fair took me breath, it did. Was from Vicar, an' said as how 'is Lordship 'ad died of pewmonia, five days back. Took some time to reach the trenches, that wire did. But I perks up, thinkin' o' Master Mark, though I was powerful fond of the old Lord. 'You just 'as to get through now,' I says. 'The Four Evangelists will see to that. God bless your Lordship.'

"Master Mark 'eld out 'is 'and, an' we shakes. 'Thanks, 'Orace,' 'e says. 'I 'opes they do their job. If those old trees fall, there'll be enough wood in 'em to make duckboards from 'ere to Berlin.' "

John felt he knew exactly what Horace meant by his re-mark about the Evangelists. It was the trees in the park, not the Saints, that he referred to. But the definite connection between them and the safety of the last Beausire eluded him. If Horace went on talking he felt he would place the story, it was so near his conscious mind.

"Why did you say the Four Evangelists will see to that?" John asked. He felt he had to know this.

"I forgot you was a stranger 'ere, sir," Horace said. "They call four big oaks in the park that 'ereabouts. While those trees stand there'll always be a Lord Beausire. If they were to fall, then the 'ouse would fall, too."

"Let's hope they stand for a good long time to come," John said. He wanted to ask more about them, but decided to wait until he got an opportunity to talk to Mrs. Hobbs. Somehow it would be easier to tell her how he had blundered into the park and the church, and to ask her where the girl lived. Horace would suspect him of prying into matters that did not concern him.

There was little further information to be obtained, save that the Court had been closed a great deal since the war, for Lord Beausire was in the Army and had been away. Now he was in India.

"But 'e retires in four years, sir. Then we'll 'ave good times again. The Court will be open, an' things as they should be. Bit run down, now, but when 'is Lordship comes 'ome for good, then it'll all be put to rights."

So there were only four years. Never mind. A lot could be done in four years.

"Has the place ever been let?" John said, watching carefully for some reaction to the remark. "It seems a pity to leave such a house uninhabited for so long. That does old houses no good, you know."

A look of horror passed over the scarred face. "Let, sir! I should think not. No strangers 'ave ever lived there, nor ever will, not as long as one stone stands on another."

It didn't sound very encouraging. Perhaps the little book would save him from the stigma of being a stranger, John thought.

One thing of tremendous importance was disclosed by one of the men in the bar. John discovered that there was a right of way through the park. A friendly carter named Meggs told him where to find the gate. One could go past those trees without the risk of being thrown out as a trespasser.

A crescent moon rode high in the sky, stars blinked down, the grass was wet with dew as John crossed the park toward those immense shadows.

Looking up into the whispering darkness, touching a great trunk, he felt a deep peace slipping down from those heavy branches, enveloping him, shutting out all fear of the future. He felt he was being swept to his Destiny by some powerful force: all he had to do was to wait patiently.

Like pearls on a rosary the events of the day slid through his mind; the first sight of the valley, the gates, the house. Suddenly the finding of that white tomb appeared in another aspect. Death was but an event in life, a constantly recurring event that did not signify an end, but the gateway to a new beginning. At the moment he had been most bitterly conscious that the barrier of death was between him and the girl who had lain so long in that quiet place, she had appeared before him, living as he was living.

Far off an owl hooted. A great star, just above the dark outline of a hilltop, looked like a burning taper held in an unseen hand. The deep and lovely sound of the bell of St. John's—he knew now that it was St. John's Church, in the village of Sudbury St. John—struck twelve times. It was midnight, and the day of his homecoming was over. Tomorrow was a new day.

Chapter Three

* * * *

THE IMMENSE AND SOMBER YEW TREES IN THE CHURCH-yard of St. John's seemed to be whispering among themselves dark secrets about the mystery of time. They cast a shadow across the famous old square tower and made a cool aisle from the little dark door beneath the tower to a gray stone wall, where another door led to the Vicarage garden.

John looked with keen interest at the wooden props that held up the tremendous lower branches of the trees, and the iron braces supporting their trunks. The slowest growing and longest living of trees, the yews must have been here for more than a thousand years.

Coming into the sunlight near the stone wall, John tried to throw off the sense of desperation that had grown upon him during his five days at the inn. He felt that behind all this beauty and ancient splendor there was something even more beautiful, something for which he had been waiting all the years of his life; yet an invisible barrier stood between him and it, and he could not break that barrier down.

The barrier was there in the sleeping silence of the Court, as he saw it morning and evening from the lower terrace, the nearest point to the house touched by the right of way. It was there in the thinly veiled curiosity of the village folk with whom he tried to talk, in the indefinable hostility he could feel beneath the courteous and efficient service of Horace Hobbs. Only in the warm friendliness of Mrs. Hobbs did a light seem to shine through it.

The church clock struck the half hour with a deep booming note that seemed to vibrate through the still air long after the sound was gone. With that sound returned all the tense excitement that had flooded him when he first heard it, high up in the wood on the hillside. He had not yet found what he had come for, but he felt it almost within his grasp. The red-haired girl had gone away, but this was her home, she would come back.

John turned his eyes toward the Vicarage wall. He knew now that she lived there, that her name was Rosalys Tremayne and she was the daughter of the Vicar, and that her dead mother had been the Miss Anne of whom Mrs. Hobbs spoke so lovingly, a half-sister of the late Lord Beausire.

The door in the wall was open now. John moved toward it quickly, eager to grasp an opportunity to look into the garden of her home. He wondered if etiquette would not demand that the Vicar call upon him—the Vicar also could not stay away for long. Etiquette would also demand that the call be returned.

Joy and excitement shimmered about him again like a golden haze. All he had to do was to wait with patience. He reached up to touch a long raceme of pale wisteria that hung down from the wall. Looking through the arch into a quiet garden, he saw an old gray stone house almost lost in climbing roses and creepers.

There was an instant impression of perfect order and meticulous care. The Vicarage garden had nothing in common with the dereliction of the great gardens of the Court. John's eyes wandered over smooth lawns like green velvet, formal flower beds, carefully trimmed shrubs, tall trees and flowering bushes. From somewhere out of sight came the whirr of a mowing machine, and the clean smell of newly cut grass filled the air.

The deep peace of the house and the garden seeped into him. He stood looking at it with a sense of wonder. He could see the tall girl Rosalys moving about this garden, entering and leaving the house. It seemed incredible that he had not known through so many empty years that she was here, living her peaceful and quiet life, waiting, as he had waited, for the ceaselessly moving fingers of Destiny to cross the threads of their lives.

Here the barrier did not seem to exist at all. He had come to this place to find her, and for no other reason. It did not matter at all that he had an ancestor who for some unfathomable reason had left this place, or that it was as familiar to him as if he had been born and brought up here. She no longer seemed to be the alabaster girl strangely come to life. Sorrow had no part in their lives. He was John Beausire, and he had come to find her, and within an hour of his coming to the valley she had stepped out of the shadows and he had heard her voice.

A French window in the house stood open. John stepped forward eagerly as he saw a tall figure dimly outlined within the room. For an instant he was sure it was Rosalys. She had returned and she would come out and call to him.

He stood, tense and still, just outside the doorway. It was Mrs. Hobbs who came to the window. His pleasure at seeing her was obliterated in crushing disappointment.

"Good afternoon, sir," she said cheerfully. "Lovely day, isn't it? I'd sooner have been working in my garden, but Vicar's books had to be done. Every three months I come up to dust them. He likes to have me see to them."

With a sense of desperation John turned to Ellen Hobbs. How utterly familiar she looked, this woman he had known for five days!

"When does the Vicar come back?" he asked. "This is too fine a day to waste indoors if tomorrow would do as well for the books."

Ellen smiled. "That's just it, sir. They come back today."

John smiled, too. "They," she had said. After all, he did not have much longer to wait. The sunlight seemed suddenly more golden, the faint sweet scent of wisteria almost overpowering.

"Today," John repeated. He was sure that Mrs. Hobbs knew how empty his days in Sudbury had been, and why, and that she was glad for him now, when the waiting was over.

"Yes, sir. The vicar comes by the six o'clock train to Taunton. Miss Rosalys is driving from London with Major and Mrs. Gregg. You'll like the Major, sir. I often thinks to myself he's the nicest gentleman of all who visit here. Great friend of his Lordship, he is. They saw a lot of each other in India."

John was conscious of unreasonable resentment that Rosalys would have old friends to entertain. He wondered if they would stay at the Vicarage or at the inn.

"Perhaps you'd like to come in and see some of Vicar's drawings of the church, sir?" Mrs. Hobbs said. "They're thought a deal of. Vicar's books on the old places of Somerset are very well known. He's writing one on Wells Cathedral now."

"I would, very much," John said, as he followed her into a long dim room with book-covered walls and heavy old furniture. "I've been poking around the church. Its age is staggering."

He had meant to take in every detail of this room. Many

hours of Rosalys' short life must have been spent here. He looked around eagerly. Then he saw nothing but the oil portrait that hung facing the huge mahogany desk.

It was of a young woman in a black velvet dress. The long white hands were loosely clasped, and the slender figure leaned forward in the big chair as if just about to speak. John felt that he had but to stand very still, to listen with all the concentration of his being, and he would hear what it was she wished to say.

He knew that Mrs. Hobbs was staring at him, but he did not care. The long blue eyes of the painted face held him. Somewhere he had seen that face, framed in silvery blonde hair, before.

He hardly heard Mrs. Hobbs say, "That's Mrs. Tremayne, sir, my blessed Miss Anne."

He felt strangely aware of a living presence. Strength flowed from it, a jubilant happiness. This girl would allow no nebulous veil to hang between her and what she knew to be her destiny. She would go fearlessly forward.

There was understanding in those eyes. Looking intently at the painting, John wondered at the artist's skill. He seemed to have caught the all-pervading tenderness, the gentle and unflinching strength of purpose, the infinite pity that had once looked from the living eyes.

Mrs. Hobbs held out a drawing in a narrow frame of ebony.

"This is the tower, sir," she said, "and the north porch. The arch of the door is said to be one of the finest in England."

John did not attempt to take the drawing. He knew that he could not go on as he had done for five days, a stranger, shut out from the hidden life of this place, knowing no more about the family from which he was descended than he had known the day he came.

The sharp thin face of a woman who had talked to him the

day after his arrival rose up before him. She had been friendlier, more disposed to talk than most. She had said boldly that
the Beausires were cursed, that in every generation something
horrible happened.

Hobbs had closed up like a clam when questioned. Now he
would ask Mrs. Hobbs.

"Tell me about Miss Anne," he said.

Ellen Hobbs smiled up at the portrait. "It doesn't do her justice, sir," she said. "She was lovelier than that."

"She is very beautiful," John said, "but not at all like her
daughter."

Mrs. Hobbs had been putting the drawing back in its place:
she turned sharply, astonishment and a shadowy fear drifting
over her worn face.

"You have seen Miss Rosalys, sir?" she asked wonderingly.
"She went up to London the day you came."

His eyes still on the portrait, John told Ellen Hobbs of his
visit to the private chapel of Sudbury Court. He heard her ex-
clamation of astonishment and turned to face her. The curious
half-veiled fear he had seen in the eyes of her son when he had
spoken about the story of a curse was in her eyes also. John determined to get the legend from her, for it interested him. He
felt he had a right to know even the superstitions concerning
the family.

"What is the story of the curse?" he asked simply, taking it
for granted that she knew and would answer him frankly.

For some moments Ellen Hobbs did not speak. Then she
gazed up at the portrait and said, "Miss Anne believed in it, but
she said the power of it could be broken."

"Sit down," John said, "and tell me about Miss Anne and
what she believed."

Ellen's eyes filled with tears. The hours spent dusting the

books had been haunted by memories. How sure Miss Anne had been, to the last day of her life, that the curse was a reality, and that it could only be broken in one way! She was suddenly conscious of overwhelming relief, as of one who is at last able to share a burden too great to be borne.

Now that John Beausire had come from America the curse would not strike again. Only now did she fully realize how great had been her terror of it.

"You have always been very close to the family, haven't you?" John was asking.

She smiled then. "Oh, yes, sir. I went in to service at the Court when I was fourteen. His present Lordship's father was Lord Beausire then."

John knew that at last he was going to get some family history. "Were you born in Sudbury?" he asked.

"No, sir. I was born in Bristol. My father kept a small shop there. One day when I was fourteen I read a story in a newspaper about Sudbury Court. I wanted to see it as I had never wanted anything in my life, and saved my money until I had enough to take the train to Taunton. I walked from there. When I saw the valley, I knew I must spend my life here. At the inn I was told that her Ladyship's head nurse was interviewing girls for the position of under nurserymaid. I applied, and was taken. My parents were very much put out, but I begged so hard they let me go."

"Were there many children at the Court?" John said, determined to keep her talking.

"Only two, sir. His Lordship's father had not been dead a year, and left a widow—his second wife—and a year-old daughter who was to be brought up at the Court. That child was Miss Anne. I loved her very dearly. His Lordship was only twenty-three, but he was married and had a son a few weeks old, Master Luke. They hoped for more children, of course, but none came. Miss Anne and Master Luke shared the nursery like brother and sister. We were very happy. When I had been there about a year I began to walk out with young Bill Hobbs of the Inn."

Ellen went on talking of inconsequential things, of picnics in the woods, of Miss Anne's fruitless efforts to get Master Luke to call her Aunt Anne when she realized their relationship. Ellen's love for the children shone through her words.

John brought her back to the thing he wanted most to know. "Did they talk of a curse then?" he asked.

Ellen's face darkened, but she answered at once.

"Yes, sir. The servants' hall was full of gossip about it. They said that his late Lordship had married again when his wife had been in her grave but six months only because he was determined to have another son. The curse had taken his eldest son, and he was afraid that something would happen to the other one, and the House would die out. He married a young girl, and a year later Miss Anne was born. He was very much put out, they said, that the babe was a girl. He died the following year, but his son by his first marriage had married and already had an heir, so the succession was secured."

"What happened to the elder son?" John asked.

Ellen shivered. "I wasn't here then," she said.

John saw that she did not want to talk about it. That did not matter. He had found out that the story of the curse went back at least two generations.

It was in telling of her own early life here that Mrs. Hobbs spoke most freely. Suddenly John realized that her words regarding her instant love for the place implied an experience somewhat similar to his own. Cautiously he tried to follow that line, almost ready to tell her at least something of the strange joy he had felt when he came for the first time into the valley.

"Was it the valley or the Court itself you felt you had to live in?" he asked.

"The valley, sir," she replied. "I felt I knew it, that to stay here I would take any kind of work. I know that sounds silly, sir." She smiled apologetically.

"Not to me," John said. "Tell me more. Did you feel you knew the Court, when you entered it for the first time?"

Ellen sat pleating the edge of her white apron nervously. She could not understand herself. Not for twenty years had she spoken of those first marvelous days after her discovery of the Sudbury valley. She now felt again that time had no importance or reality. That day fifty years ago, when she had faced her parents in the comfortable kitchen of their Bristol home and informed them she had taken a place as nurserymaid at Sudbury Court, and implored them not to prevent her going to it, seemed no further away than the day twenty years ago when, in this very room she had sobbed out her heart for her dead Miss Anne. On that day she had told the Vicar many things which she had never spoken of before or since, and he had told her she had come very close to seeing through the mystery of death. She had not understood him, and because of his own grief, had not questioned him. Now she was speaking again of those things. Why was it, she wondered. It must be the strangeness of the coming of John Beausire, or because she liked him—Ellen Hobbs resolutely shut her mind to the thought which for days now had tried to force itself into her consciousness, that from the first moment she had seen John Beausire standing in the taproom, she had loved him. She told herself firmly that that was not right or seemly, nor was it possible that she could love him as she had loved Master Luke and

Miss Anne, and later Miss Rosalys. She would admit to herself only that she liked him, that she regarded him as a true Beausire and a worthy descendant of the Lord who disappeared, about whom she and Miss Anne had talked so much, and who had become to her a legendary figure of beauty and sorrow and romance.

For a brief moment she remembered her son's sharp words as he had warned her not to talk of family affairs to Mr. Beausire. "Puts everything in the newspapers, they do," he had said. "Fine story it 'ud make about the curse, an' how there's never been a John Beausire since 1685, an' all the things as happened since then."

Then Ellen made up her mind. She was going to tell Mr. Beausire all she knew about the family. Who had a better right to know? He had been waiting patiently for her to answer his question. He might not understand that answer, but he should have it truthfully. He would only think she was an old woman who had gone a bit hazy about the past.

"You asked me if I felt I knew the Court, sir," she said. "Well, that's how it seemed to me. I can't quite explain it, but when the housekeeper showed me the great rooms I already knew them."

A great longing to enter that house swept over John. His earlier pride suddenly seemed an absurdity.

"Hobbs told me that the Court is never shown to strangers," he said. "Isn't there some way it could be arranged that I might see it? I could write to Lord Beausire, but that would take so long."

Ellen smiled. "I've been thinking of that, sir. Vicar may take you in. I feel sure he will, when he knows who you are. He acts as agent now. Mr. Bartlett died two years ago, and Vicar sort of took over."

John remembered that the woman by the forge—Meggs, her name was—had said that something happened in every generation. Now he would find out what sort of things did happen.

"Was the present Baron's father an only son?" he asked.

Having made up her mind to talk, Ellen spoke freely. She was conscious of a tremendous relief. She felt she could tell Mr. Beausire of the fear that had been tearing at her for two years or more, that the curse would strike again and that this time it would touch Miss Rosalys.

"No, sir," she said. "Since 1685 no eldest son has come into the title. His late Lordship had an elder brother, some seven years the elder, he was."

"How did he die?" John felt the cold wind of sorrow touch him. An infinite pity filled him.

"He—was killed, sir. A madman shot him, on the island in the great lake. His name was Matthew. It was a few days after his twenty-first birthday."

John sensed there was much more of tragedy and horror to that story. Some day he would hear it all. Quickly he led her on.

"It was your Master Luke who died young in the next generation, wasn't it?" he asked.

Quick tears filled Ellen's eyes. Forty-one years had been powerless to dim the horror of that day. While she lived those first awful hours again, John waited for her to speak.

It had been a lovely day. She had been hurrying to get the place tidied up, and the year-old Horace ready for the birthday tea at the Court, when her husband came to the door of the inn. She had called to him gaily, asking if the trap was ready; then, turning, she had seen his gray face, heard the mumbled words. He had said, over and over, "Ellen, my poor girl. God help you, God help her Ladyship."

Horace had been given into the trembling arms of his grandmother. She was beside Bill in the trap before she realized that Master Luke was dead.

Ellen dragged herself back to the present with an effort, thinking it was a silly thing to say that time healed everything. It didn't.

"Yes, sir," she said. "It was Master Luke then. I'll tell you about it. It happened on his ninth birthday.

"He had been given a new pony, and was wild with delight. It was a proper horse, he said. He had stopped by the inn to show it to me. I'd been married two years then, but he came every day to see me. I'd given him the present I had for him, and he had ridden on with his father, calling to me not to be late for the tea. All the tenants and farmers' families were invited."

Ellen went on in a low monotone, as if talking to herself. John saw how deeply this thing had touched her, and he loved her for it.

"They had just turned back, at the top of the South Wood, when his Lordship pulled up to pass the time of day with a carter. Master Luke rode on. He was so excited about his new horse, he couldn't stand still. The horse caught a foot in a rabbit hole and stumbled. Master Luke was thrown. He struck his head against a tree, and was quite dead when his father got to him."

There was a long pause. Bees hummed in the golden sunlight outside; the scent of many flowers filled the room. John shivered. He wanted to hear more, yet to hear it seemed unbearable. The quiet voice resumed.

"Her Ladyship was nigh out of her head with grief. I left Horace and my husband and went back to the Court to be with her. She could not bear anyone else near her. Miss Anne was eleven years old then. She grieved so that we feared for her life, too. One night when I'd sat with her until she cried herself to sleep, I went to the Queen's Room, because no one ever went there, and I had to be alone. I thought if I could cry and cry until I had no tears left I'd be calm enough to go back to her ladyship. But I couldn't cry. I just sat there in the darkness, until I heard someone in the library. It was her Ladyship, wandering round like a lost soul. She came into the Queen's Room, and we sat close together. She was quite calm. That night she told me that the family was cursed because of what was done to the Lord who disappeared, that until the place and the title went back where it belonged there would be no peace, and that she was glad the time had come, for she wished with all her heart the suffering was over.

"His Lordship came and found us there. He seemed angry. Those rooms were never used. Next day he sent for me, and told me to pay no attention to what her Ladyship said, that she was not herself now. He said he knew he did not have to ask me not to repeat it. I never have, sir, not even to my husband, or to Horace and my other sons when they were grown."

"I don't wonder that Miss Anne believed in the curse. A shock like that must have marked her for life," John said. He hoped he would hear more of what Miss Anne had believed.

"Yes, sir, it did. The Lord who disappeared and the little maid were very real to us. We grieved for them. I can't explain it, but we wanted them so much to be happy. It did not seem to make any difference that they had died so long ago. They seemed to us to be alive somewhere, and we wanted them to be together again."

"Tell me their story," John said. "I told you, I have seen that marvelous tomb."

"There isn't much of a story, sir. John Beausire was only fourteen when he inherited the estate. He was an only child.

He loved his cousin, Rosalys, who had been born in France because her parents were Stuart exiles there, and was to have married her when she was fifteen. He was somehow mixed up in the Monmouth Rebellion, and Judge Jeffreys had him transported for ten years. He was attainted—that means he was deprived of everything he had—and his cousin Mark, brother of Rosalys, inherited everything. The little maid died of grief, as is said on her tomb. It came to be believed that John Beausire had died in the Indies. I have never told a soul but you that her late Ladyship told me the family had had proof that he escaped to Maryland and founded a family there. She said he had been betrayed, that the attainder was utterly unjust, and that the cousin who inherited knew it. His present Lordship told Horace that the Lord who disappeared had married and that there were descendants, but he didn't say that the attainder had been unjust. I have always felt that every word her Ladyship said to me was true."

John wondered if it was possible that Horace felt he had come to make some claim on the family, that his coming meant trouble. There must be a way of making the man understand that nothing was further from his own mind, that the suggestion of a lease had been made only because of his desire to spend money on it, to save it. He determined to try even harder to break down Horace's suspicions, to win his friendliness.

"Horace is very fond of the present Lord Beausire, isn't he?" he asked.

Ellen smiled brightly. "Oh, yes, sir. Worships him, Horace does. You see, sir, Master Mark was born three years after Master Luke died. Her Ladyship hadn't expected another child, and she was all the rest of her life obsessed with fear that something would happen to him. She trusted Horace to look after him. They didn't want to make a mollycoddle of Master Mark, but they were so afraid for him. He liked Horace, who was four years older, and Horace rode with him, bird-nested and hunted with him. He was with him in France, too, during the war. It's been a great grief to Horace that his wound prevented him from staying on in the army as his Lordship's batman. He just lives for the time his Lordship will marry and retire."

"Is he engaged?" John asked. He thought it was odd that a man who was the last of an ancient house, as far as he knew, had not married before he was thirty-eight.

The fears and the fury that had torn her for some time now struck Ellen like a sudden wind. Her lips tightened into a thin line. John felt that Beausire must be engaged to some girl she didn't approve of. Sooner or later he would get that story, too.

Ellen looked at John Beausire. The good God has strange ways of bringing things about, she thought. Perhaps, even now, it was not too late. She remembered vividly a sermon Vicar had preached about the marvelous mechanism of the Universe. Perfect law, perfect order. Perhaps John Beausire had come in time.

She decided she would not answer that question if she could help it. She went on talking, her eyes on the portrait.

"That picture's said to be good, sir," she said, "but Miss Anne was much, much prettier than that. Vicar says that it's only because her features were so regular, and her hair so pale and fine, that the artist made her look cold. Why, she was full of fire. What she believed in she believed with all her heart."

John looked again at the portrait. It was odd, some trick of light, he supposed, but now that patrician face did look cold. All the living tenderness and strength he had first imagined in it were gone. It was just a pale fair face with long deep-blue eyes.

"You say she believed in the curse?"

"Yes, sir, she did. She was a strange girl. Dozens of offers, she had, but she was past thirty when she married. Mr. Tremayne was a chaplain in the Army then. It was the third year of the war. In a week they were engaged, and his late Lordship had offered them this living. In three weeks they were married, and Mr. Tremayne went back to the front. When she knew she was to have a child she insisted that if it was a boy it would be named John, if a girl, Rosalys. Her half-brother and sister-in-law were horrified. Those names were thought to be unlucky. There had not been a John or Rosalys since 1685. Master Mark came home and laughed at her. He said that she thought he would be killed, and her child would have to appeal for right of heritage and take the name. She cried, then, and said they didn't understand what she meant. I did. I knew she felt she would be in some way giving those two life again. She made me promise I would see to it that one of those names was used if anything happened to her."

Ellen bent down her head. Her hands were clenched in her lap. In a moment she went on.

"She died when the babe was born. Vicar got back three hours too late to see her. I kept my word. I forced her will upon them. The babe was named Rosalys. Vicar said he wanted it, too. It was his late Lordship who fought it, but he gave in when he had to."

John knew the rest of that tragic story. Mrs. Meggs had volunteered some of it, Horace also.

"You looked after the little girl, didn't you?" he asked.

"Yes, sir. Entirely for the first six months, then Vicar came home and they got a nurse. Horace was back from hospital, and I had my hands full with him. We thought he would die. The doctors said there wasn't a chance. His Lordship, Master

Mark that was, pulled him through. He seemed to pour his own young strength into Horace. He'd just come into the place, and everything was very much tangled up, what with the war taxes and such like. Vicar said it was the power of love that saved Horace. He wanted so much to live, to stand by his Master Mark."

They talked of the black war years, of the two sons, younger than Horace, that Ellen had lost, and through it, John formed a picture of a lovely little red-haired girl growing up, first at the Court, then at the Vicarage.

The afternoon was wearing on. John knew he should go, and at last, though unwilling to leave this house, he left Ellen Hobbs to her dusting and her memories.

As John walked down the village street, he began to think about the Vicar. Quite suddenly he was able to form a mental picture of the man. He must love beauty, and ancient things. It was the Vicar who cared for the old trees and who had so perfectly preserved St. John's Church. His mind went back to the beliefs of another day, even in twentieth-century Protestant England.

Though he had hardly looked at them, he thought of the drawings Ellen had shown him. William Tremayne had been touched with the tragedy of the Beausires. Had he made for himself a remote world of ancient beauty in which he could live out the years of his life?

It was not only because Ellen Hobbs had said the Vicar would arrange a visit to the Court that John wanted to meet him. He was beginning to think that the Vicar of St. John's must be a rather unusual person. John hoped that he would find a friend in William Tremayne. He decided he was not going to stand on ceremony and wait to be called on in the round of parish duties. Tomorrow he would go to the Vicarage and ask frankly to be taken to the Court, giving proof of his right to enter it.

He felt immeasurably nearer to his goal after this talk with Mrs. Hobbs. "The Lord who disappeared" had become a very real personality. It did not seem possible that another John Beausire could be denied entry to the Court, or that Rosalys could avoid him.

As soon as he stepped into the inn, John sensed a peculiar excitement. He heard Horace shouting for Sidney. A moment later Horace burst out of the taproom. He radiated happiness. Every atom of reserve was swept away.

" 'Is Lordship's just 'phoned from London," Horace said, his voice unsteady with joy. "Sprung a surprise on us, 'e 'as. Arrived back from India unexpected like. 'E'll be 'ome tomorrer. So much to do I don't know where to turn first, I don't. Where in 'ell's that good-for-nothin' scamp, Sidney?"

Then, catching sight of the boy, Horace went after him.

There was no trace of the usual sleepy quiet of late afternoon. Even the old setter, Blinkers, seemed touched by the excitement. He ambled up to John and acknowledged a pat with a hurried lick, then resumed his trotting between the kitchen door—through which John could hear the voices of the maids—and the telephone stand, where Horace was telephoning.

John waited for Horace to finish his conversation with the Somerset County Gazette. He was telling the newspaper that Lord Beausire had returned unexpectedly from India and was going to open Sudbury Court for the rest of the summer. Then he read an advertisement for maids and two footmen. John noted that applications were to be made to the Vicarage, at Sudbury St. John.

Horace hung up the receiver for a moment, then called the

number of the Somerset County Herald and repeated his story. He radiated joy.

Then he saw John, and rose stiffly from the chair. As he came forward John knew that every trace of reserve was gone. Horace was so happy that everybody and everything was included in his good will.

" 'Phoned me from London, 'is Lordship did," he said. "Said as 'ow 'e'd landed in the South of France three weeks back, but waited to get word from the War Office about something or other. Sprung a surprise on us—you bet. You could 'ave knocked me down with a feather when I 'eard 'is voice."

"It's fine that he is coming home," John said, wondering if he meant it. "He mentioned being at the Court all summer, didn't he?"

Horace nodded. "Yes, sir, till October. Of course, 'e'll go up to town, and prob'ly to Scotland for the grouse shooting, but 'e'll be comin' an' goin', and after India, that's good enough."

So there would be no chance of getting a lease this summer, John thought. Well, never mind. Perhaps some arrangement could be come to whereby work on the gardens and the house might begin. It was pleasant enough living at the inn.

The telephone rang, and a maid bobbed out of the kitchen to answer it. She informed Horace that Mr. Swain was leaving right now. His grandson was driving him over, and he'd be at the Court about six, and he'd called the agency in Bristol and would have a cook and two kitchen maids coming in early tomorrow.

Horace seemed relieved. "That's Swain, the butler, sir," he said to John. "When the Court's shut up 'e lives with 'is married daughter, over in Crewkerne. Considers 'imself on call, of course. Mighty glad 'e'll be to be back in the old place again."

The boy Sidney called loudly for "Mr. 'Obbs, Mr. 'Obbs,"

from the yard, and with a muttered, " 'Scuse me, sir, there's a power of things to see to," Horace limped across the hall toward the back door.

John went up to his rooms feeling lonely for the first time since his arrival. Pulling a big chair to the window, he sat looking down into the village street. Word must have gone around, for though the bar would not open for an hour yet, he could hear voices below. Mr. Parrett came in from the forge, wearing his leather apron; the carter Meggs followed soon afterward, and two or three farmhands, then an old man who left his horse and cart by the gate.

The sun was slipping westward. Across the road the flowering chestnut trees were already veiled in shimmering gold. Between their great trunks could be seen the grass of the park, fresh and vividly green.

Almost against his will John compared this home coming of Lord Beausire to his own arrival. Telling himself that he was being absurd, he felt a deep resentment. For Lord Beausire there would be no strange veil of unreality. He would not have to keep assuring himself that the utter familiarity of this place was imagination. He would know every soul here and would not walk alone through the villages. He could drive straight up to that marvelous house, where the front door would be opened wide to receive him. He would not have to stand and stare at it, morning and evening, from the foot of the lower terrace.

Then John knew that he desperately desired the friendship of Mark Beausire, that he wanted him to know how he had come to love this place, even in the few days he had been here, and that there would never be any claims made for anything he might be permitted to do.

The tragic story he had heard of the little boy killed in the South Wood came back to him with almost unbearable pathos.

That had happened before Mark Beausire was born, but the horror of it must have shadowed his life. There was that other story, too, of the young man who had been shot on the island.

John thought of the great lake tangled with weeds and water lilies, its unpainted boathouses filled with old and rotting boats, its lovely little islands green and shadowy. He wished now he had yielded to his impulse last night, and taken one of those boats to explore the islands, especially the one on which the small Greek temple with Ionic columns glimmered through the trees. Had the tragedy occurred there, or on one of the other two? Who had shot Matthew Beausire, a few days after his coming of age, and why?

His sense of being shut out from the inner lives of these people deepened. He wished Ellen Hobbs would come into the room and talk to him again.

A horn honked and a small blue car slid to a standstill beside the inn. John saw at first only the red-gold hair of Rosalys, her face as she turned toward Horace, who had come out and was standing talking to her; then he became aware that there were two other people in the car, a woman in a gray suit and hat, and a slender man in tweeds.

With all his strength John willed Rosalys to look up. Silently he called to her, "Rosalys, Rosalys," but he sensed that though she heard, her will was as strong as his, and she would not. Her eyes were fixed on Hobbs, who had shaken hands with the man and the woman and was talking to them.

It was the man who looked up. John saw a thin dark face with flashing eyes. In spite of his very English tweeds, he looked foreign. John met his gaze steadily. A moment later, the car shot forward again. Rosalys was driving, and now all her attention was on the narrow road, down which a heavy cart loaded with straw moved slowly.

The cart with the straw stopped beside the inn. Then came another cart, beside which a very old man plodded. John saw that his cart contained an immense white pig, covered with a thick net.

John felt that he must go down and get into conversation with some of these people. He needed to know whether the village folk liked Lord Beausire, whether they regarded him as a good landlord.

Going down the stairs he felt sure the man with the pig had been the old gaffer he had talked to one evening on the village green. He would offer him a drink and start conversation.

A group outside the door was gathering around the cart, admiring the pig, which had been scrubbed to an amazing cleanliness.

John remembered then that the old man's name was Swain. He wondered if he was related to the butler who was returning to the Court. Again that sense of resentment against Mark Beausire crept into his mind. Beausire would know all these things, while he himself did not and would be open to an accusation of prying curiosity if he asked questions.

"Good afternoon," he said, directly addressing the owner of the pig. "Fine day, isn't it?"

"Tha-at it be, zur-r," the man replied, his quavering voice rich with the slow drawl that had seemed to John, the first time he heard it, the key to many memories. The long vowels, the rolled r's, the "z" for "s," were beautiful to him.

The little group had moved back respectfully to give him a better view of the pig, which grunted indignantly while investigating with a pale snout the possibilities of raising the net.

"That's a first-rate pig you have there," John said. "What are you going to do with it?"

The bright blue eyes twinkled merrily; the broad grin

made the apple-red cheeks even more wrinkled. There was something of the serenity of Mother Earth herself about this old man.

"Fa-aten 'ee some more aga-ainst St. Ma-atty's Da-ay," the farmer replied.

"That's the big fair at Bridgwater, isn't it?" John asked. When had he heard of fattening pigs and grooming horses, preparing cattle for St. Matthew's Day? Had that come out of a book, too?

"Ay, zu-rr," came the slow answer.

"Let's go in and have a drink to the further fattening of your pig," he said. "All of you," he added, as the others stood back.

Horace stood by the taproom door. "It wants twenty minutes to opening time," he said, "but seein' as 'ow we've 'ad the best of news today, come on in."

Swain stood aside, his battered hat in his hand, for John to enter. There was no servility here, only a definite and simple recognition of their different stations in life. John felt quite sure Swain had been content with his lot all his days, and would not know what was meant by envy.

"What'll you 'ave, sir?" Horace inquired.

John took cider. He tasted the fresh cool tang of it, rich with the scent and taste of apples. Horace seemed to know what Swain and the others would have. He drew a pint of rich brown ale and pushed it toward Swain; Parrett the blacksmith received his half-and-half next, and Horace went down the line without pausing to make an inquiry.

John lifted his pewter tankard. "Here's to your pig taking first prize on St. Matty's Day," he said. The owner grinned and buried his rosy face in his mug.

The conversation became general. Soon they were immersed in talk of the best way to fatten a pig, of crops and weather, the age-old things of interest to those who gain their living from the soil.

John had a curious feeling that these simple people were gathering around him, shutting out that gray sense of isolation that had oppressed him. He thought of the hundreds of years through which cider had been made. He could imagine being parched with thirst, stifled with heat, longing for it with an almost crazy longing.

"This is good cider," he said. It seemed a wholly inadequate tribute to the drink of the West Country.

Horace replied proudly, "The best, sir. Made over at Combe St. Philip. We takes all they make, which is little enough nowadays, worse luck. This is made from Kingston Black and Foxwhelp apples, an' kept two years in a brandy cask."

"Cherry Pearmains can't be beat for cider," the blacksmith said. "That old woman at Combe St. Philip could make money if she'd attend to her orchards. Old Ben who farms for her knows more about cider-making than any man left in Somerset, I'll be bound."

They talked of apples. Winter Queenings, Russets, Golden Pippins, Nonpareils and Golden Rennets. A carter from Sudbury St. Matthew said the only way to make apples pay now was to market the table varieties like Cox's Orange Pippins and Ribston Pippins, and it was precious hard to make them pay.

Suddenly John noticed that Horace was grinning broadly.

"Come in, Major," Horace said. "Welcome back to your perch."

The dark-faced man who had been with Rosalys was standing in the doorway. He came forward and sat down at the end of the bar, where he could look down the long low room.

"Perry's my drink," he said, "and this is my particular perch."

"We've some darned fine perry," Horace replied, and shouted for Sidney to draw it. Evidently the perry was kept in the cellar.

"You've not met Mr. Beausire, have you, sir?" Horace asked.

The Major slipped off his perch and came toward John. "I'm glad a John Beausire has come back to these parts," he said, as he held out a thin and sensitive brown hand.

John thought it rather an odd greeting, but it pleased him strangely. Ellen must already have told her story at the Vicarage.

"Maybe you'd like to sit with Mr. Beausire by the window?" Horace asked.

The Major nodded. "Good idea," he said. "That old apple tree's a friend of mine, and I've never yet seen it in bloom."

They went to the table, and the perry was brought. Horace assured the Major that it was made of Moorcroft pears and aged to perfection; then he smiled at John.

"We don't encourage perry drinking," he said. "Precious little is made these days, and it's that strong it makes 'em proper peart in no time at all."

The Major laughed. He seemed intensely pleased about something.

"When I get proper peart it'll be on your Napoleon brandy, Horace," he said. "His Lordship and I will be down for a snifter of it quite frequently."

John noticed that when the Major smiled his whole personality lit up with a peculiar radiance. There was nothing unusual about his appearance: he was not noticeably tall or short, but slender and wiry, with a skin burned by tropic suns to the color of old leather, thin dark-brown hair liberally streaked with gray, quick dark eyes that could manage to give one a comprehensive and sweeping look without rudeness. Yet, once he smiled, no one who had seen him would forget him.

There was something completely disarming in his frankness. He did not beat about the bush. Directly Horace had returned to the bar, Harry Gregg said, "I'm keenly interested in your connection with the Beausires. Their family history has fascinated me for the twenty years that I have known Mark." Then he added cheerfully, "I hope you don't mind my infernal curiosity, but why on earth didn't you come before?"

"There's nothing about my coming that I would not want you to know," John said. "I did not come before because a month ago I had no idea of the existence of the place, or know anything about my father's people."

Then he found himself telling the whole story of the opening of that black tin box.

"This is it," he said. "When I saw the genealogical table in the back of it, I knew I'd been spelling my name wrong. When I arrived here, I felt the time had come to correct the mistake."

Harry Gregg took the book eagerly. He had spent the morning in London making judicious inquiries. Last night he had seen the primly worded note Ellen Hobbs wrote to Rosalys. Holding it in his hand, he had felt he was being swept into the current of some tremendous drama. Again and again he had read the last lines: "He is a true Beausire. When your dear Mother was a little girl, she would tell me what she thought the Lord who disappeared looked like, and, my dear Miss Rosalys, when he stood before me in the taproom, I could only think, 'John Beausire has come back.'"

Early next morning Harry Gregg set out to call on a man he knew who might know something about prominent Americans. When he left the office he knew all about the Boss and the great fortune made from trees. He also knew that Robert

McClaren's heir spelled his name Boser. That did not disturb him in the least. He returned to his hotel with a sense of great events about to take place.

"I'm awfully glad you showed me this," he said, as he carefully folded the thin and faded paper. "That episode of 1685 has become almost an obsession with me. There is a complete break in the family history there."

The Major paused; then he gave John one of those piercing looks that seemed to stare into the very mind.

"I suppose you've heard about the curse?" he asked.

"Vaguely," John replied, and excited anticipation swept over him. He felt that this rather odd man knew a great deal he would himself give a lot to know. "You don't think there's anything to it, do you?"

"Yes, I do," Gregg replied emphatically. "And if I knew the whole story of 1685 I'd know exactly what."

"Why don't you ask Lord Beausire?" John said. "He'd probably tell you."

Gregg smiled and lighted a cigarette. John noticed his hands. They were the hands of an artist. This man didn't look like a professional soldier.

"You don't know Mark," he said. "He's reduced not thinking about unpleasant things to a fine art. I believe the affair of 1685 was distinctly—unpleasant."

John knew that he had a friend here. He decided to get to the principal point at once.

"That's all water over the dam," he said. "I'm more concerned about the present. I'm going to make an offer to lease the place, and while I'm there I'd do everything possible to preserve it, also put the grounds and as much of the estate as I could get a lease of in order. D'you think I've got a chance?"

Harry Gregg's face was grave, but his eyes shone as if he

were immensely pleased or excited. He tapped his pewter tankard nervously.

"Search me," he said. "I've known Mark for a long time, but I've no idea what he really feels about the place. From the practical point of view your offer should be a godsend. . . . The west front's marvelous, isn't it?"

He stared in amazement when John replied simply, "I've never seen it. One can't, from the right of way, you know."

Harry Gregg thought quickly. This was carrying Mark's order that the place was not to be shown to visitors a bit far. But then, the Vicar had been away. It was odd that Horace hadn't taken John Beausire through the house. Horace could do pretty well what he liked about the place, and knew it.

There were many things to be unraveled, and during this leave he was determined to find out as much as he could about the dark cause behind those endless tragedies. He stood up suddenly, saying, "I'll be back in a jiffy. I'm going to 'phone Rosalys."

While he waited, John thought about what Gregg had said. Only now did it appear strange that he had admitted to a belief in the curse. Also, it had been quite clear that he attributed it to something that had happened in 1685.

When Harry Gregg returned to the taproom he had the air of one who had just won a victory. He spoke with elaborate casualness.

"Rosalys is going up to the Court to see the caretaker," he said. "Would you care to come up with me, and at least have a look at the west front?"

"I certainly would," John replied. He felt suddenly that he also had a share in the good the day had brought.

Chapter Four

❖ ❖ ❖ ❖

"THERE'S NO POINT IN HURRYING," GREGG SAID, AS they started off in the small car he had driven from the Vicarage. "I'd like to stop and have a squint at a part of the garden east of the drive that interests me."

As he drove down the tree-shaded road toward the gates he talked steadily. John was able to fill in the picture of village life from the remarks he casually made. The Vicar was a splendid old boy, a scholar and antiquarian, wholly impractical. He did what he could to keep things going, but since the death of the man who had been agent for many years, things had slipped badly.

At the great gates, which were open, John told Gregg of his own arrival, of how they had opened before his eyes and he had been tempted to go in.

The Major laughed. "That was old Parrett," he said. "He's the grandfather of the blacksmith and innumerable others about the place. He won't live in the lodge, prefers the cottage back of it. Opening the gates at least once a day is a superstition with him. 'Lest they stay shut,' he'll tell you."

He ran the car to the side of the drive and jumped out. "Come on," he said. "I'm going to show you something your ancestor built not long before he went away."

John followed in silence. They walked down a pathway of broken flagstones, torn out in many places. The tangled wreck of a rose pergola lay across the path, and they had to walk round it. Tall nettle and burdock plants rioted in what had been formal borders.

"This was once a rose garden," Harry Gregg said. "Very little has been spent on the gardens since the last war."

"I suppose the taxes practically ruined Lord Beausire," John said. It seemed incredible that there had ever been a time when he had not known what he wanted to do with the Boss's money.

"That's about the size of it. It's the same story, all over England. The day of the big estates is over. . . . Here it is," Gregg added, a note of excitement in his voice, as they ascended a small flight of broken moss-covered steps, walked along another paved path, and stood looking down into the ruin of a sunken garden.

Even in its desolation it was lovely. Box trees, long unclipped, grew in fantastic shapes beside the stone coping. Part of the balustrade had broken away.

"John Beausire sent to Holland for a famous gardener to make this," Gregg said. "I wish I knew who had done the stone work. It fascinates me."

Ornately carved stone seats, chipped and mossy, some piled with last autumn's fallen leaves, were against the stone walls. From one wall a fountain jutted, and opposite it there was a little covered pavilion that would serve as shelter from a sudden shower.

Harry Gregg walked quickly toward the ancient sundial in the center of the garden. Bending over it, he pointed to the almost obliterated motto there.

"In memoria aeterna erit justus," he read, then said, "Do you know what that means?"

"The just shall be in eternal memory. . . . Where does it come from?" John asked.

"The Psalms. I forget which. But there's a deeper meaning to it than the obvious one. That is that the just, or evolved, soul remembers its past lives. The memory is a sign of spiritual attainment. Few have anything of it; almost none have it with any clarity."

John shivered in the bright sunlit place as if a cold wind had blown over him. He felt the scrutiny of the Major's dark eyes, though he kept his own on the weather-stained sundial.

"Do you believe we've lived before?" he asked.

The reply came quickly, with a peculiar emphasis.

"Certainly. It's not an original idea, you know. About two-thirds of the human race accept it absolutely. It is woven into all the Eastern religions, and was taught, or at least accepted, by the Christian Church until the third or fourth century. There is pretty clear evidence all through the Gospels that Jesus knew of the belief and did not rebuke it."

John felt that this strange thought was so tremendous in its implications that he did not want to think about it now. It shed a blinding white light upon all that had been dark and obscure to him since he had come into the valley. It would explain his complete identification of himself with his ancestor.

Resolutely John turned from it as too facile an explanation. There were things he hoped Gregg would tell him. He would have a much greater power of explanation than Ellen Hobbs would, for all her willingness to talk.

"What do the symbols of the Evangelists in the crest stand for?" John asked. "And not only there. They're everywhere one turns, it seems."

Harry Gregg looked at his watch. "Rosalys said she'd be there by six," he said. "We've got half an hour. Let's sit down."

There was nothing dramatic or affected about Harry Gregg's words. He told a simple tale simply, with utter conviction and extraordinary lucidity. John felt he could see the vast preparations for the Third Crusade, feel the white flame of faith in the holiness of the cause. He could understand the heartbroken woman who had thrust aside the gift of a priceless book, and—like so many others—only turned at last to the Gospels when there was no other light in all the gathering darkness. He could accompany her in the ecstatic dream of the four Evangelists, hear their promise to her, and follow the sequence of events until that promise was kept and the Lord of Beausire and his heir returned, and four acorns were planted in the rich Somerset earth to grow into four mighty oaks.

"What do you make of it?" John asked at last, when Harry stopped speaking. "I suppose it's a legend that's grown with time, around the trees."

"I don't think so. I accept it almost literally. One has to take into consideration the mentality of the time. She spoke the only language that she knew, the language of personality, in trying to share with others an undoubtedly true spiritual experience. To my mind, one of the secrets of the survival and the terrific strength of the Catholic Church is that it has never been afraid to attach personality to spiritual truths. All that matters is that the thing is essentially true. If the tenets of the Gospels were kept, there would be no evil in the world."

"How does the curse come in?"

"Fear is a terrifically powerful magnet to draw the thing

feared. There was no hint of a curse before 1685. The first tragedy seems to have happened about 1700. Something was probably done then that caused the fear of a curse."

Watching John, Harry Gregg knew that his interest was aroused, and it would not be difficult to open subsequent conversations on the subject. There was so much he had to find out. What had John Beausire felt when he stumbled into that lovely little church? Why had Rosalys been so frightened, frightened enough to rush up to London and 'phone Mark in Cannes from there, when it had been agreed between them that nothing was to be said about his arrival in Europe until he knew whether he could wangle his exchange to the Air Force and get his leave sufficiently extended to make a visit to Sudbury. Harry felt quite sure that John's arrival had spurred Rosalys on to agree to the momentous decision made last night. The small pale face of Marian Armitage haunted him. She was deeply concerned in this, but how did it alter things for her? Perhaps she feared Rosalys might no longer be a willing tool to be used in her coldly astute plan.

But enough had been said now. John Beausire had enough to think over.

"Come on," he said, "we'd better be getting along. We'll probably not get into the house this evening, but the outside is worth seeing at close quarters."

They went up the shallow broken steps and back to the car. Harry drove slowly. Families of rabbits fed on the young dandelion shoots by the side of the drive.

"This place would take an army of men and a fortune to keep up properly," he said.

"I've got the fortune, I'd get the men," John replied quickly. He knew instinctively that the remark would be accepted as it was meant. It would never occur to Harry Gregg to think that it was meant boastfully.

The car began the ascent toward the terraces. Harry stopped it, leaned on the wheel, and staring straight ahead, as if all his being were concentrated in his slow words, he said, "I wish you luck. I'm going to give you some advice. You don't have to take it. Forget pride. Don't be offended at anything. Think only of your goal, which is to get the place, at least for a time. Remember there is order in all things, that the same force which brought you here is still with you. Mark is a queer duck, but a good sort at heart. Be determined to like him."

The car moved forward. "Thanks," John said. "You know, I'm extraordinarily glad that you're here."

Harry laughed. "The Indians have a saying that when the *chela,* or pupil, is ready, the *guru,* or teacher, appears. I've found that often works out in all sorts of ways. There's timing, orderliness, to everything. If you think I can be of any help at any time, don't hesitate to ask. You'll probably end by thinking I'm completely batty, but I'll always be glad to air my views."

Harry stopped the car before an immense dark door. "This is the main entrance," he said. "It's been shut for several years."

The house seemed like an enchanted palace. It was not a dead house: it seemed asleep. The yellow time-worn walls were covered in places with gray lichen; the weather-stained roofs and twisted chimneys seemed to defy decay. Six low steps led up to the door. Above the arch of the doorway was a stone shield.

"It is more beautiful than I had thought," John said simply.

Harry looked at it with sad eyes. "The world so greatly needs its beauty," he said. "This place is a precious heritage. It should—it must—be kept."

John did not answer. He knew that whatever influence

Harry Gregg had, great or small, would be exerted to the full for him.

"We'll get out and walk around to the west door," Harry said.

As they turned the corner of the west wing the sound of crooning doves filled the air. It seemed the whole side of the west wing was hung with purple draperies. It was covered with a magnificent wisteria in full flower, which twisted up from its thick gray roots, reached to the third floor windows, and fell over the lintel of the narrow door set deep in the wall.

"You wait here," Harry said. "I'll go and hunt Rosalys. She's probably in the caretaker's quarters at the back."

John felt glad to be alone. Turning, he saw what appeared to be a small enclosed garden and went quickly across the paved walk toward it. He felt quite sure Rosalys was there, waiting for him. He could see her mentally, in a long white dress, holding up her hands to the doves, who would perch on her arms and shoulders.

There was a dreamlike quality about the little court. John knew that this was the court of the little maid, of which Ellen Hobbs had once spoken to him. It seemed the last stronghold of the spirit of the house. He knew that once the whole estate had been peaceful and prosperous, well cared for as this was still.

Standing under the pointed Gothic archway, John saw that Rosalys was not there, but he felt no sense of disappointment. So clearly could he sense her presence that he knew he had but to wait for her to return.

The enclosed space was in perfect order. Borders, bright with spring flowers, were carefully tended. As he stepped through the arch there was a whirr of wings, and the air was filled with white doves.

John went toward the gray figure of a cowled friar which

stood on a pedestal above the fountain. Clear water splashed down into a broad basin of the same gray granite.

Slowly the doves began to settle again. Their feet were like bright coral against the gray stone and the flagged paths worn glassy smooth by the tread of centuries. In one corner an immense old dovecote—tier above tier of tiny open doors topped by a mossy ornamented roof—stood backed by the brilliant leaves of a copper beech. The coping of the enclosing wall was ornately carved, as were the seats beneath it. John looked with sharp interest at the carving of the seat-backs. Above the wall, tall lilacs completely circled the court, the faint purple of breaking buds showing through the fresh green of their leaves.

Then, almost hidden by long racemes of wisteria, John saw a circular window. It seemed to bring back memories of dark unhappy things, things that should not be thought of in the Court of St. Francis. John tried to recall whether Horace or his mother had spoken of that window, but he could not. Yet the feeling persisted that it was connected with something sorrowful.

There was a sound of steps. Again the doves rose into the air with flashing wings, to circle around the statue. Rosalys came into the court, followed by Harry Gregg. She smiled and held out her hand, but her eyes were as cold as they had been in the church porch.

"Hullo, John Beausire," she said lightly. "You should have told me who you were, and I wouldn't have shooed you out of the church so quickly."

If she was assuming this casualness, she was doing it well, John thought. Only for an instant did it seem that her eyes were not cold, but dark with fear.

"You didn't give me much of a chance to explain anything," he said.

"I was too astonished to find a stranger there," she said.

A hopeless dull anger—with himself and with her—seized him. A strange and marvelous thing had happened, and they stood talking in platitudes, as if they were ordinary people who had met in an ordinary way.

With a musical little cry, she lifted her hands. The doves came wheeling around her, perched on her hands and arms and stood on her shoulders, nestling like white flowers against her shining hair. As she lifted her face to the birds that flew about her, John felt he had seen her do this countless times before. It seemed unbearable that she should think of him as a stranger.

All sense of her identity with the girl who had died of grief so long ago vanished. She was simply Rosalys, living and radiant.

"The Court of St. Francis is one of the treasures of Sudbury Court," she said, still in the polite tone of one explaining things to a stranger.

"I like to think of it as the Court of the Little Maid," John said.

Harry Gregg had vanished. With a sense of annoyance, John thought that perhaps he had gone to find the caretaker, to arrange for them to go into the house. He did not want to go in now. He wanted to stay here.

A shadow passed over the girl's face. "The village people call it that," she said, "but in the inventories of the place it is the Court of St. Francis."

She went on talking quickly, as though she were trying to shut out other thoughts or words.

"Every autumn St. Francis is wrapped in straw and sacking: that's why he is so well preserved. He is quite old, you know."

"He was carved in 1681, or thereabouts," John said, "so that makes him 257 years old, quite young for Sudbury Court."

The startled expression he had seen before when they came

out of the church into the sunlight, flashed into her eyes again. Then she smiled and said, "I suppose Ellen told you that. She loves this place. She works among the flowers here quite often."

Slowly they walked around the bright borders. Rare varieties of narcissi and tulips bloomed here. Later there would be many roses and tall white lilies.

"I found out myself," John said. "I think these were the first things I noticed."

He indicated the deeply carved back of one of the seats. The design was a medallion, with an intricate monogram, "R. de B.," wreathed in roses and lilies, the date, 1681, beneath it.

"That was the monogram of the little maid," Rosalys said.

There was a deep silence between them. At last John took his little book from his pocket. With an involuntarily eager gesture she held out her hand. As they seated themselves on one of the benches she did not lift her eyes from it.

It was the first line of the genealogical table that held her attention, the first and the last. John watched her eyes looking from one to the other, as if those two entries were all she saw.

"There is a tablet in the church to the memory of Henrietta Beausire," she said at last. "It says, 'Widow of John, Twenty-first Baron de Beausire of Sudbury.' "

"There is no record that she left a son, is there?" John asked.

For some moments she did not answer. She stared up at the half-covered circular window, and at last said slowly, "Yes, there is. I did not know of it until last night."

John was looking at her in astonishment when Harry Gregg came running into the court brandishing an enormous key.

"I've got it," he said, his eyes alight with what seemed a peculiar excitement. "We can go in and show John Beausire his ancestor's rooms."

Rosalys stood up. For a moment John thought that she was

going to make some excuse. He was quite certain that she did not want to take him into the house. But she said quietly, "All right, but we'll have to be quick. The Pargiters are coming to dinner, so I must leave soon." She still held the book.

Only then did John realize that he had counted on spending the rest of the evening with her. He had been quite sure that now they had met again there would be no further barrier between them, for she knew that he was John Beausire. Then he tried to remember that things were going much better than he had had reason to expect a few hours ago. In a small village he was bound to see her constantly.

Harry Gregg put the key into the huge old keyhole of the dark door in the wall. They stepped over the threshold into an oak-paneled vestibule which led into a large hall, also paneled in dark wood. The door clanged behind them. John tried to realize he was inside the house, in Sudbury Court, home of his ancestors. He could think of nothing but the white figure beside him, moving with familiar sureness in the gloom. They walked through the hall, passed a dark staircase that curved down into it, then went through a doorway and up a long oak-paneled passage.

John grasped the plan of the house instantly. One could get a good idea of it from the outside. The corridor connected the three wings. The whole center wing was occupied by the great hall, and he knew that the kitchens and servants' quarters were on the north side. The gallery ran from east to west, the full length of the house. The splendid oriel windows at the east end were in the great dining room.

Through an open door at the end of the corridor, a shaft of sunlight struck down to the polished floor. Rosalys hurried ahead.

As he came up with her at the foot of the staircase, John felt again that his coming had troubled her deeply. Her face looked paler than it had in the bright sunlight.

"It is a beautiful house, isn't it?" she said softly. There was a little catch in her voice.

He began to hope desperately that she understood something of what the sight of it meant to him. It was impossible to find words to express that, so he said simply, "I did not know that a house could be so beautiful."

Instantly her eyes were veiled again and she spoke as the polite guide doing the honors of her family home. "It is perhaps the most perfect early Tudor Hall in existence," she said. "The fireplace and paneling are as old as the house—that is, about 1512. We know the house was finished then, for there is a record of a great feast held in this hall and the dining room on the feast day of St. John in 1512."

"The feast of St. John," John said. "When is that?"

She replied at once, as if the sense of strain had left her. "The twenty-seventh of December. In the old days the feasts of the Evangelists were all celebrated by a dinner for the household and tenants. That meant all four villages, of course."

The idea of the subconscious hammered in his mind. He clung to it as a defense against that queer suggestion Gregg had made about reincarnation. One could so easily deceive oneself. Yet what was the point in denying, to oneself, at least, that everything was familiar? There was always the subconscious to fall back on.

"Come on, Harry," Rosalys called, and they began to ascend the stairs.

As they passed the closed doors leading from the first landing, John still thought about the subconscious, because he could not throw off the feeling that he knew what was behind them. For instance, the long room with windows that looked clear across the park, from which the four oaks could be seen.

"I suppose many photographs and drawings of this house have been published," he said.

Rosalys shook her head. "No. A great many people have asked permission to do so, but it has never been given. Many drawings and woodcuts have been made, but only on condition that there was no right of reproduction and the original belonged to the family."

"I thought there might have been photographs in a magazine, or something," John said.

"There never have been, and there is no house like it," she replied.

They heard voices in the hall, and Harry looked down over the banisters.

"Two brats—with flowers," he announced. "Shall I ask them up?"

Rosalys waved as she looked down, then answered, "No, they'll leave them there. It's two of the village children. I asked them to try and find me some marigolds for Marian's room. They're almost over, but she loves them so."

Harry looked surprised. "I thought she wasn't coming for a week," he said.

John felt again that he was outside their lives. Marian, the Pargiters, they were just names to him.

Rosalys looked at Harry directly, and there was a curious sort of defiance in her eyes. "Plans have been changed. She's coming tomorrow. Mark 'phoned just after you went down to the Arms. She's going to have the Blue Tapestry Room again." Then she turned to John and said in apology, "Marian is Lady Armitage. She's a friend of all of us. Her husband, Sir Anthony, is my cousin's commanding officer in India. We're all going to stay at the Court."

Rosalys remembered vividly her strange sense of unreality when she came up this staircase after meeting John Beausire in the church. She thought now that she had not doubted for a moment who he was. The door of the library in the west wing had been locked then, and she began to hope with a mounting terror that it was locked now. For some reason she could not understand, she did not want to show the American the library and the Queen's Room behind it.

The strangeness of the last five days seemed more intensely with her now, as if in a moment she would know what it was that had happened. She turned to Harry, asking him if he remembered the story connected with a certain picture. Harry did, and began to tell it. For a moment she could let the impressions that had haunted her for days have her full attention. She felt that if only she would think them out, there would be nothing strange about them at all.

She had gone to the church to get some music she had left there and had been about to leave when she heard a step. Thinking it was Byers, the sexton, she had gone up toward the chancel. Then she had heard a strangely familiar voice call her name.

Now she felt again the curious shock that had gone through her when she saw that the screen door was open. It was funny how the sequence of things got jumbled when you looked back on them. It seemed now it was at that moment that she had known who was in the Lady Chapel, seconds before she stood by the screen and perceived the tall figure beside the tomb.

What had happened after that she hardly remembered. The next thing seemed to be what she felt as she entered the court and came up the staircase: that inner sense that her life had been shaken to its foundations. It was only now that she fully realized why she had been glad that the library door was locked: she had been quite sure that the stranger would have found his way there and been waiting for her. She had been curiously relieved to hear the caretaker's assertion that the library had not been unlocked for a month.

The return to the Vicarage and the wire from Mark that she found there were also hazy. She remembered only how she had decided to go up to town at once, though Mark had said he would not be there for four days. That night she had tried to reason out why the stranger had upset her so. That she had instantly connected him with the Lord who disappeared, the Twenty-first Baron, now seemed imagination. She surely had not done that until Ellen's strange little note came two days later.

Then everything had been wiped out by Mark's coming, the instant realization that he was terribly unhappy, and Marian's unspoken entreaty for kindness and understanding.

It had been in Marian's bedroom that night—in her big house in Portman Square—that she had promised she would try to help Mark. Marian's face seemed to float before her now, white and tense, with immense dark eyes, the shaded light falling on her loose blue-black hair. Marian was so terribly afraid something awful would happen to Mark.

They moved through room after room filled with exquisite furniture.

Harry stopped before the portrait of a Beausire who had followed Clive to India. He had been a younger son. He had lived several years there, picked up some strange ideas and then returned to succeed his father: his two elder brothers had been killed in the same coach accident.

Harry was speaking deliberately, with a curious light in his quick eyes. "He wrote a sort of essay on his experiences in an Indian monastery," Harry was saying. "If you are interested in Eastern philosophy, you should ask Lord Beausire to let you read it. It's in manuscript, his own handwriting."

"I'd like to," John replied.

Rosalys thought with sudden panic that she should have warned Harry: Mark didn't intend to meet the American, for Marian had thought it better not.

Harry was leading the way to the west wing now. At the end of the gallery she turned her head to look at the library door the moment it came into view. It was closed.

The west oriel was open, and a white dove perched on the embrasure. The crooning came up from the Court of St. Francis, and wisteria blossoms swayed gently over the top of the window.

John stood looking down in silence. Only the arch of the court entrance was visible: it was from the library window that one got a full view of the enclosed garden and the statue. Again Rosalys felt unreasoning panic, that she must get away before she heard something she did not dare hear. Why had she been so weak when Harry came to the caretaker's parlor to tell her that John Beausire was in the Court of the Little Maid? She had been writing out orders for the opening of the house, and had wanted to say that she was too busy, but she could not. Why had she felt that strange sense of elation as she went out to the court? Was it simply pride in the place?

Then Rosalys thought of Harry's wife, Bessie, and of how her round and placid face would suddenly assume a curiously hard and bitter look. She remembered the last time she had seen that look, as Bessie made some remark about Harry's gimlet eyes. "Oh, never try to hide anything from Harry. He sees straight through you," Bessie had said. With a quick movement she turned her own eyes from him.

A heavy depression was creeping over John. He wanted to grab Rosalys and run, away from some horrible thing he seemed about to remember. For a moment their eyes met; then she dropped her long dark lashes and turned to Harry, saying, "The door is locked, isn't it?"

Harry was standing beside a dark heavily carved door, his hand on the big silver knob. John was aware of an intense longing to enter that door, yet, an instant later, when Harry Gregg said, "Yes, it is," he felt curiously relieved.

Harry wanted to get the key and go in, and when Rosalys protested that it was too late, reminded her that she was already dressed for dinner and he could dress in a brace of shakes. But she stood firm, and they went down the west stairs into the hall below.

"You two go back to the court," Rosalys said. "I have to speak to the caretaker. I'll join you."

When they had gone out she did not attempt to go to the caretaker's quarters. She stood very still, then sat down on an old chest and stared into the shadows of the staircase. She started violently when she heard a step and saw Harry beside her.

"Rosalys," Harry said, "do ask him to dinner. Your father will want to meet him. He's a true Beausire. This, my dear, is a tremendous event."

Rosalys looked down at her white shoes. There was a streak of dust across one of them. She thought vaguely that her dress was probably dusty, too, and she would have to change.

Then she looked up, and ignoring Harry's suggestion, said, "Did you know—before last night, I mean—that the Twenty-first Baron had left a legitimate heir?"

Harry hesitated for an instant. The truth was out now, anyway, he thought. "Yes," he said. "Soon after I met Mark, in 1918, he told me about it. His father had just died. Your mother was dead, too, and you were a girl. He told me about the John Beausire in America, how his father had had him looked up when there didn't seem a chance that Mark would survive the war. We talked about the advisability of looking him up anyway, but Mark evidently decided against it, for a few weeks later he asked me to forget what he had told me. He hinted that it was something the family wanted to forget."

Rosalys was silent.

"You are going to ask him to dinner, aren't you?" Harry asked again.

Rosalys stood up. "No," she said, simply and firmly.

"Why?" Harry seemed curious and angry at the same time.

"Because it would lead to complications. Mark isn't going to receive him. He said he didn't want any American publicity hunters cashing in on the family history and dragging it through the gossip columns."

"My God, that's damnable!" Harry exclaimed. "But that's Marian, not Mark."

Rosalys looked at him squarely. "Well," she said, "what if it is? It amounts to the same thing."

Harry decided he would have to think this thing over. He would talk to the Vicar about it.

"Go out and excuse yourself," he said. "This is going to be damned embarrassing. He's staying for some time, you know. . . . Ellen likes him tremendously."

Rosalys was on the point of saying, "Horace doesn't," but she remained silent. That was another of the mysteries. What was it that Horace feared about the coming of John Beausire? He must feel it meant trouble for Mark.

The peace of evening was over the little court. John stood by the fountain and watched her enter. "Rosalys," he thought, "this place was made for you, and it is almost worthy of you."

It was when the church clock struck seven with its slow deep chime that she said she had to run. Dinner guests would be arriving in half an hour.

A sense of panic swept over John. If she went, she would seem like a dream again.

"Won't you dine with me tomorrow?" he said. Then, fearing he had been presumptuous, he added quickly, "I'd like to ask the Major and his wife, too. The four of us could drive to Bath or Bristol."

It seemed for a moment that her wide eyes were imploring him to stop, not to talk of impossible things. Her voice was hard and brittle as she said, "That's awfully nice of you, I'd have loved it, at any other time, but for the next few weeks I'll be frantically busy. I'm going to marry my cousin, Mark Beausire, very soon."

There was a long silence. Then John repeated slowly, "You are going to marry Mark?"

"Yes. We have been engaged for a long time. We had not intended to marry until his service in India was over, but now he has arranged to be transferred to the Air Force and will be in England. Good night, I must fly. Harry will come here for you."

Then she seemed to vanish. John stood staring at the tall gray friar.

Harry came sauntering around the corner of the west wing. When he saw Rosalys he hurried toward her.

"Has he gone?" he asked.

"No. Go and take him back to the inn, then come on as quickly as you can. I've got my car here."

"Then you're not going to ask him to dinner?"

"Why go into that again? By the way, I've told him that I'm going to marry Mark. It was settled last night. The announcement will be in the papers tomorrow, I think."

Rosalys moved forward, but Harry grasped her wrist. "You mean that last night you promised Marian that you would marry Mark—to shield them."

Rosalys gasped. "Don't be cruel, Harry," she said. "I—dearly love Mark."

"I know," he said. He still held her: he was trying to think.

"I've simply got to go. Buck up and get home. Father hates dinner to be late."

Harry put both hands on her shoulders. "I'm not coming in for dinner," he said. "I can't face the Pargiters tonight. Why on earth did you ask them?"

"It was arranged two weeks ago. I forgot to put them off, and then it was too late. Where are you going?"

"I'm going to ask John Beausire to dine with me in Taunton," he said. "It's about time someone showed some civility around here."

Rosalys turned and went toward the house without looking back. Harry walked into the little court.

John was standing by the fountain, looking down into the clear water.

"Congratulate me," Harry said. "I've just escaped a dull dinner party. I'm going to beat it to Taunton while the going's good. There's an awfully interesting old inn there. I wish you'd join me."

John looked at those strange dark eyes. He felt if there was one person he could bear to be with tonight it was Gregg. "I'd like to," he said. "Thanks."

It was after midnight when Horace returned from the

Court. Ellen gave him a quick look, then exclaimed, "You're dead beat, Horace. I'm going to get you a drink."

Horace accepted the whisky she brought gratefully. "Mr. Beausire was in the Court," he said, determined to get at what his mother felt about this business. It was no use quarreling about it: after all, she wanted what he did, peace for the family.

Ellen sat down in a low chair by the window. "I know," she said. "The Major took him up, and Miss Rosalys showed them through the east wing. They went down the gallery and out by the west door. He was in the Court of the Little Maid, too."

There was silence again. Might as well get to it, Horace thought. If he didn't mention it, Ma wouldn't.

"Ma," he said, "Master Mark's bin in Cannes for three weeks. Funny 'e didn't let us know, ain't it?"

Ellen spoke harshly. "Funny? Not at all. He's been with that trollop of his, I reckon, and didn't want it known."

A dull red spread over Horace's thin face, and his light eyes blazed. "I'd 'ave you remember you're speakin' of Lady Harmitage, wife of 'is commanding h'officer," he said furiously.

"I can't help who she is," Ellen snapped. "I only know what she is. Twists his Lordship round her little finger, she does. That kind never bring anything but evil."

"That's bunk," Horace said, rather regretting that he'd got into this. "Why shouldn't 'e 'ave 'is fun, with every woman 'e meets chasin' after 'im?" he went on angrily.

"Fun, you call it." The bitterness in his mother's voice startled Horace. "I've said before, and I say again, that black-haired witch will bring black trouble. She'll stir up the curse again."

Horace tried to think what to say. A bright idea struck him. "Divorce ain't the disgrace it used to be," he said. "Maybe Sir Anthony 'ud see sense, and step down to make way for a better man. Me old pal, Sergeant Hicks, knows her folk well. 'E said she'd come into a tidy fortune when 'er grandma died, and the old lady's on the shady side o' eighty. She's mighty pretty, an' she's quality."

Horace tried to put out of his mind the other things Sergeant Hicks had said, such as that the old lady could leave her money where she would, and there'd be no mercy there if certain things were known. Queen Victoria had been broad-minded compared to that old girl. He had also said that Sir Anthony was a holy terror and that if he caught on to what was going on, things would happen that would make the tragedies caused by the curse look like Sunday-school treats.

"Divorce?" Ellen shot the word at him scornfully. "Not at all. Sir Anthony won't be asked to inconvenience himself. Her ladyship will still be the wife of a very wealthy and important man, and she'll still come to Sudbury Court and have the Blue Tapestry Room, which is being got ready for her now, and she won't care a mite what that means to his Lordship's wife. You needn't fash yourself, Horace. Talk'll die down now. In a few weeks his Lordship is going to marry Miss Rosalys."

Horace sprang up. Pain shot through his right leg, but he hardly noticed it. "You don't say!" he exclaimed.

Ellen nodded. "It's true," she said. "Miss Rosalys told me herself. She did not have to tell me why. I know."

"You don't say!" Horace murmured again.

Ellen went on, almost to herself. "She's young, and beautiful as an angel; she's sweet and good, and because she loves Master Mark as a little sister would love her brother, that wicked woman, who is old enough to be her mother, is taking advantage of her to keep down scandal."

"Well, if 'er Ladyship's as old as you say she is, she ain't likely to have children. Someone 'as to provide an heir. Who better than Miss Rosalys?"

"An heir? What's wrong with Mr. John?" Ellen's eyes were hard and bright with anger. "Direct descendant of the Lord who disappeared, the Lord who was betrayed and cheated and who was the best of the whole long line of them."

Horace was glad it had come out at last. He even failed to realize that his Mother had said "betrayed," which implied that she knew more than he did.

"The attainder," he answered sharply. "The Lord who disappeared was judged a rebel and a traitor in a court of law. Master Mark's the last of the 'Ouse, and it's up to Miss Rosalys to marry 'im, if he so wills it."

Ellen sighed deeply. "She'll marry him, and wreck her own sweet life. Oh, why was Miss Anne taken? Vicar will see nothing but that it's best for the family. Well, there 'tis."

She went abruptly out of the room. She did not want to talk now.

"There 'tis," Horace repeated. Never before had he felt so conscious of the complete submission to fate, good or bad, implied in those words with which the country people greeted important events.

He went up to bed, almost relieved that the marriage he had for a long time believed inevitable would soon take place. Settle a lot of things, it would. There might soon be children at the Court, little nippers, like Master Mark had been. Great, that would be.

Looking from his bedroom window he saw to his surprise that the Major was sitting in a white patch of moonlight by the big apple tree, talking to Mr. Beausire, and that his mother stood beside them. The moon made her white hair look like shining silver.

Chapter Five

❖　❖　❖　❖

THE AMAZEMENT WITH WHICH SHE HAD HEARD THAT Mark Beausire was so soon to marry his cousin Rosalys had been nothing to what Bessie Gregg felt now, after a week at Sudbury Court. The situation seemed to get more impossible every day. It never took Bessie long to dress for dinner: she was not a woman who fussed about her appearance. She had hurried in from tennis, changed quickly and come to the little sitting room off the Blue Tapestry Room to find out what had made Marian change her mind about the American.

Bessie yanked the skirt of her black dinner dress into place impatiently and regarded herself in the gilt mirror with complete indifference. She had never been pretty, and she knew it. Her round pale face was redeemed from actual plainness by quite beautiful bluish-gray eyes. Her brown hair was so soft it never looked tidy, and it now had a streak of pure white that lay like a plume across the top of her head. The endless tennis and riding of life on an Indian station had done no more than keep her tendency to plumpness—as she expressed it—within bounds.

The door of the bedroom opened and Marian Armitage came out. Bessie turned quickly, and felt the shock of delighted surprise that Marian's rather odd beauty sometimes gave her. She thought suddenly of the endless women on Indian stations who had tried to pry out of her the secret of Marian's age. They all knew she and Marian had been friends since childhood. Looking at her now, Bessie wondered what her own judgment would have been, had she not known. Marian seemed ageless, like an ivory figurine.

There was no sign of age in the little heart-shaped face with its peculiar ivory tint that was in some lights a pale gold. Blue-black curls hung almost to her shoulders. Yet, lovely as she still was, there was no youth about her. Sometimes she looked as if she had known all things and wearied of them.

"I've bad news," Bessie said. "Harry's just come back from Taunton, and who should he run into—of all people—but Laura Paget. She and the P.D. have taken a furnished cottage in a village near here for the rest of their long leave. She asked after you, of course."

Marian twisted her ruby bracelet, watched the shifting points of the misty stars in the center of the jewels.

Laura Paget was the most vicious gossip in British India; the P.D. was the Poor Devil, the rather nice but ineffectual Civil Service man who had been fool enough to marry the fading beauty. Marian thought now of the look in Laura's eyes as she had realized that Lord Beausire was also returning to England for the summer. The Pagets had come to pay a final call before Lady Armitage left. It had been that afternoon that Marian had realized, looking at Laura, who had once been so much more lovely than she herself had ever been, how short her own time was. Unreasonably, she hated Laura for it.

"Did you tell her I was staying here?" Marian asked. She was afraid of Laura and tried to decide whether it would be safer to ignore her or to be particularly friendly and invite them for a weekend at the Wiltshire house.

"I didn't have to. She knew that already."

"What else did she say?" Marian began to think of the women Laura knew whose husbands were in close contact with her own husband. There must not be any trouble now.

"Oh, she was full of Mark's engagement, of course. Curious about Rosalys, dying to know how long you were going to stay, and if you would be here for the wedding. You know the sort of thing."

"Yes, I know." Marian looked out across the terraces to the trees of the park. She had hoped to find peace here for a little while, but it was hard to shut out the beastly facts.

She turned suddenly, saying, "Why did Harry go into Taunton? He said at lunch he was going to read in the library."

"Oh, there was something he had to look up in the Castle records. He thinks of nothing but the Monmouth Rebellion trials now. That's the latest craze."

Marian did not answer. She shivered, in spite of the sunny warmth of the room.

"I hear the American is coming to dinner," Bessie said. "What made Mark change his mind? I thought he was determined not to meet him."

"He was, but I persuaded him that that was not the best policy."

"You mean you think it would be better to be friendly? That's what Harry has said from the first. After all, he is—"

Marian's face had suddenly become so hard and cold that

Bessie stopped in astonishment. There was quivering anger in Marian's voice as she finished Bessie's sentence for her. ". . . He is the direct descendant of the Lord who disappeared, the most romantic figure in the whole history of the Beausires. He is very rich, and is stirring up all sorts of trouble on the estate by expressing his ideas on farming and sanitation. Ellen Hobbs thinks he's too marvelous. No, my dear, we're not going to be friendly, just not going to give him an opportunity to say Mark wouldn't even let him see the place. He will come to dinner once, and that ends it."

Marian got up and went over to the window. While she dressed she had thought she could not go through with it, that she would run down to the gunroom where Mark would still be talking to that awful Horace Hobbs, and when they had got rid of the man she would tell Mark that this farce must stop, that the engagement must be broken and they would go some-where, anywhere—to France, to America—until Anthony re-alized that his refusal of a divorce was merely adding to the publicity and scandal he dreaded.

But now, looking at the flower filled terrace below, she knew she must go on with it, that the decision she had come to a few weeks ago was the only possible solution. More to con-vince herself by one more repetition of the argument than to enlighten Bessie, she began to talk in a low steady voice.

"Mark is happy here. It's the only place where he is happy. There has always been something about him that frightens me. Without this place he would be a ship without a rudder. He must marry: we are horribly near to war, and he is the last of his line. Anthony won't hear of a divorce until he retires. That's four years, at least. It would be too late."

She turned misery-haunted eyes toward Bessie, and as if imploring her to understand, went on.

"Bess, I know Harry thinks Rosalys is getting a rotten deal. Perhaps she is, but not more so than life usually hands out. She loves Mark, and her whole life is bound up in this place. She will not let him waste his life: they understand each other. She will never get on his nerves. She will never be jealous of me. Only Rosalys can save Mark, now."

Quite suddenly Bessie saw as Marian saw what Mark might become. It was curious that Marian, who had always lived among hard drinking people, should so fear that Mark, if disappointed in life, bored and unhappy, would take to drink.

Marian was right about Rosalys, and about the place. This was Mark's anchor. The transfer to the Air Force and the return to England had been right. Had things gone on as they were in India, there would have been an awful crash.

Marian began to speak again, there was an iron determination in her voice. "Mark is home for good now. The estate will be put in order, as far as is humanly possible. The effort of it will pull him out of his inertia. Rosalys will help him, as only she can."

Bessie knew that, too. Mark's life had been nothing but the usual round. His military duties took little of his energy. Sport, the silly social activities of the station—and Marian: those carefully contrived meetings, a few days or even hours snatched at the ever present risk of exposure and scandal; the utter hopelessness of it; Mark's barely realized loathing of the endless lies and subterfuge. Marian was quite right: there had to be an end to it. She had done the only possible thing. Few women would have had the courage to do it.

"I'm going down now," Marian said. "Come into the hall, Bess, and sit there. I'll leave the gunroom door open. If anyone comes into the hall, just wander in."

Bessie nodded. She had shielded Mark and Marian for so long that it had become a commonplace.

They went out into the gallery. The brilliant yellow of laburnam branches flamed against the dark oak. Bessie admired the crimson Chinese vases in which they stood. They were old, lovely, belonging to another age, like the house.

As they went down a small staircase Bessie thought bitterly of the absurdity of the belief that there was an ordered plan in every life. Why couldn't Mark and Marian have met before? Marian had been married when she was very young, but the boy had been killed in the war. It had not meant much to her, she had been frank about that—a boy and girl affair the tenseness of war had rushed into marriage. Then there had been years of drifting, meaningless affairs few people guessed at—Marian had always been too clever not to be discreet—and the slowly acquired belief that money and position were the only solid things. Then Sir Anthony appeared, enormously rich, enormously ambitious. Marian had been a perfect hostess: that was really what he had married her for. Her life had been full of interest, and for five years she had been happy, in a way. With three sons by his first wife, he had not wanted children. They had seemed to suit each other perfectly. Then had come Mark—when it was too late.

Harry hurried up the stairs on his way to dress for dinner, late, as usual.

"Mark's in the gunroom, with Horace," he said. "Remind him that John Beausire's coming to dinner and will want to see the west wing. We'll need lamps."

"There won't be time for the west wing," Marian called back, but Harry was gone. She felt furiously angry with him, as if in some way he were to blame for bringing the American to the village. She could not get it out of her mind that it meant trouble.

As Marian watched Horace Hobbs pour a drink and hand it to Mark who sprawled on the wide windowseat of the gun-room, she felt, for the first time since she had known Horace, the confidence in his judgment that had always secretly annoyed her in Mark. He was no longer a lower middle-class innkeeper who somewhat presumed on his boyhood association with Mark, but a shrewd and capable ally, who knew Mark more thoroughly than anyone else on earth, because with Horace, Mark's defenses were down, and he was completely himself.

Though she drank little, Marian accepted a cocktail with a vague idea that it would please Horace if she took one he had mixed. She was acutely aware of her need to make Horace like her.

Grandmamma simply couldn't last much longer, and in four years Marian would get the divorce. With a fortune of her own she would marry Mark, who could also get a divorce. When Rosalys had said, so simply, "I want Mark to be happy," she had meant just that, and she would always mean it. There would be opposition, of course. Uncle William would be savage. Marian thought uneasily of Ellen Hobbs, who would bitterly resent what she would consider the breaking up of the life of her Miss Rosalys. She also was shrewd, with the peculiar insight of those who lived near to nature.

Mark followed the leaded diamond pattern of the window-pane with a fingertip, and said lazily, "Horace says the lumber wallah's quite a bird. Knows a hell of a lot about agriculture, and all that."

He paused. Marian knew he had not yet said what most

impressed him in the talk he had evidently been in the midst of when she came in. She smiled and waited for him to continue.

Mark went on with a forced lightness. "Moreover, he's got red hair and looks exactly like the portrait of the Twenty-first Baron. He's not flashing money recklessly around to dazzle the yokels. They like him for himself."

As Mark spoke, Marian sat very straight in her high-backed chair. There had been no time to lose. Mark had changed quite a lot even in the five years she had known him. It was absurd to say that love was blind. It wasn't: it saw with an awful clarity. She knew that Horace saw Mark as she did and that he had been shocked and puzzled.

There was a heavy flabbiness about him. He looked older than he should. It was not enough to say that the Indian sun had darkened his skin, that his hair had naturally lost the reddish tint of youth and was now a dark brown. Mark looked wearied, utterly disillusioned. He was very near the stage when nothing would matter very much, not even the place, and when the effort to keep it going would not be worthwhile.

Determination seized her. Mark should make the most of his inheritance, Mark should remember that he was Baron Beausire. For that her own sacrifice had been made.

He would be happy here. The climate of India had been all wrong for him. Now he would live properly, and in four years, when she could come back into his life, he would be the gay young Mark she had first known.

Yet, had she known him so? She tried honestly to remember when Mark had begun to change. Throughout, the bond between them had strengthened, not weakened. His need of her was more intense now than it had been even in those first rather terrible weeks when they both realized that here was something stronger than themselves, stronger than the carefully arranged plans of their lives.

The ceaseless deceit and subterfuge, the lies and dependence on people like Bessie and her own maid were becoming intolerable to Mark. Again Marian told herself that there was no other way than the one she had chosen. She turned to Horace. "Lord Beausire is home for good, Horace," she said, speaking firmly and softly. She saw the eagerness in those pale eyes that had always somehow revolted her, and knew she was on the right track.

"He is going to take the estate in hand," she went on. "You can help him as no one else can. The first thing to do is to get a capable bailiff."

Mark pushed the window open with a foot, crumbled a biscuit and flung the crumbs to a couple of enterprising sparrows.

"What a pity the American is so rich," he said, "or we might have engaged him. He seems to know exactly what should have been done from the Year One to the present day, and to be willing and eager to repair the mischief done by many generations of his thriftless kindred."

Marian held out her glass to Horace. It was an excuse to look at him. So Horace had been trying to make mischief. Mark was already bitter.

That was to the good. It would make Mark fight harder. Although it was that tendency to a sullen bitterness that had frightened her in Mark from the first, she felt now that she could use even that for her own ends.

She took the drink Horace gave her, then said, with her eyes on him, "The American may be very capable, but he is not Lord Beausire. He may look like the Twenty-first Baron, who was his ancestor, but that connection is very distant now. I think the family will survive without his help."

"That's what I say," Horace said. "I've bin tellin' 'is Lordship that if 'e'll but take 'old, an' look to things 'isself, we'll 'ave the place out o' the red in next to no time. Don't need no outsider's money, we don't."

Mark laughed. "You should have seen the list of absolutely necessary repairs old Hare stuck under my nose," he said. He stood up. "I must admit I'm curious to see him. I suppose that's really why I asked him to dinner. I'll have to shove off and dress. Stick around, Horace, or come back. I want to show you the repair list tonight."

Tall, heavily built, with regular features and hazel eyes, Mark was considered one of the best-looking men in the Army. Marian thought now that he had really been much the same when she first met him: it was only that she had a trick of imagining him as he must have been when very young.

"Buck up," she said cheerfully. "Don't leave us alone to receive the Beausire who disappeared and bobbed up again like a jack-in-the-box."

Mark laughed. "The whole thing is damned queer," he said. "I wonder if he really came because he thinks war's inevitable, and any time now there might be no family wigwam to see."

Horace put things together on the cocktail wagon when Mark had gone. He was trying to think of a way to say a few things he had on his mind. The right words would not come to him. He took up the cocktail shaker.

"Another drink, m'lady? Mild as milk, they are."

Marian shook her head and pushed aside her untouched second drink. It was foolish for them to waste time. They should be planning their campaign. Then she remembered that it was up to her to give Horace his lead.

"How do you think his Lordship looks, Horace?" she asked.

Horace stepped nearer. No time for lies now, he thought. Best to say what he thought, outright.

"Badly, m'lady. I'm tellin' you straight, it's mighty lucky he's back. Frets about the place runnin' down, when 'e's away, that's what's wrong with 'im."

"I know." Marian looked at Horace directly. He must understand that they were friends, that anything he might say was safe with her.

"But it's going to be all right now. Are you glad he's to marry Miss Rosalys, Horace?"

Horace clutched a glass uneasily, polished it and stuck it into the silver holder.

"Yes, m'lady," he said, grimly sticking to his determination to tell the truth—in this quarter, at least. Best for Master Mark, that way.

Suddenly it occurred to him that the marriage would never be taking place unless her Ladyship wished it. Master Mark was still wild about her. Best to tell her, right out, where the danger lay. She'd know best what to do about it.

"M'lady, you'd take it right if I was to tell you something that's kind o' botherin' me? You know Ma. Can't speak to 'er about anythin' that touches Miss Rosalys, you can't."

Marian did not take her eyes from Horace. She seemed to understand him for the first time, and with a wrenching sense of gratitude she sensed something of the depths of his loyalty to Mark.

"You can say anything to me, Horace, at any time," she said slowly, "and I will take it as you mean it, and it will never be repeated—to anyone."

A weight seemed to slip from Horace. Never would he hear another word against her Ladyship, he thought, not as long as he lived. Quality like the family married where it was best, but they loved where they liked. Master Mark certainly knew how to pick them.

Marian waited patiently but with a rising fear that someone would come in. At last Horace began to speak in a low and confidential voice.

"It's about Miss Rosalys," he said. "She's not 'appy, or so Ma says, an' you know Ma dotes on 'er. Then there's Mr. Beausire. 'E's in love with 'er, 'as bin from the day 'e first saw 'er, I reckon. Well—they're both young."

Horace paused, floundering about for the right words. It had seemed easy to say it right out, but it wasn't.

"Have they been seeing much of each other?" Marian's question might have sounded casual to a stranger. Horace knew she had missed nothing.

"No, m'lady, just run into each other in the villages, now an' again, but Ma lets slip where she's likely to be—seems to me on purpose—an' then I sees 'im take the car an' go off. Yesterday Ma told 'im she was goin' to see old Mrs. Bates up at St. Matthew's Farm, an' he went an' stood for an hour or more by the gate of the five-acre field, watched her go in, waited there till she came out again, then drove off, without a word to 'er."

"Your mother doesn't approve of the engagement?"

"No, m'lady. She thinks 'is Lordship's too old for Miss Rosalys."

Feeling sure of the complete candor she wanted, Marian asked directly, "What are you afraid of, Horace?"

"That Miss Rosalys will change 'er mind. What with not being first with 'is Lordship—" Horace stopped abruptly, panic-stricken. He had not meant to go as far as that.

Lady Armitage stood up. She was smiling. There were voices in the hall. "I understand. Thank you, Horace," she said. "If I were you I wouldn't mention this talk to his Lordship."

Then, with a quick smile, she went out into the hall.

Horace left the room by another door. He felt more at peace than he had for days past. Her Ladyship would know how to deal with the situation. There was nothing like being prepared. It would have been easier and much pleasanter to belittle Mr. Beausire to Master Mark, but it had been safer to tell the truth about his growing popularity. He'd only been here two weeks, wanting two days. Where was it going to end?

Her Ladyship could be depended on to show Miss Rosalys where her duty lay, if need be.

The small group gathered around the great fireplace seemed lost in the vastness of the hall. Marian watched the Vicar as he stood deep in talk with Harry Gregg. His curly silver hair framed his strongly hewn face like a halo about a head of carved granite. In the deep and powerful voice that made his most trivial remark sound extraordinary, he was telling Harry a story of how a Dorset family had fought an attainder and won their case. So Harry was still harping on that.

Marian had felt uneasy about the meeting with William Tremayne. Though it was her unfailing policy to be prepared for anything, she had been utterly unable to make up her mind whether she would tell him the truth or not. He might ask her point blank if she was or had been Mark's mistress, and what she intended to do now. This was the third time they had met during this visit. Having been away, Uncle William was particularly busy in the parish, and no awkward questions had been asked yet.

The night Rosalys had agreed to marry Mark, Marian had asked her if her father knew what was being said about Mark and herself. Rosalys had answered simply, "No, and he never will. Why should he?"

It was then that she had understood fully the strength of the girl's character. For three years she had known something of great importance in her own life and had not said a word about it to the one person whom she would naturally consult for advice.

Bessie was flicking over the pages of a magazine; Mark had not yet reappeared. Marian raised her eyes and saw Rosalys coming down the stairs in a long green dress.

The child looked well in green, Marian thought. When had she seen her before, coming down that dark staircase in a green dress? In a moment she would begin to run, and her green dress would gleam through the banisters like rippling water. She would run, in wild excitement, because John Beausire was coming home.

Rosalys did not run. She walked down quite slowly, as if her eyes were already searching the length of the hall.

Little flowering laburnam trees in green-and-gold Chinese lacquer tubs looked almost incandescent against the dark oak. Footmen moved in and out of the great dining room, in which Mark had at the last moment decided they should dine, though the little cedar room was generally used.

Mark came through the west wing door. Stopping by Bessie's chair, he looked over her shoulder. Bessie held up the newspaper she was reading for him to see the full page photograph of Rosalys, with the announcement of the engagement beneath it.

"Good, isn't it?" she said.

Mark looked at it critically. "No," he said, "I don't like it. Her eyes look like the eyes of an unjustly spanked spaniel pup."

Bessie laughed. "Her eyes are sad, aren't they? I suppose it's the way they're set. I've never known anyone who's had a happier life than she has. She says so herself."

Mark was laughing too loudly as Rosalys told him some remarks the tenants made to her when they congratulated her on her engagement. He showed plainly that he was nervous. Harry Gregg, listening to the Vicar but watching Mark, thought that Uncle William was the only one of them who was unaware of extraordinary tension.

The two footmen had turned now. Harry watched John Beausire advance up the hall preceded by Swain, and saw Mark move forward. There might have been no one present except those two.

Swain announced the guest clearly: "Mr. John Beausire." Harry wondered if he, too, felt this was a strange moment.

Mark was making conventional apologies for not having offered to show him the place before, explaining that he had been snowed under, as he always was on returning from a long absence. John Beausire was saying that he quite understood.

Looking into the unhappy face of his distant cousin, John knew that he would not need to force himself to take Gregg's advice and like Mark. He did like him. Whatever Mark did, he would continue to like him and to want his friendship. It was the dark-haired woman in the gray dress that he felt uncertain about. She was watching him as though she resented his presence here.

Mark, after his first moment of shock, was completely in control of himself. He knew now why Horace had clumsily tried to prepare him for that shock. Old Horace hadn't exaggerated: this man might have stepped out of one of the earlier family portraits. Fine faces, sensitive and intelligent, hadn't cropped up since 1685. It had been said that the French mother of the Twenty-second Baron had changed the type.

There was a long silence. Marian stirred uneasily. Suddenly Mark burst into laughter, gay and unaffected.

"Golly," he said, "I wish I'd been there when you blew into

the Arms. Old Horace's face must have been worth seeing. He told me he and Ellen nearly collapsed. You're a Beausire, all right."

A warmth of gratitude flooded John. He knew that for an instant he had seen the real Mark, even if he should never see that aspect of him again. Good-natured, gay, friendly to all the world. He wished passionately to make Mark understand that he wanted to help, not hinder.

Harry had moved quietly to where they stood, "People have such odd ideas about time," he said. "Two hundred and fifty years, more or less, is but a flash. It's not strange to me that a type should endure for that short time."

"I certainly never felt a stranger here," John said. Though he spoke to Mark, he looked across to where Rosalys stood, her eyes as green as the silk of her dress.

Bessie Gregg he had met once or twice in the village. He had also met the Vicar, who came forward now with a smile.

"Wonderful old place, isn't it?" he said, touching the carving of the fireplace affectionately. "When I think that one bomb—"

"Father," Rosalys cut in, reproachfully. "Do forget that."

William Tremayne smiled apologetically.

"Forgive me," he said, "but I've just returned from a series of meetings held to discuss how we can best safeguard the old beauties of England in the event of war. The findings weren't very encouraging."

It was at dinner that John decided to do his utmost to follow another piece of advice casually handed out by Gregg during one of their walks through the woods. He would think only of the moment, which was happy enough. Rosalys, sitting beside Mark, talked mostly to him or to Harry Gregg. But she addressed an occasional remark to himself. Deliberately he questioned her about the neighborhood. The sound of her voice gave the place names a lovely and familiar ring.

There was Norton St. Philip, with its marvelous old Inn, Creech St. Michael, Creech St. Mary, Wincanton, Nether Stowey, Crowcombe and many other lovely names.

After dinner the Rose Room seemed more touched by time than it had when he had first entered it, John thought. The pale brocade hangings from which it got its name were faded and rotting in several places.

Rosalys opened the ornate little spinet, and sitting on the gilt stool where another Rosalys had so often sat, played a seventeenth-century French tune that came suddenly into her head. It was like a sad little ghost voice calling from the past.

Harry Gregg felt elated when Mark sent for the keys of the library and the Queen's Room. As they went down the gallery he stopped and looked at the portrait of the Twenty-first Baron. There was no doubt at all about the likeness.

The west wing had not been wired for electric light. Mark explained that it was never used now, and anyway, the paneling was too valuable to be risked.

When the library door opened, John felt that he was in a dream. He could only wander around, touching a panel here, a piece of furniture there; looking up at the bookcases. He did not want to analyze or explain the deep sadness that had overtaken him. Old griefs still lingered in these rooms; old fears rustled in shadowy corners. He had felt something akin to actual terror when he passed the head of the west staircase.

"Come on," Harry Gregg called. "We're going to see some of the finest paneling in all England."

Mark was unlocking a door at the far end of the library. Astonished footmen carried in lighted lamps, lit tall candles in many silver sconces.

The door creaked dismally as Mark opened it and said something about having the hinges oiled. They all moved forward into what seemed a cavern of darkness.

Harry went in first, carrying a lamp, which he set on the only piece of furniture in the room, an immense black chest set beneath the one circular window. John recognized that window at once. It was the one he had seen from the Court of St. Francis. He was conscious of darkness, then of intense physical cold. It was as if an icy blast had rushed through the room. The walls appeared to be hung from ceiling to floor with heavy black, but when more lamps were brought in it was seen that the circular room was paneled in richly carved black wood.

"The ceiling is painted," the Vicar said. "It's quite a remarkable piece of work, though badly flaked now. We have no record of the artist's name."

Turning to look at Rosalys, John saw that she was shivering. He moved closer to her. He felt as if they were alone here, alone as they had been in the church, touched by the same sense of otherworldliness.

"What is it?" he asked. "This cold?"

She looked startled, as though surprised that he, too, had felt it.

"I don't know," she said. "Sometimes it's felt here. Nothing would drag Horace into this room, though he won't admit it."

Harry came up to them. He looked curiously pale, and his dark eyes were shining.

"Rooms take on the atmosphere of things done or very strongly thought in them," he said. "This room was once lovely and peaceful. There is something here now that is not due to the dark paneling."

The Vicar was talking about Catherine of Aragon, of the pomegranate that was her emblem and also an emblem of sorrow. John wished he would stop talking, but he went on about Mass being said here, and the light placed in the circular window shining out across the valley like a star as a sign for the worshipers to gather. Then John knew that this was the secret room of which Ellen had spoken, or the entrance to it.

Mark was standing beside a panel. "It's no go," he said. "I can't remember the trick. The directions are in the safe in Taunton."

He turned to John then and said, "I was going to show you the secret room, but I can't open it."

Harry moved a lamp nearer the panel as if reluctant to give up. John stepped forward, hardly aware of what he meant to do.

"Let me try," he said.

They all pressed around him as he knelt on the floor. A thrill of sickening fear swept over Marian as she saw his fingers close over a carved pomegranate.

"He was warned, the emblem of grief," flashed through her mind. She stared incredulously as the panel slid open.

As he looked into the blackness beyond the panel, John's only feeling was one of amazement. From the moment he had knelt down he had felt it would be simple to open the door. Almost unconsciously his fingers had sought that knob formed by a pomegranate fallen from the tree. He had felt the sudden turn of it, as he had known he would if he lifted it in a certain way and pushed along a groove.

"How did you do it?" Harry asked sharply.

Mark held up a lamp, and the light fell on twisting, narrow stone steps. Darkness, thick, dreadful, seemed to pour down them.

"I don't know," John replied. He heard Mark exclaim in a hard, choked voice, "Let's get out of here."

It seemed but an instant before they were all in the lighted library.

"We'll go back to the east wing," Mark said. "There is nothing to see up here. It's only a small stone-floored room under the eaves, with a ledge along one wall that was used as an altar at the time of the Interdiction. It's not interesting."

John looked round that splendid room. He knew he must stay now, or be shut out of it forever, that he must be stronger than the evil writhing about the strange room beyond the now closed door—that if he were not it would escape and submerge them all.

"Would you mind if we stayed here for a time?" John said. "I think this room is the loveliest I have seen in the house."

For a moment Mark hesitated; then he said, "Of course not. We can play bridge here. I'll ring for tables."

Bridge didn't go very well. It was the Duke of Monmouth, Judge Jeffreys, James II, and, though he was not named, "the Lord who disappeared," who seemed to dominate the conversation. Harry had begun it, and no one seemed to have the will to stop it.

Suddenly Rosalys jumped up. "If we must talk of the past," she said, "let it be of something pleasant. I'll show you the Journal of John Beausire."

Mark felt curiously annoyed. The book, carefully kept in a teakwood box, had always seemed particularly the property of Rosalys. As a small child she had claimed it as her own, and he had solemnly given it to her.

Taking it now from its wrappings, she felt only the desperate need to erase from John's mind the gloom cast by the opening of the secret door. She wanted his memory of this room to be a happy one. She could not bear to have him feel that the other John Beausire had been the cause of gloom and evil. He had to know him as he was.

Rosalys handed John a book bound in black leather. "Here it is," she said. "Look at it."

He did not take it. "Read it to me," he said.

Without a word she cleared a space on a low table and sat before it. John pulled up a chair. Again they were alone together.

Quietly she read of the household staff. Her voice was the music of strange and lovely almost forgotten dreams.

More than a hundred people sat down to meat every day in 1685. John began to understand the vast size of the house. It was a community. There were not only the servants, but their families and dependents.

There was the steward, clerks, lackeys of the pantry and the buttery, cooks, scullions, slaughtermen, footmen, brewers, falconers, grooms, gardeners, the armorer, twenty stablemen, maids, nurses, a chaplain and those who waited upon him, an apothecary and his apprentice.

She did not take her eyes from the book when she turned a page. John felt that though she appeared to be reading, she knew it all by heart.

A desperate terror that she would stop; that he would never hear the end, seized John as she read of a harvest carried, of a happy day on which an old friend had returned and a marriage had been arranged.

At last Rosalys raised shadowed eyes from the page. " 'Next year I shall plant—' " she had read, and then she had closed the book.

"Go on," John urged. "Next year, at Combe St. Philip, I shall plant—"

There seemed a heartbreaking sadness in her eyes, the smothering grief he had seen upon the alabaster face of the

Little Maid. "There is no more," she said, so quietly that her voice was almost a sigh. "After he had written that, he went away, and never wrote in his book again."

John wanted to tell her that it must go on. Nothing stopped like that. Their lives must go on, their love must go on, forever, like the returning spring.

He felt vibrantly conscious of life. Tomorrow they could go together to look from the hilltop at the fair sight of the cherry trees in Markscombe. Ellen Hobbs had said that the Orchard would be at its best this week.

But he could tell her nothing, for the Vicar was beside them, saying to Rosalys that it was time for him to go home.

Mark did not sit down again when the Vicar had gone. He made it quite clear that the evening was over.

John knew he would have to go. It might be a long time before he entered this room again. He loved this room; he could be supremely happy here. Harry Gregg had been right when he said that the Queen's Room had once been beautiful and peaceful.

For a moment in the hall Rosalys was beside him again.

"It was pear trees he meant to plant," John said gravely.

Marian, watching the two, knew that Horace was not imagining things. Her whole plan was in mortal danger. She wondered if the marriage could be hastened. Tomorrow she would ride with Rosalys and talk to her of Mark's need of her.

Chapter Six

✦   ✦   ✦   ✦

🌿 THE GLIMMERING FLOWER CANDLES OF THE CHESTNUT trees across the road seemed like tapers held in the hands of an unseen host, winding in an endless procession. Beyond lay the dew-silvered grass of the park, a still sea of light under the moon. Quickly John crossed the road toward it.

Almost unconsciously, John struck out across the grass to the trees. Strictly speaking, they lay between the two broad paths that were open to the public, but the villagers crossed the open space freely.

The sound of the stream and the waterfall mingled with the eerie little night sounds. The whole valley had an unearthly stillness. John felt that if he could be quiet, the tumultuous impressions of the evening would be absorbed into that stillness; all would become clear to him, and the tormenting sense of something tremendous just beyond the power of his mind would resolve itself into comprehension.

The church clock struck the half-hour like a great voice,

calling across the valley from St. John's. The Court floated in silvery light.

Beneath the oaks the shadow was a black velvet cloth. John moved from tree to tree, touching the roughness of the boles, looking up into the mysteriously rustling branches. Voices seemed to be whispering there, too softly for him to catch the words. If he could only hear what they were saying he would understand why he had known every corner of this valley, every room in the Court; he could overcome the barrier that stood between Rosalys and himself, though they both knew that she was wholly his.

Sitting on the cool dry grass beneath the great oak nearest the house, John tried to recapture the sense of peace, of complete fulfillment, that he had felt as he had heard the words written in a simple journal long ago. For that brief time there had been no barrier. She had acknowledged as he did that what had been between them was invulnerable to change or death, that John Beausire and his Little Maid had found their way back through the shadows of a passing separation to reunion.

Other impressions crowded in. Mark's sullen face seemed to stare at him again. What bitterness of memory did it call up? . . . But the bitterness was erased instantly by Mark's laugh, which brought a full tide of gaiety, good will, remembered happiness.

There was the beautiful face of Lady Armitage. She, too, was tangled in some old dream he had almost forgotten: the cold and darkness of the west wing, the horror that had poured down those narrow stone steps, a horror that was real, but not so real as the impression that had fought it, that the Queen's Room had once been beautiful and peaceful, and would be again.

It was Harry Gregg who had said that. It had not been his

own impression at all. John tried to separate reality and imagination, but could not.

The grass beyond the dark circle of the tree seemed to get brighter and brighter, to flash with an almost blinding light. John turned his eyes from it, past the distant mass of the house, to where, silhouetted against a silver-flooded hillside, the dark old tower of St. John's stood in somber majesty.

"I am John Beausire," he repeated, many times, slowly, seeking an inner meaning that had hitherto escaped him.

The meaning of the words, of all words, vanished. There was no feeling now but the roughness of the oak bole against his head, no sight but the immensity of that dark tower, a darkness that was expanding, mysteriously merging him into itself, filling all space, blotting out the moon, the stars, the valley and all within it, spreading over all the world.

Heavy drowsiness lapped about him, a slowly rising tide that rose in a great wave, dragging him down with it into a dark sea.

❖   ❖   ❖   ❖

The first gray light of daybreak made every tree and bush stand out like a black shadow. The dawn wind—laden with the scent of apple blossom—rustled through the leaves and sent down showers of snowflake petals from the fruit trees.

Horace folded the piece of sacking on which he had knelt to whitewash the back porch. He carried it to the scullery with the bucket, feeling rather foolish for having done a job that was no business of his. How could he explain to Sidney that he had been too nervous to sit around without something to do?

The boiler fire had to be attended to. Carefully he scraped out the flues and banked the fire. Just as well to do it yourself now and again, and find out that it wasn't cleaned out properly, and that was why it took so much coal to heat the water. He'd give old Jack a talking to, he would.

Then he went into the kitchen and lit the fire in the big old-fashioned range. He filled a kettle with water and pushed it down on the burning wood and coal, then went to the kitchen door to wait.

Nothing had happened, really, he told himself sharply. Master Mark had been proper put out because the American had opened the secret panel, but you wouldn't know it, unless you knew Master Mark uncommon well, the way he himself did. It was when he joked about things, pretended not to care, that you knew they'd touched him.

Things was pretty bad. For himself he couldn't see how they'd work out. Taxes going up and up, wages rising, costs rising, and things so bad half didn't pay their rents on time, always dragging behind, and all screaming for repairs that would cost mor'n the buildings was worth.

The kettle began to sing. Horace took a big earthenware teapot and a canister of tea from the dresser.

Then there were the things Swain had said. The old fool! He was a Baptist, or some such nonsense, and thought that if you broke a commandment or two you'd fry in hell for all eternity. If what Swain said was true—and he'd not lie for anything, or say what he wasn't sure of—there was no manner of doubt as to which commandment was being broken at the Court. What of it? It was Master Mark and her Ladyship as would fry, so why did Swain take on so?

A jet of steam burst from the kettle spout. Horace warmed the teapot and made tea. He knew he'd been a fool not to go to bed. There was a deal to do today, and he'd be dog tired by midday, but he couldn't have slept nowhow, knowing that the American hadn't come in.

It was a quarrel over the lease, he was afraid of. The American had been too quiet the day he came in from Taunton and told him that Mr. Hare had said there was no chance at all of Lord Beausire's leasing the Court. Still waters ran deep. Set on the place, he was, and not only the place. Everywhere you looked there was a chance of trouble. What Swain said in the privacy of the buttery, to one he knew loyal to his Lordship, might soon be talked about freely in the villages. How long would it take to get to the ears of the American, and what capital would he make of it? Even the footmen who waited on table had said he was sweet on Miss Rosalys.

Horace collected milk, sugar, bread and butter and a slab of cold bacon from the larder. Then he sat down and stared at the rapidly growing light in the window.

"Scared stiff—that's what I am," he murmured. "It's the curse. Swain knows it. The American wants the place, an' he wants Miss Rosalys. Master Mark'll give 'im neither. There'll be a shockin' row. Miss Rosalys will soon see she's bein' made a fool of. She may turn to the one nearest to hand—pride's a strong thing. It's goin' to strike again, the curse is."

Horace started when he heard his mother's voice from the hall doorway.

"What are you up for, Horace? It's barely five yet."

"I couldn't sleep," he said, and got up to take another cup and saucer from the dresser.

"Nor could I," Ellen said. She was deeply worried. Something had happened last night at the Court. That was why Horace had slipped up to his room without speaking to her. It must have been something that would reflect on his Lordship, or he wouldn't have minded telling her.

Ellen took the tea her son handed her. "Mr. Beausire came in about eleven," she said. "He put the car in, then went out again. Maybe he went up to the Vicarage. It wouldn't surprise me if Vicar talked all night, having got hold of one who loved old things as much as he does himself."

Horace was sure there was nothing in that suggestion, not with the Boy Scouts Picnic today, which tired Vicar out even after a good night's rest. There was no chance at all that the American had gone back to the Court. Not after what his Lordship had said, last thing.

Horace ignored the maddening thought that if there was trouble his Mother would not be on the side of his Lordship. He had to talk to someone.

"Ma," he said, "there's trouble brewin'. What if the American should take a shine to Miss Rosalys?"

Ellen choked down a sharp retort. It was his Lordship who called Mr. Beausire "the American." Horace was copying him. She knew why they did it. It saved calling him by his proper name. But that didn't alter the fact that he was John Beausire.

Yet, though she was angry at the way they spoke of him, she was curiously pleased that Horace had thought of that. John Beausire and his cousin Rosalys again. They do say history always repeats itself.

"I say there's trouble brewin'," Horace repeated gloomily.

Ellen spoke with more assurance than she felt. "There's no sense to that. Miss Rosalys is engaged, and she's not one to go back on her word." She paused and fixed her eyes on her son. There was more than one way of finding out what you wanted to know.

"Unless she has good cause," she added significantly. "By the way, how long's Lady Armitage staying this time? Enough fuss when she comes. In my time at the Court it was the lady of the house who had the Blue Tapestry Room, and none but her."

"Things change," Horace said. "If she likes that room, why shouldn't she 'ave it? She's the wife of Master Mark's commanding officer, she is, a great lady, and a lovely one, too."

Ellen cut a piece of bread and butter into strips with slow deliberation. Horace was losing his temper now. He'd let out all he knew, and that would be about all there was to know.

"Seems as there's some that thinks so," she said. "God only knows what the woman wants. She's had his Lordship running after her for five years, following her about like a tame poodle. I suppose they're waiting for Sir Anthony to blow up and have him cashiered for conduct unbecoming to an officer and a gentleman and drag the thing through the divorce courts. Meanwhile she expects Miss Rosalys to look the other way, go through with the marriage, even. That'd make a mighty good impression on the old lady in Wiltshire, who hates divorce and loose women and can leave her money where she will."

Horace was too angry for diplomacy. He replied without waiting to think. "If 'is Lordship or anyone else was to be cashiered for what 'e's done, it seems to me the army 'ud be mighty short o' hofficers. As to the money, the Sergeant told me 'er Ladyship was safe to get it. 'Er grandma just worships 'er, she does. An' who wouldn't? Miss Rosalys 'as good sense. She's no fool, an' knows 'ow these things are."

"Well, it isn't likely she'd be jealous of one old enough to be her mother," Ellen shot back. "But mark my words, Horace, things can't go on as they are. The engagement's stopped talk for a bit, but it'll break out again double quick when it gets round that nothing's changed."

"What do they say?" There was nothing but anxiety in Horace's mind now. No one would dare to gossip about his Lordship to him, which was a disadvantage. Sergeant Hicks had spoken as an old friend, and it was not cheerful to think of what he had said.

Ellen thought Horace might as well have it straight. She'd give him not only what Matilda had said but what she'd implied also.

"Oh, that Miss Rosalys is a poor innocent as is being took in—that is, if they're for her. If they're for his Lordship and that fancy woman of his, they say she's so keen on being Lady Beausire that she's not seeing what she's no mind to. As for Vicar, we all know battle, murder and sudden death could take place right under his nose and he'd still be grubbing in the earth for the remains of old churches and searching through old books and papers, because the only real things to him are those that happened hundreds of years back. Besides, his daughter's all he's got, and its natural he wants to keep her near by."

Horace shivered. It looked pretty bad, whichever way you looked at it.

"What do they say about the American?" he asked. Ma had a way of getting folks to talk to her. Perhaps it was because she never gossiped herself.

A strange expression passed over Ellen's face. Horace watched her closely as she spoke.

"They say it's mighty queer how he knows things, old ways of doing things as is only done in Somerset; that it's plain he loves the land, and if he'd been Lord Beausire he wouldn't have spent years away from it, wasting money on polo ponies and cars and women. He'd have been here, farming, getting the best out of the land, and helping others to. There's no swank in him, and he's making real friends around here."

Horace rose wearily. It was no use talking. You could go on forever, and it wouldn't help things.

"Now 'is Lordship's 'ome for good, things is goin' to be better," he said. Then he went out to feed the chickens.

The strident crow of a cock tore through the valley. It was answered by another from far off. John sat up, conscious of the heavenly freshness of the air and the rustling oak leaves above him, and conscious that something he had been so sure he would hold forever was already slipping from him.

Far off, above the eastern hill, the sky was a pale green, cold as ice, clear as fathomless seas. It faded so quickly that it seemed to have been color seen in a forgotten dream. Little clouds of primrose yellow gave place to ribbons of shadowy lilac. Then the whole eastern sky was flecked with a pink that deepened until it glowed with a fiery brilliance. Another moment, and the sun shot up, a ball of fire, over the crest of a hill. Pale gold spilled down the hillsides into the valley. Every leaf, every blade of grass, glowed with iridescent brilliance. The valley had wakened.

John sprang up. Something at least he could remember. He knew where to go, what to seek.

Quickly he walked through the dew, his footsteps making dark marks. In amazement he stared at the empty space of grass that stretched across to the hedge bordering the road. There were no buildings there, as far as could be seen, which was from the great gates of the drive to the first houses of Sudbury St. Luke.

John stumbled and saw that the grass dipped down in a wide and deep depression. He knew now that the farm, the barn, had been part of a strange dream, dreamed beneath the mystery-laden branches of an ancient oak. They had no reality. And Sarah? He did not know, he could not remember, who Sarah was, or why he sought her.

Slowly, reluctantly, he walked toward the road. It was early morning. He had slept all night beneath a tree. Now he must return to the inn. All that had been clear when he opened his eyes was gone from him, save the memory of some buildings and of a sweet face that every moment became dimmer.

As John entered the garden through the paddock gate, Horace was coming down from the fowl houses, a bucket in his hand. He did not know whether he was relieved or not. The American walked like one in a dream. His dinner jacket was crumpled, his hair ruffled. His face looked—Horace sought desperately for an expression and found what he wanted—as though a light was inside it. "Fair shines, it does," he thought.

"Good morning, sir. Fine day, ain't it," he said.

John stopped. He looked at Horace curiously, saw him change before his eyes. He was wearing a curious sort of jacket of scuffed and stained leather, with rough shapeless shoes of rawhide. Then that vanished, and he looked wonderingly at the collarless khaki shirt, the corduroy breeches, the modern shoes. He raised his eyes to the scarred face.

There was no scar there. The pale eyes had a familiar look of fear in them; they were topped by a thatch of unkempt tow-colored hair. John smiled triumphantly. He remembered.

"Hullo, Jerry," he said.

"Thinkin' o' some servant in America," Horace thought. "Maybe something has happened, after all. Acting queer like, though not as though he'd been drinking. Hit on the head, perhaps."

Fear seeping in again, Horace moved unobtrusively forward. He inspected the back of John's head. There was no sign of a blow. There were bits of moss on the dinner jacket and in the red hair.

"Oh, good morning, Horace," John said, as that strange face

vanished and he saw Horace Hobbs looking at him with amazement in his eyes. Then he went on into the house.

It was quiet in the hall. The front door had been opened, and looking through it he could see the scarlet tulips edging the pathway to the gate. He stood very still, his eyes fixed on the bright flowers. The thing that had been complete and coherent that first moment after he had waked was almost within his grasp again. In a second he would remember.

Sitting down on a narrow oak bench, John tried with an intense effort of his will to remember what he now believed to have been a particularly vivid dream. At sunrise it had disintegrated into fragments. The frightened face of a boy, the sweet face of a woman, a picture of an old farmhouse, the evil face of a man beneath a great gray wig, were all that remained, and he could not fit them into place.

He felt he could not distinguish between dream and reality. Was this a dream, the other a reality? It was like turning up bits of a jigsaw puzzle and seeing bits of a design on them: odd faces and things, unconnected with others, slid into his mind.

He remembered the dinner at the Court. Then Harry Gregg had suggested, and against Mark's inclination, insisted on going to the west wing. He remembered opening the panel. Then there was a wild scream. All the anguished fear of all the hunted things on earth was in that cry. Then Mark had said harshly, "Let's get out of here."

The trouble was he couldn't remember who had screamed, or why.

There were other things. One was the dark bearded face of a man. He had been kind and friendly, yet because of something he said, the light of the world had gone out. There was a pale face, framed in pale gold hair, with blue eyes through which shone a faith that was like a light in darkness, a passionate belief in eternal justice, an unfaltering love and pity.

It was all a hopeless tangle. He had just grasped a coherent picture of the Queen's Room, not dark and deserted but warm and lovely, with a table set with crystal and silver, gleaming in candlelight, and Rosalys, white-robed and exquisite, her shining hair rippling down her back. He tried to hold that, but he lost it and was in a small dark place—in stifling heat. Many men were crowded there. He longed wildly for the cool sea-scented breeze that swept over the Quantocks. He was a prisoner, yet he could see the garden of the inn: he knew he had but to step forward to be in it.

Blindly John stumbled forward. A tall woman came out of the taproom and stood in the light streaming through the open door. Here was something real again. He looked into her face.

It was Sarah. He was quite sure it was Sarah, but he could not remember what it was he wanted to thank her for. Something she had done for years, in love and devotion, because she had once promised him that she would.

"Sarah," he said hesitatingly. "Sarah."

Ellen smiled. How well he knew that smile! "My name is Ellen, sir," she said. The family always call me that. Only strangers call me Mrs. Hobbs. I'd be mighty proud if you'd call me Ellen, sir."

Everything snapped back into focus. There were no more shadows of dreams. He knew exactly where he was, everything that had happened last night.

"Why, of course, Ellen," he said. "Have you ever seen the oaks at sunrise? They're a marvelous sight. I stayed all night in the park and went to sleep under one of them. When I woke it was daybreak, and I watched the sun come up. I'm hungry. When I've had a bath I'll have breakfast."

It was Ellen who brought in the breakfast. He told her he had slept under the tree nearest the house.

"That was St. Luke, sir," she replied with a smile.

"Luke, the beloved physician," John thought. Of what evil might one not be healed if one could but sleep at will as he had slept? He thought of that strange sense of strength and power that had been his just before sleep came. That sinking down into obliterating darkness had been a descent not into nothingness but into all-embracing life. He felt again that sense of utter well-being that had been his as he stood in dream beside the farm building he still remembered. If only he could have land here, land in this valley, to farm and live on, his own land!

Before he knew it he was telling Ellen how he longed for land.

Ellen went down for more coffee. No maid should wait on Mr. John while she had a chance to do it. Horace was in the kitchen. She asked him if there was any chance that Colonel Pargiter would sell part of his land.

"Not with war on top of us," Horace replied grimly. "Thinkin' of buying rather than sellin', the Colonel is. Said to me less'n a week ago that we'd have to raise every bite we 'ad to eat, come the next war."

Ellen looked through the window to the wooded top of the hill between the villages of St. Mark and St. John. Mentally she surveyed the long sweep of land on its far side, rich land that merged into Taunton Dene.

"There's Combe St. Philip," she said. "With war so near, it's a crime for it to be wasted. Old Lucy and that good-for-nothing farmer of hers make a few barrels of cider a year and let it go at that."

Suddenly Horace saw what was afoot. "Ma," he said furiously, "are you goin' off your 'ead? There's trouble enough as it

is, ain't there? Can't you see what'll 'appen if the American set-
tles 'ere? 'E'll spend money like water, there'll be new
buildin's, new machinery, fine stock, model cottages let at five
bob a week, electricity from Markscombe Mill, all the rest that
could be done with money no h'object, an' 'e 'angin' round
after Miss Rosalys. Leave things be, Ma. Mrs. Gregg said
t'other day, when she was in 'ere with the Major, as Mr.
Beausire 'ud be bored to tears, and off, in a week or so. So 'e
will, if 'e 'as nothin' to do but walk and drive round the place."

Ellen smiled. "What did the Major say?" she asked.

Horace replied promptly. You could repeat what he had
said without passing on the inflection of his tone. "That 'e
didn't think so."

Ellen did not speak, so he went on desperately.

"There's no chance at all that Lucy Hawkes 'ud sell. That
old place is all she cares for, though it is tumbling down about
'er ears. It'll just about see 'er out, if she's lucky. She must be
nigh on eighty. Dozens of people 'ave tried to get Combe St.
Philip from 'er, an' she's sent 'em packin'. Vicar did 'is level
best, for a group as thought there was the remains of a monas-
tary or church under the ground there. She wouldn't even give
'em leave to dig. Madder than a March hare, Lucy Hawkes is,
but the place is 'ers. Ma, you leave 'er alone."

Ellen called a maid and sent up the coffee. She wanted to
think.

"Lucy Hawkes is no more crazy than you are," she said. "If
anyone should know it might bring good to have John Beausire
here, she should. She knows when the luck left this place, and
why. The Bible says there's a time for all things. Maybe the time
has come for Combe St. Philip to go back to a John Beausire."

Horace had a retort ready, but before he could deliver it, his
mother was gone.

Half an hour later, as he was working in the garden, Horace saw his mother leave by the back gate. He limped down the path to see which direction she would take. She did not take the field path toward the Vicarage but entered the lane that led to Markscombe Hill. That was the way to Combe St. Philip.

Ellen walked quickly, seeing nothing of the spring freshness of the lane. Her mind was back in the autumn splendor of the South Wood, on an October day forty-one years ago.

The color that year had been so marvelous that it almost hurt to look at it. But she had not looked long, for, finding what she had come to seek, she had flung herself down beside a newly placed flat stone a few yards from the road in the South Wood, too exhausted to weep for her Master Luke, blindly reaching out a hand to touch the trunk of the tree that had caused that awful bruise over which she had so carefully combed hair like flaxen silk.

She had known they would be looking for her, but she had not cared. For a long time she had stayed there, her face pressed to the fallen beech leaves. When she had at last dragged herself up to go, a tall figure was standing there, with a face so beautiful that for a moment she had thought wildly of angels. It had seemed to shine against the dark boughs of an evergreen.

It had been Lucy Hawkes, the woman whose tragedy had set all England talking; Lucy Hawkes, with a boundless pity in her great dark eyes.

Ellen could remember every detail of the conversation she had had with Lucy. She quickened her steps. Unless time had dimmed the memory of a very old woman, Lucy Hawkes would surely understand that here was something bigger than her own love for Combe St. Philip—her chance to break the curse that had made her life and beauty a thing of dust and ashes; to do, in a small measure, what one she had loved long ago had not had the power to do.

Ellen calculated quickly. Lucy had been eighteen in '77; that meant she was seventy-nine now. Perhaps what folks said was true, and she was crazy, and so would not understand that John Beausire must have land that had once been owned by his ancestors, that he was needed here, that his coming would bring good.

But there was hope. Some kept their wits as long as life lasted. Lucy Hawkes might understand very well how great a decision was hers to make.

With some annoyance the slatternly wife of Ben Briggs watched a tall woman come down the hillside path. The yard was filthy, and she knew it. Ben had talked about cleaning it up for weeks now but never got to it. She wished folk wouldn't come poking their noses in where they weren't wanted.

Annoyance turned to surprise when she recognized the visitor. What in the world could be bringing Mrs. Hobbs to Combe St. Philip? Reluctantly she went toward the gate.

Excuses for the condition of the place leaped into her mind. What could she do about it? Anyone could see that it would take half a dozen men to keep it going, and who was there to do a hand's turn but Ben, almost crippled by rheumatism, for the outside, and for the house and the dairy herself and that useless girl whose own mother had said wasn't all there?

Mrs. Briggs opened the gate, saying, "I've no cream, Mrs. Hobbs. It went sour overnight, and we haven't skimmed today." The last thing she wanted was to have Mrs. Hobbs see the dairy. Get after Maudie to wash it out today, she would.

Ellen saw nothing of the piles of rotting straw in the yard, the muddy trail visible through the open door of the kitchen.

"I've not come for cream," she said, "I've come to see Miss Hawkes on business."

Mrs. Briggs leaned against the doorpost. Whatever happened, she was not going to let a woman who kept her own place as neat as a new pin inside. Talk would be all over the village in no time.

"She won't see anyone," she said. "Hasn't talked to a soul for years. Why, she even has the delivery men leave stuff down by the cider mill now. Just can't bear the sight of a strange face."

Ellen looked into the huge stone-floored kitchen. Even in its dereliction you could see traces of the beauty of the house. No wonder it was said Lucy Hawkes was mad, living like a pig in a sty, shut away in two rooms, letting Briggs and his wife do as they pleased.

"She'll see me. I haven't set foot inside this place for more'n forty years, but I know the lay of it."

Before Mrs. Briggs could turn around, Ellen was halfway through the kitchen.

A fire burned in the big fireplace whose wrought-iron fireback was hundreds of years old. The figure seated beside it turned slowly and stared at Ellen as she stood in the doorway.

Ellen felt her courage ebbing fast. The old hag on the tall-backed oak settle could not possibly be the same woman she had talked to in the South Wood.

For a moment she wondered if she were not seeing a ghost. Then the dark shadows around that ancient head resolved themselves into the folds of a shawl that fell almost to the floor. A hand, more like a bird's claw than a human hand, held the shawl together. A wisp of white hair fell over a parchment-like forehead.

But the eyes were alive, the same marvelous eyes that had looked at her in pity in the wood. They were immense, sunken eyes, set in a maze of wrinkles. They were dark as a night of storm: living eyes, staring from a dead face.

Ellen moved forward. She tried to speak but could not.

Lucy Hawkes stood up, taller than Ellen, who was almost frightened to see how the ghost of beauty hung about that body's wreck.

Lucy spoke gently, as she had spoken in the wood long ago.

"Sit down," she said. "Why do you look so sad? There's an end to all things, even to grief and loss. For a long time now I've known that the wheel had turned, full circle."

Ellen shivered. Perhaps it was true what the older folk whispered—that Lucy Hawkes was a witch woman; that she talked through the long and lonely nights to departed spirits who told her many things; that death was but a little narrow stream to her; that she could look across, talking back and forth to those on the other side.

"Miss Hawkes," she began uncertainly, but the clawlike hand was raised to stop her.

"I know," Lucy said. "I saw him in the South Wood, the day he came. He did not turn his head to see me standing there. He wants a home here, and there is no other place but this."

Ellen nodded. All her carefully prepared speech, telling of the need for raising food, of the inevitable war, of all that Mr. John could and would do, of the small book of the Gospels that proved his right, went from her. It didn't matter. All that would be an old story to Lucy.

"What are you going to do?" she said at last.

"Do? We do what we must. He can have the place. Send word to the Court that the time of reckoning has come, and that it is well it is so."

Touched a bit, Ellen thought, but what matter? She seemed clear enough about title deeds, ready enough to sell. Was it hate of the present Lord Beausire, or good will toward the wanderer, that was prompting her?

All Ellen cared for was that she was bidden to bring John Beausire to Combe St. Philip, to tell him that if he wanted the place it was his. She could hardly remember a word of the conversation, except that Lucy had said she knew there was a darkness coming over the whole earth that would make all other wars and plagues look like times of light and peace. She hurried out, to meet Mr. John in Markscombe Lane at the appointed place.

◆   ◆   ◆   ◆

It was late in the afternoon when John came around to the front of the house after an inspection of his newly acquired property. He stood for a long time in the tangled garden, looking at the house. He knew exactly what he was going to do here. Old, gray, with little diamond-paned windows, the main house needed little but repairs and decoration. It was the uncovering of unsuspected beauties that had thrilled him. The long low building used as a cider cellar, filled with dusty sacks and broken farm machinery, must once have been the main hall of the house. Then there were the great open beams of the ceiling, the fine old oak staircase, that marvelous shadowy window above it which on close inspection proved to be paned not with glass but with ancient horn so thin that dim light filtered through it.

Here, over the doorway, cut into the lintel in the sprawling figures of age, were a date and those initials that marked Combe St. Philip as his own.

"J. de B. 1683," John read. That, Mr. Hare had said, was the year of the restoration, though the interior had not been finished for a year or more afterward. Tomorrow another restoration would begin. It would soon be a lovely place again.

John felt rather than saw the strange dark eyes fixed upon him. He turned and found Lucy Hawkes standing in the doorway. He was glad she had accepted his offer to stay, at any rate until a suitable cottage could be built for her.

"They'll be pleased. Made the most of the land, they say, and would like to see it well cared for again." The old voice was thin and high.

"Who are they?" John asked. Ellen had warned him not to be surprised at anything he might hear. Foolish, it might be, but quite harmless.

"The old monks. They still come back, sometimes. Their great church stood down in the west orchard. This was the hospice for the pilgrims. It will be filled again by seekers for safety, they tell me."

John smiled. He thought of Harry Gregg and his earnest insistence that we know almost nothing of the forces that surround us. Who could say what was real and what was not? "I'm glad they'll be pleased," he said, and Lucy nodded gravely.

They could not be more pleased than he was, he thought. Today he had become the owner of an old house, which that other John Beausire had loved and restored, and of five hundred acres of Somerset land.

Harry Gregg leaned over the gate and called to John as he came out of the house. John was extraordinarily pleased to see him and to fall in with his suggestion that they should go on to Markscombe Farm for tea.

"Their raspberry jam should be written of reverently," Harry said, "and Devon couldn't beat their clotted cream and splits. Come on. From the hilltop we can see the 'fair sight,' which will be at its best now."

They drove down a narrow lane between towering elms and ascended the steep road through the wood. When they came to the top and looked down, John knew his ancestor had written truly. A fairer sight could not be found on earth.

The gabled old house of gray stone seemed buried in breaking waves of white that threatened to submerge the scattered farm buildings, edged the wide mill pool, lined the side of the swift stream below the millrace.

"Rosalys may be here," Harry said casually as John drove down the rough road into that mass of whiteness.

There were cherry trees everywhere. They towered over the gate with its wrought-iron Lion of St. Mark, held white draped arms up to the little windows, sloped down to the pool and stream.

The great oak water wheel turned slowly. It had turned so for four hundred years. Its predecessor had been turning when the Conqueror came. It was mossy now; water dropped from it. Great flowering branches, so thickly hung with pure white pendant blossoms that they seemed luminous, were etched against it.

Harry went into the house to order tea. The newly painted white board, with its black lettering, "Markscombe Farm, Teas," had seemed an incongruous note, but to John it was a welcome sight, for it meant he was free to come here. He went down to the mill pool.

Swallows skimmed and darted over the pool in a mazy dance. Dragonflies, living jewels, flashed over the still water. A kingfisher was a streak of blue that might have dropped from some heavenly sky.

Then John saw Rosalys standing by the little bridge that spanned the stream to the mill house. He went toward her quickly.

She did not move. When he approached her, her eyes were wide and deep. She raised them to the great flowering branch above her head and smiled.

"John Beausire did well to plant cherry trees here, didn't he?" she said.

John nodded. The door of the mill house was open. Inside, it was cool and dark and misty with the dust of ground meal.

If they could stay alone, they could slip back into the enchantment that they had found so briefly in the church, and again last night while she read from a book written long ago. John thought with a wildly rising hope that if they found that place often enough, even for a few moments, the time would come when there would be no turning back, when it was the utter wrongness of their separation that would drop away.

The sadness of her eyes hurt him as she looked, not at him, but at the turning wheel.

"I hear you have bought Combe St. Philip," she said. "I am glad. It could be as lovely as this, if it was cared for."

"It will be," he replied eagerly. To tell her of all he meant to do, of the beauty he had seen hidden in that decaying old house, would be the best part of it all.

But another figure came down the path, a woman in a yellow dress, her black hair gleaming in the sun.

"Oh, hullo," she said, "I hear you've become a landowner. God help you! It's no fun these days. Come on, Rosalys, Mark's waiting by the house with the car."

"Good-by. Good luck at Combe St. Philip," Rosalys said, and followed Lady Armitage up the path.

John watched them go. Harry Gregg was coming down through the cherry trees. John tried to think that it was enough to have seen her and heard her say she was glad he had Combe

St. Philip. If only he could see her, just once again, she would admit what she already knew.

That she did know he loved her, he had not the shadow of a doubt.

He wondered why he could not get it out of his head that it was Lady Armitage, not Mark Beausire, who stood between them. If reports were true, she should welcome the breaking of the engagement.

Harry Gregg stood halfway up the sloping orchard, signaling for him to come up to the house. John went, knowing that he would tell Gregg what he wanted more than land, more than a lease of Sudbury Court. He felt curiously sure of sympathy, though Gregg was Mark Beausire's friend.

Chapter Seven

❖ · ❖ · ❖ · ❖

MARIAN SLOWED THE CAR AS SHE ENTERED THE SOUTH wood. In the green coolness, with the heady scent of honeysuckle drifting through it, the reckless drive from the Wiltshire home of her grandmother seemed to take on the quality of a nightmare.

The tall spires of the foxgloves, the fragile blue of harebells, pale stars of dogroses flung over the fallen trunk of a tree, brought no joy in their beauty, but only a hideous reminder that the summer was at its full now, and soon it would be autumn.

It was the terror of approaching autumn that had caused her to make the mistake last night of trying to find out something about her grandmother's will. She had received no information whatever about the disposal of the huge fortune, only a direct question as to the date on which she would return to "dear Anthony."

Marian wondered if she could make a funny story of last night's interview to amuse Mark. He had been depressed and moody for weeks now.

But the thing hadn't been funny, it had been horrible. The old woman, her ghastly scrawny hands deliberately laying out solitaire cards as she talked, had made it quite clear that gossip had reached her, but while there was no open break with Anthony, she would overlook it, though October was the last possible date she would consider correct for the return to India.

Then the old wretch had discussed Rosalys with Aunt Lydia—who looked more dessicated than ever this summer— and because what they had said had hurt her so much, and she hated herself for admitting that it did, Marian thought of it again, trying to analyze it for any particle of truth.

Grandmamma had said that the girl was not modern at all. That, of course, was meant as a compliment. Then she pointed out that she had been brought up by an unpractical and unworldly old man, seeing little of girls of her own age; that her whole interest was in the place, and the marriage was in every way suitable. Beausire would probably settle down.

Aunt Lydia had murmured, as if a little shocked at her own daring, that reformed rakes often made excellent husbands; then she had blushed a deep and unbecoming crimson, thereby admitting she had heard gossip, too.

The clock in the car hardly seemed to move at all. Marian knew that Mark would not be at the gates, waiting for her, until the appointed time. She had come at such a pace from Wiltshire that she was early.

It had been easy in the spring to believe that when autumn came the courage to make the necessary break would appear. The necessity for the break increased daily, now that autumn approached, but there was no sign of increased courage.

For ten days she had not seen Mark. It had seemed a brilliant idea to lengthen the time between those desperately sought meetings—against the time when the interval would be a year, at least. But ten days had been almost intolerable.

How would it be possible to endure four years of almost continual separation?

Marian pulled herself up with a jerk. Today was going to be gay and happy. Slowly the car descended the steep hill. The crested gates were closed. Marian felt small and somewhat contemptible before them. She was ten minutes early.

She sat very still, hoping old Parrett would not come from his cottage and open the gates. Stonechats seemed to be chirping everywhere. They clicked like Aunt Lydia's steel knitting needles as Grandmamma talked last night. What fools those old women were! Didn't they know that there was more than one kind of love, and that Rosalys loved Mark, and was part of the anchor that would keep him from being washed out on a tide of physical and mental ruin? Uncle William was no fool. He saw things as they were. He knew there was something solid in the love Mark and Rosalys had for each other, bound by the love of the place. He knew it would wear better than some silly love affair she might have with a boy of her own age.

Marian knew she was not being honest with herself, that there was a far greater danger. She saw the two red heads together in the lamplight of the library, bent over an old manuscript book. Mark had come into her own life too late. Had John Beausire come to Sudbury too late for Rosalys?

An Airedale came round the curve of the road, and when the dog recognized the figure in the car, it broke into a joyful trot. Marian called, "Jamie, Jamie," excitement almost choking her. Her eyes were on the road.

In a moment Mark turned the corner. This at least had worked. Mark, on his usual morning walk, had come upon her, apparently by accident. They would go up to the Court together, taking some time to do it.

Mark leaned on the door of the car, and his hands covered hers. Marian looked into his face eagerly, as if she could discover there how things had been going. That was useless: he was only thinking now that they were together again and could be alone until they had to go to the cherry-picking fete at Markscombe.

"We can leave the car in the Lodge Wood," Mark said, and got in.

Marian backed out into the road, and turned. As she drove the car into the broad path between great beech trees, she made up her mind that for a few hours, anyway, there should be nothing but Mark, nothing but the joy of being with him again.

"Where's everybody?" she asked, as they started to walk into the wood.

"Getting ready for the fete," Mark replied. "Bess and Rosalys are decorating the mill house for the tea. Funny thing, but no one knew when the cherry-picking fete was started. Harry buzzed round trying to find out this morning. Swain didn't know, and Ellen didn't. Uncle William said the basket of cherries as token rent was given as far back as 1660, for there's a record of it being done that year."

"The entire population turns out for the cherry fete, doesn't it?" she said, wondering if she was going to look absurdly overdressed in her rose-colored Lanvin frock and rose lizard shoes. Pretty awful if everyone else turned up in tennis clothes.

"Yes. It's the big shindig of the year. This year there'll be a bigger crowd than ever. They'll all want to see the American."

"How's he getting on?"

Mark laughed harshly, then began to speak in a voice that attempted casual amusement and only succeeded in sounding bitter. "Oh, he's running the valley now, from the other side of the hill. Soon we'll all be speaking with a twang and chewing gum. He has the entire population paying court at the inn every evening, unless he elects to receive on the village green at St. John. It must be quite funny. He advises on farming, quite forgetting that three months ago he'd never seen Somerset and probably wasn't aware of its existence. He's talked Pollard into having a power plant put in at Markscombe. He's probably paying for it, too, though Horace couldn't get anything on that. Every cottage that wants it is to have electricity. He knew damn well that I couldn't refuse permission."

"With the water power there is at Markscombe, it should have been done years ago."

Marian gasped when she had spoken, amazed at her own tactlessness, but Mark did not appear to have noticed it.

"Combe St. Philip's a sight to behold," he went on. "All done in period furniture. The old cider cellar's now a perfect Tudor hall. They found some amazingly fine things under the mess. Architectural magazines have been sending people down to photograph and write up the place."

Marian knew that Mark had to talk. She tried to think of something to say that would please him.

"He'll get bored with it," she said. "After all, when the restoration's finished, he'll have nothing on earth to do."

Mark turned angrily. "You can bet your life he will," he said. "He plans a cannery, American style, that I understand will feed all Bristol, not to speak of Sudbury. Chicken houses of the most modern type—and of course the most expensive—are going up from the end of the orchards clear down to the old Sykes cottage on the Taunton road. Dozens of laborers' cottages are being built, and a huge piggery. Mrs. Pargiter told Uncle William that she can't keep the Colonel away from the place. The American encourages him and talks to him about feeding problems if there's war. There will be war, of course."

Marian saw the bright green of the grass through a mist of tears. Mark had been hurt. He had been unfair, and that was not like him. The American didn't chew gum, and he didn't talk with a twang.

The rooks in the elms seemed to be crying, "Mark, Mark, Mark." She knew that the misery of this moment was but a small foretaste of the years to come. She gathered together every scrap of courage she had ever possessed and spoke calmly and firmly.

"Combe St. Philip was never anything but a small manor of the estate. You are Baron of Sudbury. Mark, get a first-class bailiff and a good agent—progressive men, not old dodderers like Bartlett. You must take the Air Forces training, of course, but you'll be able to be here a good deal. You can put the estate in order in four years. War *is* coming: you will have to raise food, and the gardens and park must go."

Mark nodded. He was silent for a time, sitting beside her, twisting the rose topaz bracelet on her wrist. He said suddenly, "That's not all. He's after Rosalys. Ellen's in with him. Horace swears she lets him know where Rosalys will be."

Marian tried desperately to crush the wild little hope that sprang to sudden life. Even if Rosalys married the American, she could not marry Mark. Yet there would be time, time to plead with Anthony once more, to threaten a flaming scandal that would be even worse than a quick and quiet divorce.

But this hope was only a ghost. Mark would never be happy unless he could live here and keep the place decently. He had to have an heir, and there was no time to lose. War might come almost any day.

In the afternoon sunlight the valley looked as if it could never know anything but peace and prosperity.

"We ought to go," she said. It was half-past three, and Mark was due at the fete in half an hour. They would have to go back to the house to 'phone Rosalys at Markscombe, so she could come down the lane and get into the car, to arrive with Mark.

"Not yet," Mark said. "It won't matter if we're a few minutes late. Let's go to the tower."

Terror gripped Marian as they walked across the grass. Mark couldn't let her go—and he must not let the place go. There was no way he could have everything he wanted. In her heart she knew that it was the place, the life he had been brought up to, which would mean most to him. That would last: her beauty, her physical hold on him, would not.

"Harry's to blame for a good deal of the excitement over the American," Mark said, as though he could not get away from that one subject. "He's been talking to Ellen. They gave each other meaning looks at evening service last Sunday, and stood gaping at the tomb afterwards. Uncle William preached with vigor and vim on the unfailing justice of the Lord, and Harry sat and positively purred out loud. I think he's converting Uncle William to his rattlebrained theories. I've always liked him, but he has a slate loose. Went nutty over this spiritualistic stuff he's always boning up on. Bess loathes it. He really believes the American is—John Beausire—the 1685 John Beausire. Same soul, new body, don't you know? Memory more or less intact. If it is, I can expect some dirty looks when we meet today. They've been grubbing up old Monmouth Rebellion records at Taunton Castle. There was more there about John Beausire than I had any idea there was. . . . If the theory's correct, I hope that when I move on to my next body, it'll have the sense to turn up where it can inherit several millions in the currency of the most financially stable country in the world."

Marian looked into the little roofless room of the tower. What did anyone know? Less than five hundred years ago, living, loving humans had walked up and down these twisting broken stairs, where now only the ivy climbed safely. Where were they now? Living and loving again, or gone like the Castle smoke?

"I'd not bother about the cash," she said. "Money's not everything. Please concentrate your attention upon acquiring as exciting a body as you managed on this trip. That's purely self-interest, you know, for I shall be around—also in a nice new body. Would you like blue eyes, golden hair—natural, of course—and about, say, five foot seven, for a change?"

Mark laughed. "Thanks for the compliment," he said. "Isn't there some proverb about making the most of the old before you get new?"

He pulled her toward him. She watched the flame of sudden passion light up his eyes. It would be easy to die, she thought, if a time came when it no longer lighted for her.

Mark spoke thickly but with unwonted fluency. There was fear in his voice.

"I want no change in you," he said. "I never want, or shall want, anyone else. You, as you are, can make me really feel. No one else ever did, though I tried to think they did. Marian, don't leave me. I can't go on without you. Rosalys will always understand, but that won't be enough."

Marian drew in her breath with a gasp. "Don't think about the future," she said. "We have today and tomorrow. We can meet in Bristol tomorrow."

"No, no," Mark said. "We'll go up to town tonight."

Marian did not reply, but raised her lips to his again. She

knew that she would go—after telephoning a careful story to Aunt Lydia, to be relayed to Grandmamma.

* * * *

The big kitchen of Markscombe Farm hummed with excited chatter. Village girls, pretty in their waitress costumes—flowered muslin of the Charles II period, with high white muslin mob caps gay with cherry-colored ribbons—jostled each other for a look into the dim old mirror hanging on a wall.

Mrs. Pollard, mistress of Markscombe Farm, hurried into the kitchen. Her plump fair face showed anxiety, and instinctively five pairs of eyes turned to the window. No sign of rain. The day was perfect.

"You had better get down to the Mill," she said. "His Lordship's not arrived yet, but Vicar thinks we should start tea."

There was a general movement toward the door. Mrs. Pollard went back to the small room used as an office. On the table stood the big decorated basket, its bright ribbons and glistening fruit glowing against dark wood. Once more Mary Pollard rearranged the neatly separated piles of cherries in their beds of leaves. There were Bigarreau Napoleons, Black Hearts, dark almost to blackness against pale Queen Anne's for contrast, May Dukes, bright scarlet sour cherries for their color. She was proud of the basket this year. Where in all the world could one find better cherries than in the Markscombe Orchard?

His Lordship was late. She didn't like to start tea until the speech had been made and the cherries presented, but Vicar said it wouldn't do to wait.

As she left the room, Ellen Hobbs came down the passage from the hall. She brushed past Mrs. Pollard as though she didn't see her. Her eyes blazed, her lips were set in a hard line. Miss Rosalys had been sitting in the hall for half an hour, watching the gate for his Lordship. Two hours ago he was seen walking near the tower in the park with Lady Armitage.

The uneven-floored hall, with the broad staircase of gray stone winding from it, looked cool and shadowy as John entered it from the kitchen passage. Rosalys stood by the front door, her white dress and big hat sharply outlined against black oak, looking down the path toward the gate.

Before she turned he sensed her tense anxiety. For the first time he felt the fear of the curse that always seemed to hang over Horace and Ellen. Harry Gregg was probably right, and fear was the only source of trouble.

Rosalys smiled. "Mark's late," she said. "He never can remember how time goes."

John leaned against an old sea chest. His only thought was to keep her talking. He had come absurdly early, because Ellen had said that she would be here, but she had been surrounded all the time by chattering women and girls.

"Why is the cherry fete held for the benefit of a Sailor's Home?" he asked. "Do you think John Beausire had that in mind when he planted the orchard here?"

"He had a good friend who was a sailor," Rosalys replied. "A son of Markscombe. Captain Pollard sailed his *White Heron* to the Indies three times to search for John Beausire."

John nodded. He and Harry Gregg had found that story in the dusty, time-darkened old records in Taunton Castle.

"The *White Heron* is a marvelous name for a ship," he said. He remembered the galleon-shaped cloud that had floated above him just before he entered the valley, and his thought of a white bird and a dark-bearded man.

Pollard, the farmer, was also tall and dark. He must be a descendant of Captain Pollard, the old seadog who had failed in his search. But had he failed? Who was to know?

Rosalys went on talking, as though she feared silence between them.

"The Pollards are a seafaring family. One or more of the sons have gone to sea in each generation. Two were lost during the last war, one at Jutland, one in a minesweeper which blew up off the Cornish coast, very near the place where the *White Heron* was driven ashore and smashed in the early years of the eighteenth century."

Dim voices of the past were calling. Sometimes they were so clear that one could almost hear their message, but just as it was about to become comprehensible, a harsh voice from the present cut across it.

Now it was a quick step. The Vicar came up the paved path beside the house and entered the hall. It was obvious that he was distressed and angry.

"We'll have to start tea," he said, then turned to John. "I'd be greatly obliged if you'd say a few words to open the fete. Lord Beausire usually does it, when he is here. When he is not, I arrange for some person of standing to do it. You are a newcomer among us, owner of one of our oldest and most storied farms. It would please them greatly if you would."

"What can I say?" John asked. He was not sure whether he wanted to do it. There was something terrifying in the thought of speaking to these descendants of that other John Beausire's tenants, as so many of them were.

"Oh, just give them an idea of what you plan to do at Combe St. Philip and make them understand that you have come to stay, not bought the place for a whim."

In the last hour the Vicar had seen clearly something that he had for weeks tried not to see. This ignoring of the existence of

John Beausire that Mark insisted upon was entirely wrong.
The man had every right to be here. It was already obvious
that he was doing immense good, good that in case of war
would be a godsend to the parish.

"All right," John said. "Do you mean now?"

"Yes. You speak from the mill. Let us go down."

Rosalys did not move. Her father spoke to her with a nervous sharpness in his voice.

"Come on, my dear," he said. "You are only making Mark's
carelessness more obvious by waiting for him here."

Rosalys went without a word. She had forgotten Mark. It
was so strange and wonderful a thing that John Beausire was
back among his people. Yet there was mockery in it. How far
back did one remember? She could not remember when she
had begun to save cherries for John Beausire, throwing them
into the stream for the running water she was assured would
somewhere find the sea to carry them to Maryland, the place
with the lovely name, where he was, and would of course find
them. Surely when she had been nine or ten she had not believed that, but she had gone on taking a few cherries from
the basket every year, throwing them into the stream, watching them vanish in the rippling waters. She had never
stopped it: it had become a little private ritual, an offering to
the memory of childhood dreams. She did not even think
whether she would do it this year: she could think of nothing
but her terror that Harry would remember the silly thing and
tell John Beausire. Her eyes wandered among the crowd
gathered down near the mill. She must find Harry and warn
him not to speak of it, but she knew, as she saw him talking to
Ellen, that she would not have the courage to do so. It was so
silly. Ellen knew, too. When she had been very small, Ellen
had helped find the fattest and brightest cherries in the bas-

ket. If only she could think of a casual and diplomatic way of telling them both that such childish things shouldn't be mentioned!

◆　　◆　　◆　　◆

Mark turned the car into the narrow road leading to Markscombe Farm. A gaily painted wagon, drawn by four splendid gray Percheron horses, almost blocked the way.

It was a tight fit, though Meggs, the driver, pulled the horses as far as he could toward the side. He took off his cap with a broad grin. Mark kept his eyes grimly ahead, but Marian saw that the side of the wagon had "John Beausire, Combe St. Philip, Somerset," painted on it in bright blue letters. The harness of the horses was decorated with scarlet ribbons and the wagon piled with large empty round baskets.

Mark spoke savagely as they neared the gate. "The American's probably accepted the basket of cherries by now. He's sending a cartload into Taunton schools and hospitals."

Marian blamed herself bitterly for allowing Mark to be late. She still felt shaky from that moment of shock when she had looked at her watch and seen it was already half-past four, and then they had to get back to the car.

Horace was by the gate. He pushed past the eager Scouts to open the car door. "Tea's almost over, m'lord," he said, with reproach he was unable to stifle in his voice. "At half-past four Vicar said to start."

"That was right," Mark replied. "I was—unavoidably delayed." He looked up at the gray old house, not daring to catch the laughter he was sure was in Marian's amber eyes. Had he looked, he would have seen no laughter there.

"I suppose the Vicar made a speech," Mark said. He felt he

must go on talking to Horace, to wear down the unspoken reproach.

"No, m'lord, Mr. Beausire did. They say he made a first-rate speech and the folks are mighty pleased with it."

Mark's face hardened. This was high-handed of Uncle William—a revenge because his suggestion that the unfriendly attitude to the new owner of Combe St. Philip was wrong had not been well received.

"What did he have to say?" he asked.

"He spoke of farmin', as 'ow it was the oldest and noblest way of makin' a livin' and 'ow the English farmer had a tough row to hoe these days, what with foreign and Colonial competition, some countries being subsidized by their gov'ments into the bargain, but that things would surely mend, they 'ad to, and that now, with war a possibility, the land must be worked for all it was worth, without a thought if there was money more'n a bare livin' in it or not."

"Did he speak of himself?" Mark hated to show interest, but it was easier to ask old Horace than anyone else.

"Just said as 'ow glad 'e was to be 'ere, an' though it was nigh on three 'undred years since 'is hancestor left the Sudbury Valley, that 'e'd felt at 'ome from the start. Then 'e thanked us all for being so kind to 'im an' sat down."

A curious thrill of guilt stabbed Mark. He felt surprised, as though it had happened to someone else. He'd done the needful, asked the man to dinner and shown him the Court. After all, it was nearly three hundred years since his ancestor had left the country—attainted.

He found there was peculiar satisfaction in the mental repetition of that word. "Attainted." There was something final and utterly damning about it.

They were going down the orchard now. Marian caught

the gleam of long white tables beneath the trees. She knew that in a moment all eyes would be upon them, and that they had been incredibly foolish to come together.

As they passed the first of the small tables, specially reserved for private parties, she bowed and smiled stiffly to a woman seated there. She had always believed she could put up a show of easy naturalness whatever happened, but now she wasn't so sure.

The woman at the table almost rose from her seat, then sat back, peering through a lorgnette as she exclaimed, "Marian Armitage and Beausire have the nerve of brass monkeys! He's frightfully late, and now turns up with her. We'll walk down toward the mill. They'll see us, and have to ask us to join their party. After all, we belong to the same clubs in India."

Henry Paget thought for a moment of refusing to go, but twenty years of marriage to Laura had taught him that doing what he was told to do at once saved a good deal of useless unpleasantness. He merely remarked mildly, "It's a private affair in the mill. They ask their own friends. If they had wanted us, we'd have had cards. The Greggs are staying at the Court, that's why they're there."

Laura Paget's big china-blue eyes were still on the mill bridge. Beausire and Lady Armitage had not crossed it yet. The girl in white must be the fiancée, and the man in clerical black her father. Harry Gregg was talking to a tall man with reddish hair.

Henry Paget was vaguely curious about that man, the American. What strange aberration could make a man with money leave a vast new country like America, seething with life and youth and hope, to bury himself in this hole, which was as dead as its past?

"If the girl has the sense God gave geese, she'll drop Beausire and hook the American," Laura said. "Money's the only thing that matters these days. She's only a parson's daughter, so a title would be something, of course, but it's cash that counts, and Beausire hasn't too much of that."

She stood up, and they began to walk through the tables toward the mill.

The mill house looked as it always did on cherry-picking days. The sunlight streamed through the high narrow windows, casting great shafts of golden light across the wooden floor, lighting up the immense rafters.

Marian was aware of the semicircular table and the long one below it, gay with the pink roses Harry and Bessie had taken from the Court. A shaft of light struck the big basket of cherries. Rosalys stood beside it, her hand on its ribboned handle, but her eyes were on John Beausire, who was talking to that old bore, Colonel Pargiter, a local landowner who had a passion for raising pigs and a grim and seemingly hopeless determination to make them pay.

The youngest Pollard boy, in the uniform of a Cub Scout, had presented the cherries, and Mark had replied in his flippant and rather charming way. They might resent Mark's actions sometimes, but they couldn't help liking him.

The dusk of evening was already in the mill house, though the top of the combe was still bright with sunlight, when Rosalys walked out to the bridge, watching the group that moved slowly up the orchard. The hardfaced woman who must once have been very beautiful was still talking to Marian.

On one side of the bridge the mill pool lay, wide and still. Rosalys turned and looked down at the five broad slabs of mossy stone over which the water fell into the narrow swift stream. She slipped quickly into the mill house again.

The cherries made a splash of color in the dusk, and Rosalys moved toward them. They held memories in their crimson depths. Mark should have taken them, but he had forgotten.

A bat shrilled a high clear call, almost too high for dull human ears to hear, as it skimmed out for the evening hunt. Rosalys took three cherries from the basket, looked at them as they lay like great rubies in her hand.

Passionately she wished to be a child again, to be able to believe she could throw them into the stream and they would reach far-off Maryland. She wished Ellen could take her hand and talk to her about John Beausire, who had first planted a cherry orchard at Markscombe.

There was no sound of footsteps, only the creaking of the wheel, the singing of a blackbird somewhere outside, but she knew that John had come into the mill house.

Turning, the cherries still in her hand, she saw him standing in the doorway. As he came forward into the shadowy place she saw him again as she had first seen him in the church. There was the same sense of something infinitely more real than this life, the same utter conviction that she had always known his face, and then when he had spoken she had known the sound of his voice was utterly familiar.

Then she was only aware of one thing, that they must not stay alone here. She had known today with complete finality that if she failed Mark now something dreadful would happen to him.

Quickly she moved toward the door, brushed past John, and safely out on the bridge, managed to call out, "There's cherry bounce being served at the Farm. Come on. Mark says it's the best part of the show."

Almost instantly John was beside her. In the orchard, figures still moved among the trees. Marian was with Mark.

They were talking to Harry and Colonel Pargiter. Mrs. Pargiter and Bessie stood near.

"Have you saved some cherries for John Beausire?" John asked.

Rosalys stared at the stream. Tears stung her eyelids. It was Ellen who had told him. She knew that. "No, I'm not a child now." She tried to laugh, but the sound came out perilously like a sob.

"Please give me those in your hand," he said.

She knew he was not joking. If he had spoken lightly she might have been able to hand over the cherries with a smile, but it was a desperate demand, an insistence on the recognition of something that must be forever unrecognized.

"No," she said. "They always went into the stream."

Mark's voice cut across the quiet orchard. Rosalys saw him standing by the big tree near the path. The golden rays of sunlight caught clusters of crimson cherries above his head.

"There's Mark," Rosalys said. "He wants me."

With a quick gesture she flung the three cherries into the stream and ran.

Chapter Eight

* * * *

WILLIAM TREMAYNE NEVER DID ANYTHING BY HALVES. Having become convinced that Mark had behaved abominably, that his attitude to the new owner of Combe St. Philip was unreasonable and rude, he saw to it that everyone in Mrs. Pollard's great hall who might not be up to date on village news was made aware of the exhaustive preparations being made for the war that was sure to come.

Marian listened with mounting anger. She knew that someone must stop him. Quickly she crossed the hall in search of Rosalys, and found her at the foot of the stone staircase. If only Uncle William could be led into discussing that! No one would be much interested in hearing about it, but it would keep him off Combe St. Philip.

Mark came up to Rosalys then, and his voice sounded bitterly angry as he said, "There'll be no war. Not yet, at any rate. Preparing for it has become a sort of hobby. It stirs up excitement."

Marian saw Rosalys turn sharply, stare at Mark for a moment in utter amazement, then regain her self-control and go on talking to a small gray-haired woman, whose lips compressed into a thin line of disapproval as she said, "That's not the opinion of most military men. My brother, Brigadier General Kenyon Kent, thinks it may come at any moment and has warned us to prepare."

Mark turned to her with a smile. "You shouldn't bother, Cousin Alicia," he said. "Surely the whole district will be able to depend on Combe St. Philip."

A taller, heavier and older edition of Miss Alicia cut in icily, "We shall feel much happier having Mr. Beausire there."

Marion touched the last stone baluster and said rather breathlessly, "Every time I come here I feel more covetous of this staircase. Early Tudor, isn't it?"

For a moment the Vicar seemed to be rising to the bait, but Miss Theodora had something to say, and she meant to say it. "We need landowners who stay on their estates and prepare the land for maximum production—landowners who know something about the land." She then gave Marian an icy stare, and continued, "We also need landowners who will uphold the moral standard. With civilization in danger of collapsing entirely, those in high stations should remember that there are still some things that are not done." She turned to her sister. "Come, Alicia."

Marian knew that the sooner she got Mark out of this place the better. The old devil had been right. There were some things that were not done, and Mark was suspected of doing at least some of them. Yet it was a rottenly unfair remark, bawled out for as many as possible to hear.

She tried to talk amiably to people who came up to her, but her mind was on Mark. How could he stay on the land when he was in the army? But she knew what the woman had meant. There had been long leaves spent abroad, leaves in England when he had been at the Court for only a few week-ends, usually with a gay crowd from London. While he had been at Aldershot he had seldom appeared here. They had read of his doings in the gossip columns of the papers.

Laura Paget was rattling on about news from India, promotions and retirements, marriages and scandals, and Mark joined a group at the door who were talking of landing fields. Ned Pollard said that Mr. Beausire was going to make a landing field near Combe St. Philip and would have his own plane, but that he had said the best place for a field was in the park, between the Lodge Wood and the lake.

"I didn't know he'd been through the park," Mark said. "I suppose he has pretty well surveyed the whole place."

"The cut to St. John goes through that stretch of the park," Harry Gregg reminded him quietly, and tried to change the conversation.

Marian saw Mark's eyes turn to Rosalys. Then he turned to Harry and said, "We'd better push off now. I don't want dinner held up, for I may have to go up to town tonight."

They had not been at the cherry-bounce party for half an hour. It was the custom to stay considerably longer. Marian left Laura Paget in the middle of a long story and went over to Harry.

"Harry, make Mark stay. He can't get out of this yet," she whispered.

"Better for him to go," Harry replied.

Marian hoped Mark would speak pleasantly to the American, but something she could not repress, something deeper than her common sense and innate courtesy, rejoiced when Mark did not seem to see him. She had an utterly unreasonable feeling that she was fighting for Mark's position, that she had to hold it for him against this stranger who was winning the friendship and good will Mark had lost.

The Vicar was standing at the gate as they drove off. He felt disturbed and unhappy. It was no longer possible to ignore obvious facts. Mark was still in love with Marian Armitage. The affair that he had guessed at, but had thought of as something in the past, was by no means over.

Was it possible that Rosalys could find happiness in such a marriage? When he had been asked formally for his consent to the engagement, the thought of what that marriage could secure for her had persuaded him to consent. All men of Mark's age and position had something of a past. So few marriages turned out happily. As a priest he knew that better than most men did. At worst it was divorce, at best a compromise with life, an acceptance of disillusion and disappointment.

He remembered his thoughts as he had sat down to write to Mark. It would be the best and happiest thing for her: the love she had for Mark would last as long as life lasted—unless she should ever meet a man she could love with the fullness of which he knew her to be capable. So few found a real and lasting love.

If there was war, Mark would probably be killed. He was marrying for an heir. There was nothing essentially wrong in that.

Now, quite suddenly, he made up his mind. He would not be a party to this snubbing of John Beausire. Rosalys was innocent, but she was not ignorant: no parson's daughter who had taken an active part in village life could be ignorant. She probably knew very well what was going on.

As he started up the path to the house, he realized that if his daughter decided to break her engagement, he would be enormously relieved. He also knew that if she decided to marry

Mark, nothing he or anybody else could say would change her mind.

❖ ❖ ❖ ❖

The car had just come out of the Lodge Wood when Mark noticed a few small lumps of coal on the right of way through the park to Sudbury St. John.

"I wish to God they'd be more careful going through the park," he said angrily. "It's ridiculous the way the cuts are used. There's a perfectly good road going around. Yesterday I saw tree branches covered with straw."

Rosalys looked at him steadily. This was a new Mark, sullen and petty, thinking not of a few wisps of straw or lumps of coal, but of John Beausire walking through the public right of way, telling village boys what could be done with the hundreds of acres of rich land.

"I'd stick up a notice at the pub that those who used the cuts should be more careful to leave the place tidy," Harry said. "Horace could find out in no time at all who carted coal and straw recently."

Marian could not decide whether it would be better for her to depart at once, and leave Mark in this frightful mood of his to Rosalys, or to stay and try to get him out of it herself. If she stayed, Rosalys might be furious—there'd been enough talk already, and there was a limit to what the girl could be expected to stand. If she went, they might have a violent quarrel that would not be easily patched up. She clenched and unclenched her hands and wondered if there could be anything in Harry's wild idea that a soul treated with bitter injustice in the past could return to seek justice in another body. That something was happening she knew. She did not need Harry to tell her that. The tension that had existed since Mark entered the Mill House and saw John Beausire standing there, the center of a group, was like an evil vapor. If there was going to be an outburst, let it come quickly.

Mark turned to Harry Gregg directly they entered the hall, and said something hurriedly about having to telephone; then he went quickly toward the gunroom, as though he had remembered something important that must be done.

Marian looked across the hall to where Rosalys stood alone. It was there that the only hope lay. If Mark and Rosalys quarreled now, it would be fatal. Quickly she went toward the girl.

"Rosalys," she said urgently, "I'll go or stay, just as you wish, but for God's sake be careful with Mark this evening. He's frightfully put out. It was a bit thick—that stranger making the speech."

The coldness of the eyes turned to her was terrifying. They were stone gray, somber as November dusk.

"It was a bit thick that Mark didn't turn up until nearly five o'clock," Rosalys said. "He knows very well that tea has to begin at four, at latest, for all to be served. How can he blame the people for responding when they find someone who understands their problems and is interested in them?"

"He's furious with himself about being late. Don't rub it in. Go to him now."

Because she did not want to talk to Marian, Rosalys went slowly toward the gunroom.

Mark looked up at her as she entered and said with a new sharpness in his voice, "I've 'phoned Edwards to close the cuts. He'll have 'No Trespassing' boards up this evening. I'm not going to have the place made into a thoroughfare. It should have been done years ago."

Rosalys stared at Mark in utter amazement. "What have you done?" she asked, understanding all too clearly.

"Closed the cuts. You heard what I said. Come on, I need a drink."

Without a word she followed him across the hall. She knew why Mark had done this senseless thing.

John Beausire would not be able to walk through the park woods now, or find a boat in the dilapidated boat house—as Ellen said he often did—and row out at dusk to one of the islands. She wanted desperately to go to him, to tell him not to mind, to say that now all the beauty of the place was worth nothing, it had been killed. She did not care whether Mark would be angry or not, she would go to Combe St. Philip and see what John had done there, as he had asked her several times to do. Combe St. Philip would be alive, untouched by the evil of a curse.

By the door of the west wing she hesitated, knowing she could not bear to talk to Mark tonight, feeling uncertain of herself, almost afraid of being alone in the Vicarage.

Swain came through the doorway and went to Mark: he said that Edwards had 'phoned and was holding the wire. He could not believe that the message his wife had given him was taken down correctly and wanted personal confirmation from his Lordship.

"I'll speak to him," Mark said angrily, and went toward the gunroom again.

Rosalys followed, and while he waited for the call to be switched, she said quickly, "Mark, I'm dead tired. I'm going home to bed. Call me early tomorrow, won't you?"

To her infinite relief he said at once, "All right, little one. You did too much for that damned shindig. I'll call you before breakfast. We might go up early and swim in the mill pool."

He bent down and kissed her cheek lightly, thinking of Marian and how much trouble and explanation this would save. He'd go up to town tonight, call Rosalys from there tomorrow and make some arrangement for the afternoon. He turned to the telephone.

Marian was on the point of going in search of Mark when she saw him come out of the gunroom alone.

"Where's Rosalys?" she asked sharply.

"She's tired, so she went home," Mark replied. "Edwards made a fool of himself. I'm not at all sure that I shan't get rid of him. He tried to tell me that it wasn't legal to close the cuts."

Marian knew that Mark already regretted his burst of temper, but would not rescind his order now. It would make an already difficult situation almost intolerable. "I'd thought of that," she said. "Those paths have been open to the public for some time. You should have called Hare first."

"I have just talked to him," Mark answered. "He said I could do it."

Marian knew that Hare had said a good deal more. The old man had probably been furious. She did not dare think what the Vicar would say.

"Let's start for town now," Mark said. "I'd like to get away from the place tonight. We could dine on the way."

A cold panic she could not control gripped Marian. For a moment she felt helpless in the path of oncoming disaster, knowing that quick action was the only hope, but not knowing what course to take. To go with Mark to town, and leave Rosalys alone with her father, who would be furious, and with Ellen, a willing intermediary between the Vicarage and Combe St. Philip, was unthinkable.

"Mark," she said urgently, "you've made a mistake. Face it, and rescind the order. Call Edwards now. We can't afford another row. Being late this afternoon made a frightfully bad impression. It upset Rosalys more than I would have thought anything could."

"I'll not rescind the order," Mark said. "The little one will get over it. She's a queer little thing, but she's devoted to me and to the place. She won't take it seriously."

It was the way Mark took Rosalys for granted that made the whole thing frightening. He simply could not or would not understand how wholly justified she would be in breaking the engagement.

Marian knew that if the mistakes of today were to be patched up she must do the patching. Having once decided what to do, she spoke with determination. "I'm going to the Vicarage," she said, "and I'm going to tell her that we are thinking of going to town tonight, and that if she does not wish it, I will go home."

"You make too much of the whole thing," Mark said irritably. "She has accepted the situation. Let it go at that."

Marian already had her hand on the bell. "I can't. I tell you, this afternoon was serious. I'll be back in an hour, if you are to stay. If she agrees, I'll go on, and we can meet at the usual place in Bath."

"She's a strange child," Mark said, repeating his words as though trying to convince himself. "Completely sexless, though her beauty blinds most people to that fact. I'm quite sure she never would have married—otherwise."

Marian wanted to laugh wildly. She did not know if Mark's blindness was funny or terrible. She went quickly to the door.

Once in the car she began to think clearly. Marian always thought best when driving, and would drive for hours when she had a problem to solve. Now she had only the few minutes it would take to get to the Vicarage.

Her whole angle of appeal must be altered. The portrayal of herself as a tragic Queen Iseult, of Mark as a sorrow-haunted Tristan, which had worked so well in London, was now ridiculous. Mark could no longer regard himself as the last of his line. He had an heir, and a very satisfactory one. Rosalys might well say now that they could wait the four years until a divorce might be obtained. While Mark lived he was Lord Beausire; nothing could take that from him. If John and Rosalys married, their heirs would inherit, even if Mark outlived John.

There was only one thing to do now, and she knew, as she turned the car into the Vicarage drive, that she was capable of doing it.

Rosalys was sitting by the open window, looking out into the tranquil garden. Marian closed the door, and came to the point quickly, before the startled girl had time to speak.

"I had to see you," she said, slinging herself down in the Vicar's enormous leather chair.

"Why? I thought everything had been said in London."

It was not a promising beginning. Marian knew she had a fight on her hands—a fight she could not afford to lose.

"Things have changed. I'm going to be perfectly frank with you. I'm leaving Mark in October—perhaps sooner—for good."

An almost eerie fear lapped about her, a superstitious terror that fate or something might take her at her word. She condemned herself for a weak fool, and plunged on.

"I've been thinking things over very seriously lately and have had a frank talk with my grandmother. There would be no question of money from her if Anthony divorced me, or even if he let me divorce him, which he would not do. If I got a divorce and married Mark, we would be deadly poor. I couldn't face it. I think—I know—he's getting tired of me. I'm not a young woman, my dear. One can't have everything in this world. I chose money and position—which Anthony gave me. I can't wait four years for a divorce, living in a hole-and-corner way, then marry Mark with a cloud of scandal attached and face what we would have to face. You see that, don't you?"

The eyes whose coldness had frightened her an hour ago were now soft with pity.

"I don't believe that Mark's getting tired of you," Rosalys said. "He loves you. He told me so."

Marian saw now how to follow up the advantage of this softened mood.

"I know, my dear," she said. "But Mark's only real love—and that has been the tragedy of his life—is the place, and all that it implies. My mind is made up. Perhaps it would be fairer to say that I can't face what sticking to Mark would mean."

"Does he know?"

Marian could almost see a dark mist of despair around the still white figure beside the window.

"No. I want you to realize first what it would mean if you did not stand by him now. If you do, in six months or less, he will be happier than he has ever been, managing the place himself, being here as much as he can. If you do not, he will go from one woman to another. He will spend money he hasn't got, neglect the place, gamble, take to drink. In a few years he will be a wreck, physically, morally and financially. Mark's life—his soul, if there are such things as souls—is in your hands."

There was a long silence. High and clear, children's voices drifted in from across the garden.

"You do understand, don't you?" Marian asked at last.

When Rosalys turned to her, Marian wondered why she had not remembered before how the girl had looked in London. It must have been in London that she saw her so, for surely she had seen that white, mask-like face, those deep dark eyes, that frozen look before.

"Yes, I quite understand. You love Mark, but not enough to give up anything for him."

It was like a knife thrust. Marian knew she must accept it.

"You could put it like that, I suppose. I have loved him as I have never loved anyone before and most certainly never will again. It's best for him, too. He'd loathe all the mess of a divorce, even if I could get one. I see that now."

Rosalys was silent again for a long time. Marian bore it as long as she could, then said, "You will marry him, won't you?"

Rosalys turned again and faced her. "Yes, I will marry him, and I'll do my best for him. I love Mark—and with all my heart I pity him."

"You give me your word?"

"Yes. I give you my word that I will marry Mark, unless he asks me to release him. I will marry him at any time he wishes."

Marian wanted to run, to get away from this room as quickly as possible, but she could not go yet.

"He has to go up to town tonight. Air Force business. Do you mind if I go, too? It would be easier to make him see things as they are, in London."

Cold fear sprang into Rosalys' eyes.

"You mean you are leaving him now—this week?"

"No, no," Marian replied quickly, thinking she had not got that renewed promise any too soon. "I'll see him a few times, until September. I shall go to Paris for a couple of weeks' shopping before I sail."

Rosalys replied in the same toneless voice of heartbreak,

"That would be best. Go to town tonight, do whatever you wish. I am very tired. I would like to be quite alone tonight and tomorrow."

As Marian kissed her, she felt horribly near tears. She had achieved exactly what she came for, and it was rather awful. She left the room quickly.

Rosalys stood up. It was no use putting it off. Tonight was only the beginning of the shadow life that might go on for sixty years or more. Would it be more bearable, or less, because a bright and radiant light had been kindled for a moment, then gone out, leaving only the knowledge of how cold and deep the darkness was?

✦ ✦ ✦ ✦

The taproom of the Arms was packed. Conversation buzzed like a swarm of angry hornets.

"Dow-an right sha-ameful, tha-at it be." Old Swain's quavering voice rose above the clamor and was greeted by a chorus of affirmation.

Horace's eyes were continually on the door, as he hoped desperately that someone would turn up to explain this inexplicable thing. He had just returned from his dash to the Court, where he had been informed by Swain that the matter was beyond his understanding and that his Lordship had just left for London, driving himself.

Orders were getting mixed: someone who ordered half-and-half got cider; ale was shoved across to a carter who never drank anything but beer, but was too furious to notice the difference tonight.

Harry Gregg stood in the doorway. He grinned cheerfully at Horace as he came forward and gave his order.

"Ma-aster Ma-ark allus was a young fool, an' tha-at bla-ack-'aired ba-agge 'asn't taught 'im no sense, neither."

Horace put down the Major's whisky with care, then seized a pewter mug and banged it on the bar until the glasses rattled. He looked furiously in the direction from which the voice had come. It was old Parrett. Since his unemployed son had got well-paid, steady work at Combe St. Philip there'd been no holding him.

"None o' that," he said harshly, "not in this 'ouse. 'Is Lordship 'as more on 'is mind than the likes of you knows of. Riskin' 'is life this very moment, 'e 'is, practicin' flyin', for to defend people like you from 'Itler's bombers. Maybe none o' you 'as ever seen a bomb go off, or 'eard it. I 'ave, mor'n I like to think of now. In the next war you'll all get it, and then maybe you'll remember, if there's anything left o' England, that it's to 'is Lordship and men like 'im we owes it."

Horace paused for breath. Harry smiled at him and the thought that sprang into his mind seemed to Horace to come directly from the Major's intense eyes. "Maybe 'is Lordship is planning to build an airport right in the park. Would the Gov'-ment allow all the village idiots to come gaping at it while they was laying out the land? Maybe when war comes, and planes go up right out 'o the park, you'll be mighty glad you used the road 'round for a bit."

There was a dead silence. It was broken by the excited laugh of a young farm hand.

"Now Mr. John's coom we ca-an look for things to be lively," he said.

So it was "Mr. John" now, Harry thought. Poor Mark, did he think he could hold back destiny with a few painted boards?

"Is Mr. Beausire in?" he asked Horace.

"No, sir. Maybe 'e's gone back to Combe St. Philip."

"If he comes in, tell him I'm looking in again in about an hour, and I'd like to see him. I shall walk around for a bit: it's too fine a night to stay indoors." He gave Horace another encouraging smile and went out.

A dark figure was leaning over the gate of St. John's Wood. Harry knew at once that it was John.

"Hullo," he called.

John turned. The newly painted board set between the boles of two beech trees seemed glaringly white and out of place among the dark and rustling leaves.

They stood in silence for a moment, looking up the wood road.

"No more walks through the park and home woods," John said at last, with a hard little laugh.

Harry was about to say he believed Mark would rescind the order in a few days, but decided there was no point in not facing things as they were.

"Mark has made a crashing mistake," he said. "The tenants are furious. I've just been talking to some of them at the Arms."

John stared into the unearthly beauty of the dim wood, trying to realize he would not see the house again—not for a long time, anyway.

"Harry," he said, "can you convey to Mark that I know this has been done because of me, and that if he will open the cuts, he can rest assured that I will not enter the park?"

Having decided on truth and not diplomacy, Harry made no attempt to deny John's statement. "I'll do my best. He's gone up to town, but he'll be back tomorrow."

"Thanks. I don't want the people penalized for me," John said.

Harry felt for his pipe. "Got a match?" he asked, finding none in his pocket.

John pulled out a package, and as he did so a tiny object fell to the ground. He stooped and searched for it.

"There it is," Harry said, seeing a dark speck within the small circle of the light. The earth about the stile was trodden to the smooth hardness of wood. He picked it up, saying, "This is a cherry stone. What did you drop?"

John held out his hand for it. "That," he said, and for a moment he considered telling Harry of his hour-long search among the stones of the mill stream for spots where three cherries might have been caught.

But he decided there was no point in it. Harry couldn't understand the sense of loss, or the wild triumph when the first scarlet flash had been sighted among some reeds, and later two more by a big stone.

Harry jerked his head at the board with its arrogant "No Trespassing" sign. "John," he said, "you're not going to—clear out, because of this?"

John answered instantly. "No. Nothing could make me clear out. There's a hell of a war coming, and I'm going to do what I can to see these people through it. My belief that I belong here hasn't been altered by Mark's not accepting me."

"You don't hate Mark, do you?" Harry asked. "If I were in your place, I'm afraid I should."

"No," John said. "The strange thing is, I feel I only met the real Mark for an instant, and that was when he laughed as he spoke of Horace's shock at seeing me. Let's go back to the Arms. Old Horace will be badgered by the villagers tonight, for he won't hear a word against Mark. We should be there to help him out."

As they walked down the road Harry made a mental note to be written later into his record book. This book contained every authentic record of Beausire family history during the

life of the twenty-first Baron and through the following years,
with every scrap of family or village tradition concerning "the
Lord who disappeared" and "the Little Maid of Sudbury," and
with notes on his own views of the development of the story.
Now he would add that John Beausire, in his years of exile and
suffering while he waited for the release of death, had reached
a very high point of spiritual development, which would give
him tremendous power in a future incarnation.

"Harry," John said, as the lights of the inn gleamed through
the shadowy branches of the trees, "were you born in these
parts?"

"Lord, no," Harry replied. "Haven't I ever told you where I
sprang from? I was born in a midland slum. I'm a T.G. of the
last war, you know."

"What's that?" John asked.

Harry laughed. "Temporary Gentleman," he said. "I came
up from the ranks. Once you asked me why I was so sure we
had knowledge not gained by our physical selves. I hadn't time
to explain, but I'll have a shot at it now. You see, I've had the
experience myself. My people came of fairly decent middle-
class stock, but before my birth they'd sunk into abject poverty.
My mother had been a schoolteacher, and was better born and
reared than my father. She taught me herself. My father was a
fanatical Nonconformist lay preacher. To him everything that
had beauty or gaiety was of the devil, the very personal devil in
whom he so strongly believed."

Harry smiled, stopped by the white gate of the inn and
leaned against it as he went on.

"I was never allowed to hear music. Of course, in those days
we didn't have the pictures—at least, not in mill-town
slums—and attending a performance of the third-rate pan-
tomime that came once a year to a near-by town would have

been out of the question. No books or papers were allowed in the house, for they, too, reeked of sin. I never played a game, for other children might have led me astray. I was harangued incessantly on the horrors of hell, and before I was seven I was quite sure no one could escape it. My own ultimate entry there was a foregone conclusion. But I lived in a private world of beauty. I knew of color, of music, of fine and lovely houses, rare jewels, the exquisite perfection attainable by the human body at its best. At twelve I went to school, but as I had an evening job, and did all the housework and cooking, there was no time for dissipation or evil companionship. At fourteen I went into the Mills. My father gave up his job and worked night and day at his preaching and soul saving. Sometimes he would come in, drenched to the skin, after an open-air meeting, and fling himself down as he was, praying aloud for the souls he had failed to drag from the burning. We lived on the few bob a week that I made.

"When I was nineteen, war broke out. I joined up at once, and in 1916 I got a commission. In 1918 I met Mark, who had just succeeded to the title. We have been friends ever since. He pulled the wires that got me into the regular army after the armistice."

"Did you feel you knew him, when you first saw him?"

"Most definitely. I was scared stiff when I was told I was to share a billet with Lord Beausire. Then, when he came in, it was only Mark. I felt an immense pity for him, though he had everything the world could offer, and I had nothing. We got on, though really we have nothing in common. In that first week he told me things—family stuff, you know—that his old friends had never heard."

John was thinking of the appalling bleakness of Harry's early life. "According to your theory, what on earth could you have done in a previous existence to get such a rotten deal in this one?" he asked.

Harry laughed. "Oh, I've no memories whatever, and am not in the least curious about the past. It's the present, the use one makes of it, that matters. I probably neglected an opportunity—a talent, or a chance to help others. The teaching is clearly expounded in the Gospels. Parable of the servants and the talents, you know."

They entered the inn. The taproom was still full, though it was near closing time. For John things seemed to have come to an impasse. Harry wondered if it would be war that would open the way for him, as it had done for himself years ago.

Chapter Nine

✦ ✦ ✦ ✦

GREAT HERRING GULLS FLASHED PALELY AGAINST THE dark hillside fields as they flew far inland to escape the storm. The rising wind lashed the orchards of Combe St. Philip, and sudden gusts of rain spattered the old house.

John stood in the doorway of the restored hall, watching two men pile small camp cots on a hand truck. The beds would not be needed now: two days ago a pact had been signed at Munich.

Combe St. Philip had been prepared to take in fifty children and their attendants. The cots were to be put away, as similar makeshift beds were being put away in every small country town and village in England. John wished he could believe that they would not be brought out again.

Already the events of the last two weeks had begun to take on the misty quality of a dream. John felt now that the only reality had been his brief meeting with Rosalys under the dark shadow of the yews in St. John's churchyard, when with her deeply shadowed eyes raised to his, she had implored him to go back to America. The knowledge that she recognized the

347

strange bond between them, that she loved him and wanted above all else to know that he would not be dragged into the approaching horror, had been a light in the darkness.

While all England waited, tense and still, for the outcome, John had lived in a sharp expectancy of his own, waiting for a call, a letter, a message, that would summon him to her.

But no word had come. Mark had been at his post; Harry and Bessie were somewhere near London; the Court had been closed. John had thought of it as plunged into a deep sleep that might suddenly become a flaming nightmare.

It was under the yew trees that he had known it did not really matter, that there was an inner life of the soul invulnerable to loss, which could draw from death and suffering only the immense benefit of tremendous spiritual experience.

John turned to go inside. The Vicar stood framed in the doorway, a dark raincoat flung carelessly over his broad shoulders, his thick white hair wind tossed.

"Hullo, John," he said. "I have to go to Markscombe, so I looked in to see you."

"Can't you stay to lunch, or come back?" John asked. The face of his friend was worn and haggard. Looking at the deep new lines graven there, he realized something of the strain the Vicar had been under. There had been days of intense activity, sleepless nights tortured by the vivid memories of another war.

"I'd like to. I hoped you'd ask me. Can you have it early?" the Vicar said.

"Of course." They left the hall and went out into the neatly kept garden.

"Any news?" John asked. It was always the same on these welcome visits that were becoming more and more frequent—the sickening fear of being told that Mark and Rosalys were to be married at once. When the fear was overcome for the time, he could begin to draw the Vicar into one of those long conversations on the many things that interested them both.

"No. Mark's coming down, today or tomorrow, but only for a couple of days. He's still stationed on the east coast, but hopes to get to Salisbury or thereabouts soon, now that the immediate danger is over."

"Has Lady Armitage sailed for India yet?" John felt that while this woman, whom he had no reason to dislike, but did, was still in England, he was safe.

"No. She's in London. She was ready to drive an ambulance in the London streets."

When lunch was over in the small paneled room, the Vicar looked at the rain streaming down the diamond-paned window and was even more reluctant to go on to Markscombe. The utter weariness that had plagued him for two days now was like a heavy weight.

"You can't go yet," John said. "It's pouring cats and dogs. You can 'phone Markscombe."

The Vicar gladly agreed to wait. He looked out of the rain-dimmed window to the shadowy outline of new buildings. John Beausire, whether he was owner of Combe St. Philip for the first or second time, had done a marvelous job here.

They had talked for a long time of the war that must inevitably come, when the Vicar said suddenly, "John, I fear the future."

"You mean you think we can't lick them?"

"No. I don't know why, for I know how slim our resources are, but I don't fear that. It's the aftermath. It's when the suffering, stunned people, hungry, shabby, cold, unutterably weary, laden with debt, face the future, that the time of real danger will be upon us. You see, so few people really study history or think deeply. This house reminds me of many fears. It was an Abbot's house. The monasteries became corrupt, as all the world was. The people allowed a selfish and wicked King to destroy them, forgetting what they had been to England— guardians of the light of culture through the dark ages, schools, hospitals, law courts. Because a few of the monks were evil, self-seeking men, innumerable saints were martyred."

John, fascinated by that mournful voice, also saw a vision of old and lovely things that had served their purpose being smashed into nothingness, when they should have evolved slowly into finer form.

"Why is it people are so ready to condemn the past?" the Vicar said. "Few seem to realize that we have means now of mass education, of medical miracles on a tremendous scale, of vast production of human necessities, that even twenty five years ago would have seemed like the imaginings of a mad-man. Will they say that old and tried forms of government have failed, because they have not yet accomplished that great advance in human welfare that should now be possible to them? Do you think they will have patience, John, those war-battered peoples? God grant they do, for any one who thinks knows the human race is on the verge of a new era that could end in the pit of destruction, or in what those old monks would have thought of as heaven on earth."

The Vicar stood up. He reached out a long arm toward a bookcase and he took down a volume.

"John Locke's *Essay Concerning Human Understanding,*" he said. "He probably wrote most of it at Sutton Court, quite near here, while he was the guest of his friend, John Strachey. Locke and Strachey were contemporaries of your ancestor, John. John Beausire must have known them. Here's the paragraph I want. Listen.

" 'That there should be more species of intelligent creatures above us than there are of sensible and material below us, is probable to me from hence, that in all the visible corporeal world we see no chasms or gaps. All quite down from us the descent is by easy steps, and a continued series of things that in each remove differ very little one from the other.' "

As he closed the book, the Vicar said, "The Law of the Universe is evolution, always upward, slowly, steadily. It will be a supreme tragedy if one tyranny is destroyed only to raise up another."

John knew he did not dare to think of next month, to say nothing of five or ten years hence. He was beginning to realize that now the time of stress was over, he would again be lucky if he saw Rosalys from a distance, and would depend on Ellen for word of her.

It was late in the afternoon when the Vicar rose to go. He felt he would be willing to concede much to Harry's theories, if Harry would only explain why John Beausire had come back this year, instead of a year or two years ago. As he went out again into the rain the unhappy eyes of his daughter haunted him. The more one saw of life, the more inexplicable it was.

By sundown the wind had risen to gale force. As John stood beside the door, watching the wildly tossing branches, the contractor for the new buildings turned the corner of the house and came toward him.

"I've been looking for you, sir," he said. "Just before the men knocked off they found something that may be of considerable interest."

John went with the stout little man down the leaf strewn path. Directly opposite the doors of the restored hall, Hodges stopped and pointed to what appeared to be an immense iron trough, connected to the remains of iron pipes.

"That's the bath where the pilgrims washed before entering the hospice," he said. "We've found others, among the ruins of monasteries. It proves this was the hospice, not—as Mr. Tremayne thinks—the Abbot's house."

Lucy's insistence that she had talked with the spirits of those old monks, and that they had told her this was the hospice, became intensely interesting. The Vicar, who was considered an authority on old Somerset, was quite sure that the farm was the remains of the Abbot's house, because of its traces of beauty and richness, so Lucy had not got her views from him.

"Has this thing been uncovered, say, in the last fifty years?" John asked.

Hodges laughed. "That ain't been seen by mortal eyes for three or four hundred years," he said. "I'll be getting back to Taunton, sir. I wanted to show it to you."

When John went in, the house was very quiet. So thick were the old walls that the sound of the rising storm was shut out. He decided to look for Lucy Hawkes and tell her of the find.

The old woman was sitting staring into the flames of the kitchen fire. She was still at the farm, though John rarely saw her. At first he had tried to tell her his plans, but she was obviously past all interest in Combe St. Philip.

"Miss Hawkes?" he called from the kitchen door, not sure whether the darkness in the corner of the high backed old settle was a form or merely a shadow.

Lucy did not answer, but she turned, and he saw her dark eyes burning in the parchment-like face.

"Sit down, sir," she said, as he approached the settle. "It's a wild night, but good will come of it."

Lucy often said incomprehensible things. John had come to understand that she lived in some strange world of her own, and it was not hard for him to believe that she saw and heard things others did not.

"They've found an iron trough near the hall doors," he said, "several feet down. Hodges thinks it was used by the pilgrims for washing before they entered the house, and that it proves the old hall was a part of the hospice."

"Aye," Lucy said, "I've known that for many years. I told Vicar, but he'd have none of it. He said only in the Abbot's house would you find such stonework. That's not so. In those days they gave their best for the poor. They knew God sees all."

She lapsed into silence but for once seemed content to have company. Usually she moved away after a few words.

"Miss Hawkes," John said at last, "did they tell you to let me have the place?"

It was a bold move. She might resent it as mockery.

Lucy answered simply, "No, sir. I did that because I knew the time had come to break the power of the curse. My life was blasted by the curse of the Beausires, blasted as was the old walnut tree the lightning struck last year."

John did not speak. He knew that if she wished to tell him, she would.

Suddenly she began to speak again. Her clawlike hands lay limp on her knees; her shawled head seemed merely a face, peering out of darkness.

"Sometimes I've thought of telling the whole bitter thing to Miss Rosalys, but she's a creature of light, and has no part in darkness. Her father told me that it was all forgotten, that she did not know."

The old voice went on. "It was in the summer of seventy-seven it happened. My brother farmed Combe St. Philip then. He'd married a Pollard of Markscombe. Henry Pollard was wild for me, and my brother and his wife were set on the marriage. But they did not know that all that summer Matthew Beausire, the eldest son, had been my lover. I made believe that in the autumn I'd marry Henry, just to keep them quiet. He began to get Markscombe ready for me, and I knew something awful was being done, but all of life was in those hours in the woods with Matthew Beausire. I would have wrecked any life for one more meeting with him.

"Sometimes I cursed my parents, dead then, for having educated me above my station. They had been proud of my beauty, and sometimes I blessed them for that.

"In June, Matthew went away. I wandered in the woods and fields like a lost soul. When word came that he was betrothed to an Earl's daughter in London, I thought I would die.

"But I had to see him once more. He came back in September, with the girl. She was all pink and white, with gold curls, simpering and smiling. I stood—it was at the St. Matthew's Day Fair at Bridgwater—and looked at them, sure at that moment of my beauty and its power over him. He gave me one long look and I knew that at least once more I should be in his arms.

"That evening, at dusk, I ran over the fields to the hollow stump at the end of Markscombe Lane. I had not been mistaken: there was a note there, telling me to be at the willow tree by the boathouse at moonrise.

"I did not dare return to Combe St. Philip, for fear of being questioned and followed. I lay beneath a hawthorn hedge, watching for the moonglow over Sudbury Hill.

"It was only then that the picture of that meeting at St. Matthew's Fair was clear to me. I saw the silly doll face, framed in feathery gold curls, heard the tinkling laugh of the Earl's daughter, and I saw the blood rise in the fair face of Matthew Beausire, and then drain away, leaving it white and tense. I saw his blue eyes blaze as they met mine. And I knew what I had not known at the time, that one of the horses being walked slowly down the paddock, just a few feet from where Matthew Beausire stood, was led by Henry Pollard, and that Henry's sullen black eyes were fixed on us.

"I knew that I would be missed, that Henry would know to whom I had gone, but I did not care. When the crest of Sudbury Hill was lighted by a silvery glow, I got up and ran, and fearing that I would be seen if I took the road round the hill, I cut through Markscombe. Perhaps Henry saw me then."

Lucy drew her shawl more closely about her with a curious gesture of terror. For a long time she sat transfixed by remembered joy and grief. When she spoke her voice was low and urgent.

"Sir, you've asked me more than once why I let you have the place. I'll tell you now. The last words my love said to me told me that there would be no peace or happiness for the Beausires until the bitter wrong done in 1685 was righted.

"Matthew was by the boathouse," she went on. "Without a word he lifted me into the little boat hidden in the reeds and rowed out to the island. At first there was nothing but the flaming joy of being together. The sleeping swans were spirit birds to me, the marble summer house set in the gardens of paradise.

"It was hours later, and the lake a sheet of silver, when Matthew told me that we were going away together, that his father was urging that his marriage be hastened, as the doctors feared his brother would not live long. Then he told me why the House of Beausire was cursed, and it was a bitter tale. The Lord who disappeared had been betrayed by his own people. All he ever did was to offer Christian charity to the hunted and oppressed. But he escaped the slavers, and reached Maryland. When he knew his little maid was dead, he would not return.

Years later, he married, dying soon after, leaving an unborn child. When his widow came to claim that child's rights, she was murdered so that she should not tell her story to the King."

For a moment the picture seemed to be in the dancing flames, then within his own mind, but John saw again, clearly and distinctly, the pure calm face, framed in pale hair, with its long blue eyes filled with love and pity, that had looked down from the Vicarage study. He felt elated, like one who finds an important clue in a mystery, but he could not keep his mind on it, for fear of missing something Lucy said. Her voice was so low and broken he had to listen intently.

"Matthew said he was weary of it all, and he could not face the marriage, and we would make plans, quietly and quickly, and be married in Bristol, the day a boat sailed for Maryland. He would find the descendants of John Beausire there, and before we made ourselves a new life, we would tell them the tale he had been told when he came of age, not many weeks past. He felt that his brother would not live, and that if he stepped aside, the wrong might at last be righted, for after his father's death the title of John Beausire's descendants would be clear."

John thought quickly. In 1877 his grandfather had been practicing law in Baltimore, a well-to-do bachelor of forty-two. The following year, to everybody's astonishment, he had married Mary Beaton, a girl of twenty. In 1880 a son had been born to them. Had that late marriage been prompted by a sudden desire for an heir?

The dark haunted eyes were staring at him again. "Henry Pollard found us there, just before dawn. We did not hear him as he rowed over the lake. I knew nothing until the whole world seemed to split apart with one shot, and I felt hot blood gush over my bare breast. As if in a dream I saw Henry take my blue muslin dress from the floor where it lay, and tear strips from it. I made no protest or outcry when he bound me to one of the twisted marble pillars, with no covering but my long dark hair. No word was spoken between us. Soon I knew that I was alone again, and that Matthew lay on the white marble floor. There was a thin stream that looked black in the moonlight flowing from beneath his head.

"I saw the moon go down behind the trees. At the first gray glimmer of dawn another shot seemed to rend the whole valley. I watched the marvel of sunrise, strangely calm and still, feeling that Matthew was alive, beside me, wholly mine now, and that we had escaped the power of the curse forever. Then I slipped into a mist of darkness.

"I remember a hoarse shout, and one of the gamekeepers running up the slope, and how he flung down his gun as he knelt beside Matthew.

"It was many weeks before I was clear-headed again. They told me that Henry had shot himself to death beside the pool in the Lodge Wood, the round pool where the lilies are now."

Suddenly Lucy laughed. It was the laugh of a happy girl, going through dewy fields to meet her lover. John watched her in astonishment: the years seemed to have dropped away, and her face was almost luminous, the splendid eyes shining.

"It was more than fifty years ago, that September night," she said. "Now, all the bitter years are gone. It was but yesterday. Soon, soon shall I step out of this worn body, as I stepped out of my blue muslin dress, and I shall be with him again, young, happy, all old griefs forgotten, only the joy of meeting real."

John remembered all the strange things he had heard of her. Harry Gregg was convinced she had supernormal powers, and the Vicar had obviously been puzzled more than once.

"Tell me," John said, his thoughts finding words almost before he was aware of it, "do you know that conscious life continues after death?"

There was infinite pity in the answer.

"When Matthew Beausire died I sought him where he was. I found I had strange powers. Oh, if the world would believe me, old as I am, I would go up and down the land, telling of what I know. Grief for the dead would vanish, as the dew does when the sun comes up. But they would not believe. I think each soul must find the way for itself. Not long ago I told Vicar that soon there would be such a torrent of grief for the dead, the young and splendid dead, that it would break down that thin veil between the two worlds."

"Then you think we must have war?"

"Yes, sir." Suddenly the somber darkness of the eyes lit again, and Lucy spoke quickly, with a ringing assurance that was oddly convincing, "But do not fear it, sir. You will know how quickly passing is all earthly grief. Nothing can destroy the life of the spirit, it is of God."

Without hesitation John answered her, speaking frankly of what had been in his mind for weeks now. "I can honestly say I do not doubt that now. But this life, this now, is good. I want that, too."

Lucy smiled brightly. "This life is good, if we have made it so," she said. "For you it will be. I said the darkness was nearly over for me. For you it is over also. I knew, when I watched you in the wood, the day you came, that you would find all you sought."

Then, before he could question her further, she left the kitchen, walking across the stone floor with surprising speed and agility. John went back to the small paneled room he used as an office.

He turned on a light and looked at the two pictures in narrow black wood frames that hung behind his desk. One was an old print found by Harry Gregg after a long and patient search through Bristol print shops. It represented the yard of the Beausire Arms, Sudbury St. Luke, and was dated 1795. The other was a very beautiful pencil drawing signed by William Tremayne and titled, "The Abbot's Barn, Glastonbury."

John looked at them a long time. He knew he had seen every detail of the first one as he had stood at the front of the inn on the day of his arrival. It was all there—the galleried buildings surrounding the yard; the mounted blocks and hitching posts where now was a neatly cultivated garden. And, stumbling across the dew-wet grass of the park, beyond the dip that had once been the duck pool of the home farm, he had seen those two barns, vanished long ago, that had been faithful copies of the barn that still stood at Glastonbury.

◆　◆　◆　◆

Mark sat in the foyer of his hotel in London and wondered if it was because he was getting old that he felt so little sense of relief. This time three days ago they'd been digging trenches in London parks, sandbagging priceless old buildings by the light of flares. Women and children had been pouring out of almost undefended cities. Then there had been some excuse for feeling that life was over; now there was not.

Perhaps it had been the overwhelming realization that England was in actual danger that had made things which used to be of tremendous importance seem to be utterly insignificant. Nothing had seemed real but the desperate need to make the most of the little time left for training, and the hours spent with Marian at the cottage she had taken near the base. It had been a mad thing to do, of course, but there'd been nothing else for it. The hotels and inns were crowded with people from the cities. Bessie had stayed at the cottage, but Mark knew how futile the attempt at convention was.

This morning Marian and Bessie had gone up to town. At five o'clock he was to telephone, to find out where he was to meet Marian if he had got leave. He had got three days. There was still nearly an hour until five. For the first time in his life Mark tried to think things out.

Every day for the two weeks she had been at the cottage, he had meant to tell Marian that things couldn't go on as they were, that something must be done. But when he had seen her small tense face, and felt her clutching hands that betrayed the terror she tried so hard to conceal, nothing mattered but the two hours or so they had together.

Three days ago he had flown over the Sudbury valley. As he had looked down on the great house, surrounded by the four villages clustering round the park, he had had a strange sense of elation he tried now to recapture. All difficulties and entanglements had seemed to have been miraculously smoothed out. He had known quite clearly that he could not marry Rosalys and that Marian must leave her husband, if not with a divorce, then without it.

Beyond the Mill he had looked down at the far side to the long lines of new buildings at Combe St. Philip.

All the things he had heard in the last weeks had seemed to jump into his mind at once. He knew that men who had reason to know believed that England's survival would depend on two things. One was the strength of the wholly inadequate Air Force; the other was food.

Then he had seen the coming of the American in a wholly different light. It had seemed a marvelous piece of luck. He had wished he could ground the plane, find John Beausire and tell him of the desperate struggle that was to come.

All day that sense of friendliness toward John Beausire had been with him. Next day Horace had come to the base, and he had cautiously tried out the idea on him. He remembered now how he had tried to appear casual as he said, "I've been thinking of seeing if that American would still like a lease of the place. I'll have as much as I can do in the next few months without bothering about it."

Horace had been shocked, had argued furiously against it. Then a subaltern had burst into the room with the news that Chamberlain had signed a pact.

No more had been said about the American, but he had known that Horace was against the idea. That night he had tried it on Marian. She had violently opposed it, implored him to be sensible, to leave things as they were, to marry Rosalys in November.

Mark tried now to think of Rosalys. It was odd how when he was away from her she ceased to be an individual, but became a part of something real and lovely that was always there to return to, however long he had been away.

If he asked her to break off their engagement, she would marry the American. He didn't know why he was so sure of that, but he had been sure since the day of the cherry picking.

Thinking of the cherry picking reminded him of the cuts. It had been a relief when Uncle William 'phoned that they had to be opened, as no one could spare a drop of petrol now and the right of way through the park cut off three miles between St. John and the road to Taunton. He had said of course to open them.

It was twenty minutes to five. As he waited for his telephone connection he felt curiously glad that he and Marian had thrown caution to the winds during the last weeks. There would probably be an uproar of scandal, and the devil to pay. It might be to the good. Anything was better than going on like this.

The familiar voice of Marian's butler said that her Ladyship was not in town, but that Mrs. Gregg was in the house and would take the call. He had no time to be astonished before Bessie was saying that Rosalys had telephoned about three asking Marian to drive down for the weekend, so she had started at once to arrive before dark.

Mark hung up the receiver with more bewilderment than anxiety, though it was a beastly day for driving. He wished Marian had gone by train. She probably felt they might as well be hung for a sheep as a lamb, and had decided on the weekend at Sudbury.

The man who brought his car around said the storm was getting worse and the roads would be in a shocking state.

Rain lashed the windshield, and trees tossed their branches fretfully. When he was clear of the suburbs Mark put on speed. Every yard of the road was familiar. In Taunton people muffled in mackintoshes struggled along, trying to keep umbrellas braced against the wind.

As the car ascended the slope of the Quantocks, Mark's mind began to clear. Things that had been vague and shadowy for days now stood out in bold outline. He knew that all his life, or all that he could clearly remember of it, he had waited for two things. One of them had been Marian. He had realized at once that she was quite different from any woman he had ever known or would know. Now, after almost five years, he could not imagine getting tired of her. The other thing was the war that would soon come.

He wished the American had come years ago, when he had

been a child. He could have got used to the idea then. Perhaps the best thing would be to do nothing at all until the war did come—just put off marrying Rosalys, being with Marian whenever possible, coming home for a day or so at a time, as he was doing now.

Mark tried to push from his mind all the nagging obstacles to that plan. Marian would have to go back to India in November, or there would be some sort of showdown. People who knew said it would be a year before there was war. Rosalys couldn't be expected to wait a year, meeting the American about the place, as Horace said she did.

A numbness seemed to creep over his brain. The two realities were still there, Marian and the war that was to come, but everything else seemed meaningless.

The long, heavily lidded, clear hazel eyes of the American seemed to be peering at him through the dusk. He saw the man as he had first seen him, advancing down the hall; felt again the shock of surprise, which even Horace had not prepared him for, when he looked into the young man's face. Mark knew that he was not going to have the courage to take the best way out. Marian was against it, and so was Horace. Besides, you couldn't treat a man the way he'd treated John Beausire, and then, when the bottom seemed about to drop out of everything, coolly ask him if he'd like to take over.

Mark tried to persuade himself it was because no sane man in the position of the American would take on Sudbury Court now that he wasn't going to risk a snub, but he knew it was because of that sudden outcry from Marian when he had suggested it, the look of stark horror that had flashed across her face as she exclaimed, "Mark, no!"

The car began to climb Sudbury Hill. Odd bits of the story Harry had so carefully pieced together flashed like pictures into Mark's mind. He imagined that the other John Beausire was exactly like the present one. There would have been the secret trial, the hustling to the slave ship, the brutal voyage, ten years of slavery.

Mark thought of his time in the trenches. Because he was so young, and had only got in at the end, he'd had only three months of it. It had seemed an eternity, days without end, nights when it seemed that dawn would never come. How did anyone ever stand ten years of hell?

What had the Mark Beausire who inherited thought of, during the years before he knew his cousin was dead? Had he thought of the slave ship and the plantations as he rode about the place? There was no doubt at all that he and his wife had engineered the arrest.

But why bother about what had happened hundreds of years ago? It had all been pretty foul, but things were different then, and nothing could undo what had been done.

But couldn't it? In some sort of way, if John Beausire had the Court for a time—

The car skidded, lurched. Mark put on his brakes. It lurched again, the front wheels sinking forward as if into a hollow in the road.

Leaning out, Mark saw that the headlights cast a bright path of light down the almost sheer side of Markscombe.

Knowing that the slightest movement might send him crashing down into the combe, Mark sat quite still, leaning out, staring into the shadowy depths below the light. He noticed how the wind had risen, how much harder it was raining. He knew exactly where he had missed the road and branched off onto the narrower one that ended in the bridle path which twisted down the side of the combe. He had been thinking, not attending to business.

Before he sprang clear of the car a single thought filled his mind. "Mark Beausire was a fool to jump Markscombe Mill. He should have gone to Maryland, brought John back, gone to the King, claimed amnesty for him, and full pardon."

Then, as he struck the rocky side, slipped, and sprawled against it, clutching the bush he felt under his hands and trying for a toehold, he remembered that when the horse and rider leaped into the combe, it had been too late to bring John Beausire back from Maryland.

Very slowly at first, then faster and faster, the car began to move. Mark turned his head and watched it go, feeling only anger at his own stupidity. Cautiously, step by step, he began to descend the side of the combe. Someone in the mill might have seen the accident; if so, before it was known that he was safe, it would be all around the valley that the curse had struck again. Rosalys would hear it, and Marian.

Almost unconsciously he began to move faster, missed his foothold and slid for several feet, then checked himself. With any luck, the miller had gone home, and in the high wind, the crash had not been heard. There might be time to get to Markscombe first.

Odd pictures from the past flashed into his mind. There was the day he had been fishing with Horace, not half a mile from here. He had been about nine, and all that morning had been thinking about the curse. Now he could remember quite clearly how he had reasoned it out. He had been at boarding school for a year and no longer thought of the curse as an animal, fierce and of unknown species, that would some day spring upon him from a dark corner. No one had ever known how he hated and feared the dark. His childhood had been shadowed by nebulous fears of which he could not speak.

As they fished, he had very cautiously mentioned the curse

to Horace, and had been enormously relieved to find that Horace knew all about it and to hear him explain that Master Mark was quite safe, because only one was taken in each generation.

From then on the curse had seemed less formidable. "Being took" was something mysterious, which, though it entailed death, was not so simple, and happened only to Beausires touched by the curse.

Looking below him, he saw he was not yet half way down the combe. The lights of a car flashed through the elm trees of the Combe St. Philip road. Mark saw that the car was not moving, and tried to shout into the wind, for he was convinced that it was Marian. Scrambling now in reckless haste, his only thought was to let her know that he was safe.

Instead of touching slippery earth and loose stones, his foot dangled in space, and he knew he had landed on top of the big boulder that overhung the narrow path a few feet above the stream. Turning to gauge the distance for a jump, he looked straight into the upturned face of John Beausire.

For an instant Mark felt only relief that the car he had seen was not Marian's. Then he thought that he had never seen a face so clearly as he saw the one looking up at him through the dusk.

It was a young face—Mark thought of the eighteen-year-old boys at the base—yet it had a strength and character they would not have for years.

It seemed that they stared at each other for a long time. "It's the American," Mark thought, trying to break through the strange unreality of this meeting into commonplace fact. The American had been on his way from his place to the Inn, had seen the car go down, and of course had come to help possible survivors.

The American said something, but Mark could not hear what it was. Then, with a sense of intense surprise which he knew to be unreasonable, he saw John Beausire step nearer, brace himself against the side of the rock, and hold out his hands.

They were long slender hands, but Mark knew they had unusual strength. Part of his mind tried to reason out how he knew, but another part was concerned only with the knowledge that if he took those hands, something of tremendous importance in his life would have occurred, something that was tied up with those early years of fear. He had a curious sense that these hands were stretched out not only to help him down to the safety of the level path, but to drag him out of all the chaotic, fear-haunted restlessness of his life.

His own hands felt like lead: he had to make an effort to raise them; then he felt a firm grasp, and jumped.

"That was a narrow squeak," John said. Mark was faintly surprised at the friendliness of his voice. He had an unpleasant sense of guilt as he suddenly remembered the cherry picking and the cuts.

"Couldn't have been closer. I just jumped in time." Then, anticipating the unspoken question, he added, "I was alone in the car. I missed the South Wood road at the fork."

"I was on my way to the Arms," John said. "My car's in the elm wood. I'll drive you home."

"Thanks." Mark was grateful for the distance between the elm wood and the Court. He would have time to decide what he was going to do. You couldn't accept help from a man in an emergency like this, and then not ask him in for a drink. Yet if John Beausire entered the Court again . . .

They slipped through the wide gates. As they neared the bridge John remembered that it was just here that Harry had told him to think only of the moment. That was what he would do. Mark would probably ask him in. An hour ago he had talked to Ellen on the 'phone, and she had said that Rosalys had gone to the Court and was staying the night there. He would almost certainly see her. He would be in that hall again, and she would be there.

The car ascended the terrace. Almost before Mark realized it they were before the house. The wind shrieked through the twisted chimneys and tore around the corner as if in a frenzied effort to uproot the vast shadowy bulk of Sudbury Court and fling it into the air.

For a moment after the car stopped they sat, staring at it. Mark had a strange sense that it would ride out the other storm that was fast approaching, the storm of the worst war in the history of man. He wished he could convey this to John, but instead, he said, "It's a fine old place, isn't it? We've got reason to be proud of it."

John answered very quietly, "I have always been proud of it. I think it is the loveliest house in the world."

Mark was strangely excited, as if he were about to enter upon a new and brighter life. He would ask John Beausire in for a drink. They would talk, and he would see how things panned out. He would not allow the thought to form in his mind, but he knew that if John asked again for a lease he would agree. There was a satisfying sense that the whole matter was no doing of his. He'd never have approached John Beausire, after what had happened during the summer. John had just turned up.

"Let's go round to the West door," Mark said, "I've got a key in my pocket."

Because he could not explain that he didn't want to disclose his presence to Swain, Mark said nothing. He wanted to be alone with John a little longer, to see if this feeling of peace would last. It might be only relief at having escaped so lightly from what could have been a beastly mess.

"Come in and have a drink," he said, as the car stopped. He was glad when John got out of the car. For a moment he had thought he was going to refuse. Now he wanted to go through with this thing: talk to the American, hear his plans for war, find out if he really intended to stay through it.

A surprised footman who passed the west hall took their coats and an order for drinks in the gunroom.

"Miss Rosalys and Lady Armitage are in the Rose Room," he said, "Shall I announce your arrival, m'lord?"

Mark shook his head. "I'll be there shortly," he said. Marian was safely home. Somehow he was certain that what he had to settle now was as much her concern as his, that now, after this, she would be wholly his, with no more separations, no more fears, no more bitterness or humiliation of deceit.

John took his drink from Mark's hand. Mark wished the whole damned thing weren't so beastly familiar. It was like drinking with Harry, or someone he knew frightfully well and was fond of.

"Thanks for helping me out," he said.

John smiled. "I'm afraid I only saved you a tedious walk," he said. "But you certainly had a narrow escape. I saw the car go, and it looked distinctly—unpleasant."

Mark put down his drink. They mustn't waste time in formalities: they must talk and plan. John probably wouldn't want the house now, but he should have the land, start to cultivate it.

"We've all had a narrow escape," he said, "but I trust my personal one is more permanent."

John's face darkened. "I know," he answered. Then,

quite suddenly, he understood that he had to do the talking. He knew what Mark had in his mind and that he should be surprised, but that he was not: he could only think it was something which had to be settled between them, as quickly as possible, for somewhere in this house of dreams Rosalys was waiting, and when it was settled he could go to her.

"And I am going to stay through it," he said firmly. "I am doing everything with that end in view. Combe St. Philip will be quite ready when it comes."

Mark stared at the flaming logs in the fireplace. Fires always seemed better and brighter at Sudbury than anywhere else. "I wish I could say the same of my place," he remarked.

John moved a step nearer. Why were they standing, as if waiting for some momentous thing to happen?

"My offer for the place still holds good," he said, "on any terms you wish."

It seemed a long time before Mark answered. Then he said slowly, "It is accepted. You can make better use of the place than I can, and lately—since Munich, you know . . ."

"Yes, I understand. Will you let me have it for five years? I will undertake to give it back in absolute order, with everything possible done to preserve the house."

Mark tried to think of Marian—of Horace. But there was something else, a sense of peace, with him now that was infinitely stronger than any objections they might raise.

"You can have it for five years. No rent. Just keep it up. Farm it for all it's worth. Don't spend money on the house. Speaking between ourselves, from what I know of—their air power, I don't think it's any use spending money on old houses. It will have to go. But the land will remain."

"The house will, too." John did not know why he could

speak so confidently, but he felt sure of what he said. "Then it's settled?" he asked.

"It's settled—and I'm damned glad." Mark held out his hand. When John took it, Mark knew that his strange thought while he had stood on the rock was still there. John was in some way pulling him out of darkness and danger into light and safety.

When Mark went up the corridor toward the hall, he knew he must tell Marian what he had done. He wondered if she would ever understand why he had done it. Would she be surprised when she heard that John Beausire had a lease of the whole estate for five years; that he, Mark, had practically promised that he was going to break off his engagement to Rosalys tonight, and that John was waiting for Rosalys in the library in the west wing?

He felt quite sure that she had known for a long time that this had to come.

John walked in the opposite direction, following the butler, Swain, who wondered what on earth was happening now. John could think only of getting to the library and taking that journal written long ago from its box—he had asked and received permission to do so—for he knew that he would not realize what had happened until he read those faded lines. That it had happened he had no doubt whatever. Today was October the first. Mark had not said it in so many words, but he had surely given his consent to the marriage of his cousin, John Beausire, and Rosalys.

In the Rose Room Marian became more and more restless. "Mark's late," she said. "I'm getting worried. Are you?"

Rosalys raised her eyes. There were blue shadows beneath them. "I think he'll be here soon," she said. "If he doesn't come in half an hour, I'll call the base."

"I'm going to look for a book," Marian said, after a moment and went out of the room. Somehow, alone, it was easier to think.

She did not go to her room, the Blue Tapestry Room she had always loved. She went down into the hall.

It seemed vast, empty. It waited for something to happen. Marian felt it about her as a sentient thing. She looked down at the little lights and shadows that slipped in and out of the sable hem of her tea gown, at the long, loose, sable-edged sleeves of crimson velvet as soft and dark as the petal of a rose. She had chosen that, and her best emerald earrings, which brought out the pale gold of her neck, because tonight she must look her best.

The logs blazed in the fireplace. Marian drew back so that the heat would not flush her face. A cold terror, like a dark sea kept in check only by the dike of her will, seemed about to break over her. Now, she had to let Mark go or risk losing him forever: she had to let Mark go, and she had not the strength to do it.

He would come in by the main door. Again and again her eyes traveled down the length of the hall, watched for the two footmen, closely followed by Swain, who would appear as if by magic to open the door.

Then she turned her eyes to the door of the west wing. The men would come from there. Surely they were coming now.

The black wave broke over her. Mark stood there. His hair was damp and ruffled, his light uniform mudstained. He came toward her slowly, not taking his eyes from her face.

The logs were a wall of fire behind her. Marian stepped forward. She knew that she no longer controlled Mark's destiny; from now on he controlled hers.

When at last Mark left the little cedar room to go upstairs, Marian knew that all her carefully made plans were dead as door-nails. She could not tell whether she was glad or sorry, for she could not feel at all. But Mark was going upstairs now to tell Rosalys she was free.

It seemed a long time before Rosalys came down the stairs. She walked slowly, like one in a dream, tall and slender in her white dinner dress. When she had crossed the hall, Marian looked into her face and felt curiously ashamed. She knew she had tried to do a brutal thing.

"Mark says he wants to break our engagement," Rosalys said. "I think he does not need me any more." There was a deep stillness about her.

In hurried, broken sentences Marian tried to explain. Mark was so hopeless at explaining anything. But as she spoke she knew that Rosalys would understand quite as well as she did what had happened to Mark.

"I know," Rosalys said. "I must go now. John is in the library, waiting for me."

"What have you got in your hand?" Marian asked.

She saw that Rosalys no longer wore the sapphire Mark had given her, and thought perhaps she carried the ring.

Rosalys opened her hand. Marian felt a strange thrill of fear as she took a ring from her. It was an old ring, a square emerald set in old and tarnished gold. It was a signet ring: "J. de B." was engraved on it, and the crest of the Beausires.

Marian dropped the ring back into the outstretched hand. It flashed green flame as the stone caught the firelight.

"Mark gave it to me—for John," Rosalys said. "He found it among his personal papers when he went through them a few days ago."

Marian nodded. Mark had made his preparations for death.

A few days ago he had been saying cheerfully that his life was not worth a crooked six pence.

She stared mercilessly at Rosalys, taking in every tint and line of the lovely young face, the deep shining eyes and bright hair.

"Rosalys," she said, "I did my damnedest to make you marry Mark. I was quite willing to sacrifice your life to his— even this afternoon I still wanted it. But, if you had married him"—pausing, she gave a hard little laugh that was more like a sob, then went on—"My God, how I would have hated you."

"You wanted what I did," Rosalys said gently, "to make Mark as happy as he could be."

Marian watched her go across the hall and up the wide staircase.

◆　　◆　　◆　　◆

The gallery looked immensely long and dark. Only a few lamps were burning. Rosalys felt suddenly weak and exhausted, as if all life had drained from her. She thought she had done this very thing, not once, but many times: she had walked down this gallery in the evening, telling herself that John would be waiting for her in the library, or perhaps in the Queen's Room beyond it.

But he would not be there. There would be only emptiness and silence, or the little crackling sounds of a wood fire. Now, though Mark had said he was there, she was afraid to go on.

The painted faces of the dead seemed to stare down at her in pity; the lights blurred into one misty glow as tears stung her eyes. With dragging steps she went forward, and the length of the gallery seemed endless.

At last she turned the corner into the wide space between the west staircase and the library door, and as though fear urged her forward, she ran across the polished oak floor and flung open the door, clinging to the great silver knob.

The room seemed a blaze of light. John stood there, his hands held out to her, as in hazy dreams she had so often tried to convince herself that she saw him.

Chapter Ten

❖   ❖   ❖   ❖

THE HUNTSMAN'S HORN RANG THROUGH THE VALLEY. Though he had risen with the others before daybreak, Harry Gregg had no intention of joining the cub hunt. He reined his horse to a standstill at the top of the South Wood, and watched the sun come up on the feast day of St. Luke. The autumn beauty of the woods seemed almost unbearable, as if they tuned the senses like a violin string, higher and higher.

Two horses, a black and a chestnut, emerged at a walk from the South Wood. Harry waved his crop in greeting as he recognized John and Rosalys. Then, turning again into the wood with a sudden determination to find Marian, who was not out with the hunt, Harry thought of the pitiful letter—one of the treasures of his record—that had been written on another St. Luke's Day, October 18, 1687, by a dying girl who begged the nuns that had cared for her in her early childhood to pray that she might go soon, for she had come to believe lately that Diana was right, and that John was no longer in this world. To the letter—written in French—there had been a pitiful postscript which had told how she tried to mount a horse, to ride to the South Wood, but was too weak to do so, and perhaps it was better so, for the memory of that last ride with her cousin John, the day before he had gone away, was too bitter to be borne now.

Harry rode up to the great gates. They were open now. They had been cleaned and the splendid old stonework of the massive pillars repaired. The lodge windows were open, and a furniture van stood beside it. John had engaged a lodgekeeper, who was moving in with his family.

The pale gold of elm leaves showered down with every passing breeze, but the drive was free of weeds. For nearly three weeks now a small army of men had been at work on the place.

Harry asked the groom who came up to him whether a horse had been sent around for Lady Armitage, and was relieved to hear that no order for one had been received. This morning might be his last chance in some time to have a talk with Marian.

As he reached the head of the west staircase, he saw her. She was sitting on a low stool in the gallery, staring at one of the portraits. Harry was not surprised to find that it was the Lely portrait of Diana, the wife of the Baron who had killed himself in 1700.

Marian started when he called to her, rose and said sharply, as if seized by sudden fear, "Where's Mark? He should be in by now."

"He will be, soon," Harry replied. "A lot of people turned out. The woods are a sight to behold. You should ride today, Marian."

"I may, later," she replied, her eyes still on the portrait.

Harry also looked into that bright painted face with its bold black eyes. The dark curls were twined with pearls; ropes of pearls fell among the laces of the tight pointed bodice of brilliant yellow satin.

"She was a thorough bad lot," Marian said, "but Mark says she is his favorite ancestress. Anyway, whatever she did, or didn't do, she seems to have loved her husband."

Harry nodded. Marian had been bored with most of the records he had tried to get her to read, but almost against her will she had followed the story of Diana. "We are told on the best authority that love covers a multitude of sins," he said, "so there is hope for her."

"She must have suffered horribly," Marian said. "I can't help imagining how awful it must have been to watch her husband become the wreck he apparently was in the end. Come, let's look at his picture. It was painted in 1680, the year they were married, you know."

The splendid portrait of Mark Beausire, also painted by Sir Peter Lely, in the year the famous artist died, was lighted by sunshine pouring through the east oriel window. Looking at it, Harry was again startled by its likeness to the boy who had entered an almost derelict farmhouse in France one bitter day in November, 1918, and had said, "I'm Beausire. I believe we're to share this billet. We haven't had much luck, have we?"

There was no doubt in his mind at all. Diana and her husband, Mark, had come back to work out their salvation, under much the same conditions as when they had failed so miserably before.

There was only one weak link in the record. He could not find out what had been his own part in the episode of 1685, and yet he was certain that he had had a part in it.

"Harry," Marian was saying, "you knew Mark long before I did. Did he ever look like this?"

Harry answered slowly, picking his words with care.

"When I met Mark he was only eighteen, but he had been through a veritable hell, and had just heard of his father's death. Also, Horace was on the way to a base hospital, horribly wounded. But still, I saw something in Mark of what Lely saw in his ancestor. Perhaps this expresses it better: Mark, untouched by the tragedy of the war, his childhood a normal one, not shadowed by fear of the curse, would have been like this."

Marian nodded, as though the explanation satisfied her. "You know," she said, "when I first met Horace I loathed him. I suppose it was because Mark had talked so much about him that I expected—oh, something quite different. It's only since we've been home this time that I've realized how the man adores Mark, and one can't take a thing like that lightly."

"I should say not," Harry replied. Horace presented no difficulty. He slipped into his place without doubt. The half-witted boy Jerry, who had died with the twenty-second Baron, had worshiped his master and served him with untiring devotion.

Marian was looking particularly well. The reddish purple of her perfectly cut tweed suit brought out the peculiar tint of her skin admirably, she wore little make-up, much of the tenseness had gone from her face.

Harry remembered that if he wanted to hear about Marian's plans, this was his last chance before she went back to town.

"Marian," he said directly, "what are you going to do?"

Marian indicated the broad window seat. "Let's sit here," she said. "I've been wanting to tell you how things are panning out. I'm beginning to see the light.

"Mark did the right thing in letting John have the place," she went on. "At first I was wretched about it, far more so than I let him know. Now I see the sense of it. It will add generations to its existence."

"That's what I tried to make Mark see," Harry replied. "Is there any hope of a divorce?"

"Not this year. Anthony came home in a frenzy of rage, but I don't think he had any clear ideas as to what he intended to do. Laura Paget wrote a damnable letter, you know, saying my affair with Mark was public gossip. Anthony was completely flabbergasted to find Mark was still engaged to Rosalys. It was frightfully sporting of the child to keep up the fiction for days and give me time to deal with the situation. It saved my bacon."

Harry wondered if Diana had been as coldly calculating, when she had been laying out her plans. Probably she had. For all her youth and beauty, the portrait had caught a hardness in her face.

"What did you settle with him?" Harry could not quite understand the situation as Bessie had explained it. The engagement of John and Rosalys had been announced a few days ago.

Marian did not reply at once. She looked down at her brown suede brogues, a curious expression flickering across her face.

When she spoke it was with bitterness.

"You know," she said, "I never hated Anthony until we met to discuss the situation. I begged for a divorce, and thought at first that it was for my sake he wouldn't hear of it. Mark was still officially engaged to Rosalys at the time, you know. Then, slowly, it dawned on me what was in his mind. He was quite sure that there would be war, in a year at most, and that as Mark had got into the Air Force, his life wasn't worth a damn—certainly not worth going to all the inconvenience of a divorce for. He said in his best judicial manner that we must consider things for a year, then talk again."

"And Mark?"

Marian knew instantly what Harry meant. She wanted to tell him of the strange peace that seemed to have come to Mark since the signing of the lease, but it would be difficult to put into words.

"Oh, Mark thinks of nothing but the Air Force now," she said. "I thought he'd be furious at Anthony's attitude—that sitting tight, waiting for him to be killed—but he wasn't. He is quite sure that nothing can separate us now. The future, beyond the war he's so certain will come, doesn't seem to mean anything to him at all."

Harry nodded. He couldn't explain to Marian that souls often know their own destiny, and accept it, though unable to explain it consciously. That Mark knew his, Harry hadn't a doubt.

The sound of voices floated up from below. Harry watched Marian running down the stairs and thought of her and of Mark. The last threads of the pattern were being woven. Mark would die. Perhaps in a few days or hours of selfless courage he would atone for much. Marian had changed little. The process of evolution could be very slow. She would fight to the last for what she wanted, and when that slipped irretrievably from her grasp, her darkness would be absolute. She had no spiritual resources. Coming of a long lived race, with tremendous vitality, her body would not let her rest. For some years yet she would keep some semblance of beauty. She would long for the fullness of life that she would never know again. To her the separation from Mark would be final and unbearable. She had had little real happiness, and soon she would begin to pay in full for the past.

✦   ✦   ✦   ✦

The dinner guests left early, for they were motoring to London. Mark moved about the library restlessly, obviously anxious to follow. Marian had gone on, for appearance' sake, but he would meet her in Salisbury and they would go on to town together.

"Let's go and see what old Horace is doing," he said. "He's poking about in the secret room. He wanted to see how the roof had been repaired."

Rosalys and John followed Mark into the Queen's Room. Harry, who had begun a game of chess with the Vicar, looked toward the door. The Vicar caught the look.

"Come on," he said. "This can wait."

The Queen's Room was no longer dark and desolate. Fine old furniture, brought from various parts of the house, lightened its somberness with bright brocades and rich lacquer. Crimson velvet cushions were heaped on the dark old chest. A wood fire burned in the huge fireplace, and brilliant autumn flowers lighted dark corners with splashes of color. Harry had returned to the Court only the previous night, and he had not seen the Queen's Room since John had had it furnished. Yet he knew that he had often seen it as it was now, that he had had long and interesting talks here, eaten meals, sipped marvelous wine from a crystal glass. He saw John standing by the open panel across the room, heard him call out to Horace, but it was the ceiling that held his attention.

Suddenly he saw the design in that flaked and faded painting: the whirling spheres, the faultless order of the Universe. Law, unalterable, was expressed there. There had been references, in the journal kept for several years by Diana Beausire, to a French artist, Amadis Dupuis, the man who had done the stonework of the Dutch Garden and many other things in the house and grounds, and who had carved the lovely tomb of the little maid. Though there was no record of it, Harry knew that he had also painted this symbolical design on the ceiling of the Queen's Room. He crossed the room with a sense of elation. The last piece in the puzzle had been put in its place.

The cause of his beauty-starved youth and childhood was at last clear to him. Amadis Dupuis must have neglected his talent, failed to pass on to the world the beauty that he could have created. Perhaps he had worked only when it pleased him to do so, as when he executed commissions given him by his friend John Beausire. Harry knew that now he had received the clue, he could work out the thread of his destiny.

Horace held the electric torch close to the roof and tried not to notice the trembling of his hand. He had felt ashamed and foolish when his Lordship asked him if they'd made a good job of the roof of the secret room.

"I was just going up to see," he had said boldly, and, hell or high water, that is what he was going to do.

The panel had an ordinary knob on it now, cleverly fitted into the carving. He had walked in boldly, trying to stifle the dank terror this place always evoked in him.

He peered through the slit beneath the eaves. The great golden Hunter's moon was just coming up over the trees. An owl hooted, and he shivered with fear.

But Horace did not intend to let himself off lightly. He inspected every nook and cranny before he turned to the narrow stone steps that would lead into light and human companionship again.

"Musty old place, this is," he muttered, when he honestly felt there was no more to see.

Light flooded the space at the foot of the steps. The panel had been opened wider. He started back with an unconscious gesture of terror as he saw a figure standing there. Then, as it advanced to the first step, he saw that it was Mr. John.

"Hullo, Horace," John called. "Is it all right up there?"

Horace descended a few steps and stood staring down. "Yes, sir," he replied, but did not move. His torch threw a golden circle near his feet.

Mr. John looked very tall. His head was thrown back, and his face looked white, almost luminous, his hair dark. Horace felt he had seen him stand just like this before.

And he was slowly aware that he felt quite different about him. He was no longer angry that Mr. John had the place. There was an air of strength, of power about him. While he was here, things would not go wrong. He would make the place what it should be: even in three weeks he had done a powerful lot, and there was a heap more to come.

Horace came down the steps slowly. He would have been furious had he been told so, but in those moments he saw John Beausire as a superior being, one who was capable of leading them through all the dangers and difficulties to come. He had complete confidence in the American. It was a rare piece of good luck that he'd come when he did.

Horace saw Mark standing beside John, or just behind him, outside the panel. He quickened his steps. "It's all fixed up," he said. "The roof'll be tight for many a long day to come. They made a good job of it."

When he was in the Queen's Room he looked around with approval. "This is as it should be," he said. "What's the use of having the finest paneling in England in a room as is too gloomy to bide in for more'n a brace of shakes?"

Mark laughed. "It's not gloomy now," he said. "If you like, Horace, you can drive me to Salisbury and bring the car back."

Horace beamed. "I'd be mighty glad to," he said. "There's several things I 'as to speak to your Lordship about."

As Harry went upstairs he wondered if anyone else had felt that curious sense of finality when they came in from the terrace after seeing Mark off. Mark had gone, as he had gone several times since John had taken over the place, with a casual remark that he would be back for the weekend, or the weekend after it, anyway, and the tail light of the car had disappeared down the slope, and John Beausire had turned and walked back into his house.

Light gleamed from a room that was seldom used. Passing, Harry was struck by curiosity, and peered in. It was the little sitting room, furnished in faded gilt and brocade, that was said to have been used by the little maid. The door into the bedroom beyond was open. Harry went toward it.

A tall figure leaned against the faintly glimmering gilt bedpost. Harry absorbed every detail—the canopied gilt bed, the rich faded furniture, the heavy silk curtains now faded to a dim gray—before he recognized Ellen Hobbs.

He spoke quietly, afraid of startling her, for she seemed deeply sunk in thought.

"Ellen," he said softly.

Turning, she peered toward the door, then smiled. He saw that she held something white in her hand.

"Come in, sir," she said. "I'll light a few more candles and show you something I think you'd like to see."

As Ellen moved about the room, Harry had the sense that she was utterly familiar with it. Yet that was not possible, for this room had not been used in generations.

Soon candles were glowing from every corner of the room, reflecting their little points of light in old gilt and glass. The windows were open, and the night breeze rustled the curtains gently.

Harry looked with wonder at Ellen's face. It was radiant. Her eyes were like stars, and her silver hair shone purely in the candlelight.

"Look, sir," she said. "Miss Rosalys is to wear this for her wedding." She held out what she had in her hand. Harry saw a small cap of exquisite old lace, yellowed with age to the color of ivory.

Ellen went on talking, and her voice seemed but an instrument for joy. "They're to be married on St. John's Day," she said, "very quietly, by the Vicar, of course, in the chapel. I am going to dress her for her wedding."

Harry began to think about another woman. Sarah, her name had been, Sarah Giles. There was little in the historical record about her, save that she had been the widow of the Farmer Giles whom John Beausire had been deported for attempting to save, and that she had been the young Lord's foster mother, and had loved and tended the little maid with a great devotion, dressing her for her burial.

He thought of the bitter vigils those two would have kept in this room, of the times without number they would have gone to the chest to look at wedding finery that was at last to be used as a shroud. He thought of the anguished prayers, the days of hope, then the black days of despair, and the tragic end.

And it seemed that he saw Sarah, a little lace cap in her hands, not smiling, as Ellen had been, but weeping in unendurable grief, and that he remembered trying to make her understand that life and love go on forever, for they are of God and cannot die. He could not remember whether she had understood or not, for Ellen was telling him joyfully of the servants being engaged for the Court and of the plans Mr. John had for redecorating these rooms, though he would live with his wife in the west wing, as his ancestor would have done.

When he emerged from his own room, the Vicar was crossing the gallery.

"I thought you'd gone back to the library," he said, as Harry came up to him.

"I'm sorry," Harry replied. "I saw a light in an unused room, went in to investigate, and slipped back into the past."

The Vicar was becoming accustomed to Harry, so he merely smiled. "A happy fragment of the past, I trust," he said.

"On the whole, yes. I think I had a lesson on the truth of the saying that though grief endureth for a night, joy cometh in the morning."

Without another word they turned toward the library. Harry wanted a chance to talk to the Vicar. The Vicar was beginning to worry him. Wasted opportunity was an awful thing. Here was a man with a voice that was a God-given instrument of beauty, and a vast knowledge of that great mystical heritage of the Church; a man who knew the "Communion of Saints" to be more than mere words in the prayer book, from personal experience of that communion; who knew that miracles took place, because they were as well attested as any facts that have come down through the ages, and were still taking place today.

The Vicar must be persuaded that never in the history of the world would faith be so needed as in the decade that was to come, and that those who had it, either by the Grace of God or by a long and determined search for it, must share the light that had come to them.

Moonlight flooded the Court of St. Francis: chrysanthemums glowed like pale fallen moons; the fountain waters were sparkling jewels; the leaves of the bushes gleamed with silvery softness.

The Vicar turned from the window. The sight of the two forms moving across the court into the shadow of the lilacs filled him with fear.

"Harry," he said, "I shall be enormously relieved when St.

John's Day has come and gone. It would be unbearable if anything went wrong now."

Harry stood with his back to the fire. His slight form and thin dark face seemed to have taken on a strange dignity, and he spoke with a peculiar force. "Nothing will go wrong. They will be married on that day. I think that they will live long and happily here, whatever happens. I think that John will become Lord Beausire. He does not desire it, but I think that it will happen."

The Vicar was interested. He had never heard Harry speak like this.

"Why do you think that?" he asked.

"Because I have seen the almost completed pattern. Sit down, and I will show you what I have seen, and what will logically follow."

It was late when the Vicar left. His mind was so full of chaotic thoughts which had to be put in order that he decided to walk. Harry's voice, rising and falling, ringing with authority, seemed to follow him still.

That strange record of the Beausire family history was a haunting thing. How clearly Harry had shown the working out of the Law through it! It was not difficult to believe that a girl who had had the courage to journey over wild seas to a strange land, to seek justice for her son and for the dead, and who had met cruelty and death, should return, her faith and love undaunted, to give physical birth to one on whom she had showered her love and pity in the past.

It would explain much of the seeming waste of that short life that had ended in 1918. As Harry had said, we could see only the tangled threads from the wrong side of the tapestry. The completed picture was on the other side. Annie's life had not been wasted. She had accomplished that one thing she had sworn to do: obtain justice for John and his Little Maid. Unconsciously the Vicar turned and crossed the drive, making for the oaks.

As he walked across the broad expanse of shining turf he became aware of the beauty of the night. Surely, there had never been so still and lovely a night as this one of the Feast of St. Luke.

The moon hung low, like a great, red-gold shield. All around it there was a rosy flush, as though some heavenly dawn were breaking. The woods were burnished. A passing breeze turned the vastness of the oaks into massed banners of shimmering gold, then died away, leaving utter stillness again.

In the library, as Harry had talked, the cold fingers of grief for Mark had touched him, but now the Vicar found himself thinking of the future with a strange impersonality. Great changes were coming. John could accept them, Mark could not.

As he walked up the white road, the village of St. Luke seemed asleep. Here and there a light gleamed from an upper window. The Vicar thought of Horace Hobbs as he passed the Inn. What Harry had said was true. Horace, led by his devotion to Mark, was growing, mentally and spiritually. He had developed initiative, courage, a shrewd common sense, in the years he had done his best to help in the management of an impoverished estate. If Mark was killed, it would be terrible for Horace.

After a short and futile effort to thrust the thought from him and see only the heavenly beauty around him, the Vicar accepted the realization that the whole horror of war, greatly intensified, was again upon the world. He thought of his own years of utter darkness following the last war. How much more bearable it would be if all the world could believe as Harry believed, in that other body, that ethereal finer replica, immortal, invulnerable, which would slip out of each battered, mutilated or starved physical body to live—on another plane of being, but to live, with mind and soul untouched, because it could not die. It mattered little if one believed that it would again take on a body of flesh. In the Father's House there were many mansions. The Universe was too vast for human comprehension. Through what worlds of beauty and order might the soul not go?

And yet, it was a fascinating theory that a life cut short might return to receive joy denied, or to atone for evil done. There was justice in it, and God was Justice.

Now, in the loveliness of the quiet night, it was not hard to believe that John Beausire and his Little Maid had returned to receive what had been taken from them, and enriched with spiritual development attained by their courage and self-sacrifice in the past.

It was when he passed the entrance to St. John's Wood, still sunk in thought, that the Vicar saw a glimmer of white among the trees.

He stopped for a moment, staring at the moonlight beauty of his daughter.

She stood looking up, the satin-lined hood of her white cloak a radiant frame for her face, which seemed luminous in its pale purity of outline.

John was beside her. They were watching a bird or sleeping squirrel, in a tree.

The glimmering aisle of the broad path struck straight as an arrow through the wood, narrowing into shadowy darkness. The Vicar went on up the road, feeling as confident as Harry Gregg that all would be well with them now.

THIS EXCLUSIVE EDITION

has been typeset for The Reincarnation Library in
Granjon with Aquinus and Neue Neuland Ornaments
and printed by offset lithography
on archival quality paper at
Thomson-Shore Inc.

The text and endpapers are acid-free and meet
or surpass all guidelines established by
the Council of Library Resources
and the American National
Standards Institute.

Book design by Carla Bolte